CRIMINAL JUSTICE, LAW ENFORCEMENT AND CORRECTIONS

BUREAU OF PRISONS (BOP)

INMATE REENTRY, FEMALE INMATES AND APPROPRIATIONS

CRIMINAL JUSTICE, LAW ENFORCEMENT AND CORRECTIONS

CRIMINAL JUSTICE, LAW ENFORCEMENT AND CORRECTIONS

BUREAU OF PRISONS (BOP)

INMATE REENTRY, FEMALE INMATES AND APPROPRIATIONS

MELODY KELLEY
EDITOR

snova
New York

Library of Congress Cataloging-in-Publication Data

ISBN: 978-1-53615-292-0

Published by Nova Science Publishers, Inc. † New York

CONTENTS

PREFACE

Intellectual disabilities have long been a concern for both practitioners and academics alike. With the introduction and advocacy of concepts to the public in recent decades, and the normalization and valorization of intellectual disabilities, humanistic concern has become the dominant trend in providing interventions and services for people with these issues.

Today, various ideas for societal inclusion of those with intellectual disabilities have been introduced. However, many practitioners and academics have criticized these ideas as idealistic, and in many ways, inapplicable for actual social inclusion of people with intellectual disabilities.

The situation is particularly serious regarding those intellectually disabled individuals presenting various forms of self-harm, aggression, disturbing behaviors, and emotional fluctuation (SADE: S =Self harm, A = Aggression, D = Disturbing behaviors, E = Emotional fluctuation). In many instances, social exclusion, labelling, punishments, deprivation of rights, physical restraints, as well as psychiatric medications are commonly used in controlling intellectual disabled clients with SADE.

A thorough understanding of intellectually disabled clients has revealed that their self-harm, aggression, disturbing behaviors, and emotional fluctuations (SADE) are closely related to their unfulfilled needs, developmental traumas, abuse, neglect, and abandonment in their lives. These individuals have problems in expressing their views and emotions, as well as having severe attachment needs.

Based on the writers' substantial experience, clinical practice, and supervision in working with intellectual disabled clients with SADE, this book is the first to formulate and consolidate the communication, emotionality, intimacy, and trauma based interpretation and intervention for intellectually disabled clients with SADE. This book provides methods for effective, humanistic, normalized, and integrated recovery of these individuals.

Chapter 1 - This is an edited, reformatted and augmented version of Hearing before the Committee on Oversight and Government Reform House of Representatives, One Hundred Fifteenth Congress, First Session, Serial No. 115–95, dated December 13, 2017.

Chapter 2 - As of September 2016, the Federal Bureau of Prisons (BOP) incarcerated 10,567 sentenced female inmates, representing 7 percent of the total BOP sentenced inmate population of 146,084. Though female inmates compose a small percentage of the nationwide incarcerated population, correctional officials have recognized that in some areas female and male inmates have different needs and BOP has adopted gender-responsive programs and policies that account for these needs. As a continuation of prior U.S. Department of Justice Office of the Inspector General (OIG) reviews examining BOP's management of certain subpopulations of inmates, including aging inmates and inmates with mental illness in restrictive housing, OIG initiated this review of BOP's management of female inmates, specifically BOP's efforts and capacity to ensure that BOP-wide policies, programs, and decisions adequately address the distinctive needs of women. The authors decision to initiate this review was also informed by members of Congress and public interest groups recently raising concerns about what they consider to be deficiencies in BOP's current management of female inmates.

Chapter 3 - The Bureau of Prisons (BOP) is the largest correctional agency in the country in terms of the number of prisoners under its jurisdiction. BOP must confine any offender convicted and sentenced to a term of imprisonment in a federal court. Changes in federal criminal justice policy since the early 1980s spurred growth in the federal prison population. The total number of inmates under BOP's jurisdiction increased from approximately 25,000 in FY1980 to over 192,000 in FY2016. While the federal prison population in FY2016 is nearly 7 times larger than what it was in FY1980, the number of inmates under the BOP's jurisdiction peaked in FY2013 at approximately 219,000 inmates. The federal prison population has decreased each fiscal year from FY2013 to FY2016. BOP's appropriations increased by nearly $7.149 billion from FY1980 to FY2016, which was the peak of BOP's nominal appropriations. Between FY1980 and FY2016, the average annual increase in BOP's appropriations was approximately $199 million. Its appropriations decreased by $340 million in FY2017. BOP's annual budget is divided between two major accounts: Salaries and Expenses (S&E, i.e., the operating budget) and Buildings and Facilities (B&F, i.e., the capital budget).The nearly continuous increase in BOP's appropriations is in large part driven by a nearly unbroken year-by-year increases in the S&E account. Funding for the S&E account has continued to increase even though the prison population decreased from FY2013 to FY2016. An increasing per capita cost of incarceration might explain why funding for the S&E account has not decreased along with the prison population, but it might also be due to the fact that the prison population has not decreased to a point where BOP can reduce staff and shutter prisons. The nominal per capita cost of incarcerating an inmate in the federal system has increased every fiscal year from FY2000 to FY2016, from approximately $22,000 per inmate to nearly $35,000 per inmate. After adjusting for inflation, the overall cost of incarceration was relatively flat from FY2000 to FY2012, but in recent fiscal years increases in per capita costs have started to outstrip inflation. A comparison of requested and enacted funding for BOP's S&E and B&F accounts shows that Congress has been somewhat more likely to fund the Administration's request for prison construction and less likely to fully fund the Administration's request for operating the federal prison system. From FY1980 to FY2017, appropriations were lower than the Administration's request for the B&F account 16 times while appropriations were lower than the request for the S&E account 24 times. One concern among some policymakers is that BOP's expanding budget is starting to consume a larger share of the Department of Justice's (DOJ's) overall annual appropriations. A review of funding for DOJ and BOP show that since FY1980 both BOP's total budget and the S&E account have, in general, encompassed a growing share of DOJ's annual appropriations.

In: Bureau of Prisons (BOP)
Editor: Melody Kelley
ISBN: 978-1-53615-292-0

Chapter 1

OVERSIGHT OF THE BUREAU OF PRISONS AND INMATE REENTRY*

Committee on Oversight and Government Reform, House of Representatives

Wednesday, December 13, 2017
Washington, D.C.

The committee met, pursuant to call, at 10:05 a.m., in Room 2154, Rayburn House Office Building, Hon. Trey Gowdy [chairman of the committee] presiding.

Present: Representatives Gowdy, Jordan, Amash, Gosar, Massie, Walker, Blum, Russell, Grothman, Hurd, Palmer, Comer, Mitchell, Cummings, Maloney, Norton, Clay, Connolly, Kelly, Lawrence, Watson Coleman, Demings, Krishnamoorthi, Welch, Cartwright, and DeSaulnier.

Chairman GOWDY. Good morning. The committee will come to order.

---

* This is an edited, reformatted and augmented version of Hearing before the Committee on Oversight and Government Reform House of Representatives, One Hundred Fifteenth Congress, First Session, Serial No. 115–95, dated December 13, 2017.

Without objection, the chair is authorized to declare a recess at any time.

I will recognize myself for an opening statement, and then the gentleman from Maryland.

First of all, welcome to our witnesses. Thank you for being here.

A criminal justice system that is both fair and perceived as fair, that is both respected and worthy of being respected, is one of the foundations of our country. Next door, even as we are meeting here, the Deputy Attorney General is appearing before the Judiciary Committee. Last week, the head of the FBI appeared. Two weeks ago, the Attorney General himself appeared at Judiciary.

So while Judiciary does have principal jurisdiction over matters related to our justice system, Chairman Goodlatte and, frankly, Ranking Member Cummings deserve our appreciation and gratitude for recognizing that this issue cuts across several aspects of government, and a hearing in this committee could be and, hopefully, will be constructive as well.

Our justice system must both be fair in reality and perceived as fair. Our justice system must be proportional. It must protect the innocent. It must punish those who have not conformed to societal norms, with those societal norms being reflected and codified in what we call the law.

Fair, even-handed, proportional, just, equal in intent and application, those are expectations. Those expectations are lofty. Some might argue they are aspirational, but I would rather aspire to fairness and fail than set any lower standard.

Part of our justice system includes correction, rehabilitation, and acknowledgment that the vast majority of those who are incarcerated will be out, back in society. So for the benefit of all—society as a whole, those who are likely to come in contact with those former incarcerated folks, and those formerly incarcerated themselves—we must find a common sensical plan rooted in fact and evidence for reentry, for assimilation, for rejoining an ordered community and avoiding the tyranny of recidivism.

It is in all of our interest these reentries be successful. It is in all of our interest these transitions back into society are successful. Those leaving incarceration for reentry into society will often find society has changed.

Anyone reentering society, even after the shortest of absences, will find things have changed dramatically.

Speaker John Boehner was not in prison, although he may have felt like it when he was the Speaker of the House. He recently reentered society after a lifetime of public service. And hearing him tell stories of clicking on the wrong Uber ride and sharing a ride with lots of different people that he did not intend to share the ride with, hearing him tell stories of not being able to find the latch that opens the gas tank on his car because he hadn't driven in years, those may be funny stories because he is a quick learner, and he had people to help. Imagine having to get a job to pay your restitution. Needing clothes for an interview. Needing a ride to an interview. Knowing how to interview. And dreading the whole time when the question comes up of "Have you been arrested or convicted?"

I doubt anyone will ever accuse me of being soft on crime. To the contrary, there would be very few Members of Congress ever who have sent more people to prison. As much as I believe in law and order and respect for the rule of law, we also have a deeply held conviction that paying your debt to society pays the debt.

We are a nation of second chances. We love redemption stories. It would be nice if our criminal justice system produced more of them.

With that, I would yield to my friend from North Carolina. Mr. WALKER. Thank you, Mr. Chairman.

Families are the building blocks of communities. It is hard to imagine anything more disruptive to a family than losing a parent or a spouse to incarceration. To have a loved one removed from your life and sit in a prison must be an overwhelmingly difficult experience for both the inmate and the family.

I can still remember as a young child, being the son of a pastor who was also a prison chaplain, still sitting on the bunks of those inmates, in many cases hearing the sad stories. Now make no mistake, I firmly believe that when people break the law, there must be consequences, and incarceration is oftentimes the appropriate consequence.

However, the justice system and the Bureau of Prisons also have a responsibility to help rehabilitate that person and help the inmate have a successful reentry back into our communities. This makes sense from both a public safety perspective and borne out of compassion for our fellow citizens.

Because what is clear is that virtually all of the inmates in Federal prisons are going back and returning to their communities and their families. When they are released, the question should be asked. Will they be better, or will they be worse?

See, redemption has always been an American ideal. We need former prisoners to integrate back into society, restore stability to their families, and contribute to their communities. Inmate release preparation and programming is essential to developing and restoring hope—hope that they will never return to prison, hope that they will find a job, hope that they will one day be able to support their family, and hope that they will build a good life after prison.

For that reason, rehabilitation and reentry efforts must be real, and they must be effective. Three weeks ago, I spoke in Winston-Salem, North Carolina, at a wonderful nonprofit organization, the Winston-Salem Prison Ministry, doing a great job. But the Bureau of Prisons must also make successful inmate rehabilitation and reentry a priority. The Bureau must also evaluate its programs and reentry decisions so that their effectiveness can be measured based on evidence of success.

We have got to figure out what reentry and rehabilitation strategies work best. Does release to a halfway house improve an inmate's chances at successful entry? Are some halfway houses more effective than others at assisting inmates to succeed? Would placing more inmates directly into home confinement reduce recidivism? Do certain education or life skills tend to lead to more successful inmate recovery?

These are all questions I look forward to discussing today. I believe that evidence-based assessments are essential to determine what programs work, especially those that work well at reducing recidivism and what programs simply do not work very well.

I am grateful for all the witnesses here today. Appreciate your expertise. Reducing recidivism and improving inmate reentry services is a challenge, but it is one we must all be committed to achieving.

With that, Mr. Chairman, I yield back.

Chairman GOWDY. The gentleman from North Carolina yields back.

We will now recognize the gentleman from Maryland, Mr. Cummings.

Mr. CUMMINGS. Thank you very much, Mr. Chairman.

I want to thank you, Chairman Gowdy, for calling today's hearing to discuss the Fair Chance Act and other ways to address barriers faced by formerly incarcerated individuals.

This is a very important hearing to me because I live in a neighborhood where many of these people return, and I see what they go through. While they may spend time in prison, they find that there are so many barriers to their moving forward that they remain in prison in a sense until the day they die.

Congressman Walker, I want to applaud you for what you said and what you do in this area, and you said some very important words. You said whatever we do with regard to these folks, we have to be—it has to be real, and it has to be effective. These are people's lives.

They come home, can't get a job. Can't do anything. And in many instances, not trained to do anything and coming into a world which is not the world they left. So, therefore, this is a critical hearing and the latest in our committee's efforts to examine these questions.

I also appreciate this opportunity to hear from the new Director of the Bureau of Prisons, General Mark Inch, and we welcome you to our committee. Study after study has shown that finding and keeping a job is the single most significant factor for reducing recidivism and for helping formerly incarcerated individuals successfully reenter our society.

I used to run voluntarily a reentry program, and we found that if we could get a person a job and could direct them away from the corners that sent them there, and get them more involved in their families and give them some kind of support group, they were usually successful. Steady and meaningful employment is a proven way to give these people a real second chance and to increase the contributions they make to our communities.

Unfortunately, many people who have paid their debt to society are never given a fair chance at getting a job. You try not having a job for a month or 2 months or 3 months. Try it. And no source of income. Try it. And you got to feed three children. Try it.

And every door that you knock on, people are saying, uh-oh, yes, you may have served your time, but we got to put a bar up. So you can't get past this bar because now you have this record. Many employers automatically screen out these applicants, even those who are highly qualified. These individuals never make it to an interview.

The Fair Chance Act is a bipartisan legislation that I introduced with Representative Darrell Issa to address these challenges in the Federal Government. In the Senate, Senator Cory Booker and Senator Ron Johnson have shown strong bipartisan leadership on this bill, and the Homeland Security and Government Affairs Committee approved the bill earlier this year by voice vote. And again, Mr. Chairman, I thank you for all you have done to try to push this along.

Our bill allows Federal agencies and contractors to ask about criminal histories at the final stages of the hiring process after a conditional offer has been made, rather than automatically screening people out from the beginning. It does not require any agency or contractor to hire anyone if they don't want to, and of course, it includes important exceptions for national security, law enforcement, and positions for which criminal history information is required by law.

Unfortunately, we are not at the forefront of these efforts. We are actually lagging behind. Already 30 States and more than 150 cities and counties have instituted, and I quote, "ban-the-box" policies. These include States ranging from California, Colorado, Connecticut, Kentucky, Indiana, and Utah. That is right, I said Utah.

In addition, companies like Walmart, Koch Industries, Target, Home Depot, Starbucks, Bed, Bath, and Beyond have embraced ban-the-box, as well as the number-one employer in Baltimore, Johns Hopkins University and Hospital, where we have about 30,000 employees. They have made it a part of their mission to address this issue in this way.

I want to thank Glenn Martin for being here today to discuss the proven success of ban-the-box policies. Mr. Martin is a leading advocate for the formerly incarcerated, and he knows firsthand what it is like to face barriers to reentry.

We must also face the reality that our Federal prison system is not doing enough to prepare inmates for reentry. That is very, very important. There is a bipartisan consensus in Congress and among States that we must do more in this area. Recent reports from the Department of Justice Inspector General, the Government Accountability Office, and the Charles Colson Task Force on Federal Corrections have raised alarming concerns about the lack of sufficient services and a failure to track and measure the effectiveness of existing services.

If the system is providing ineffective service in areas such as employment skills training, postsecondary education, healthcare, and substance abuse treatment, Federal inmates will have great difficulty readjusting to life outside prison when they are released.

I am also concerned about the recent reports of closures of Federal residential reentry centers, or halfway houses, and the cutbacks in other transition services, including at a Baltimore location. We need to know more about the reasons for these closures. If the Bureau of Prisons is not tracking data on these services or measuring their effectiveness at reducing recidivism, then it cannot know if its programs are working or if cuts are, indeed, justified.

We cannot do our work effectively and efficiently if information is not available or does not exist. I am heartened that the Bureau agreed to implement many recommendations to improve reentry services and better track their effectiveness. I look forward to hearing from Director Inch, Inspector General Horowitz, and Ms. Maurer about the progress of that implementation.

I also want to thank Cynthia Roseberry for her work on the Colson task force. I am particularly interested in the task force's recommendations to improve BOP oversight, including the creation of a new performance, accountability, and oversight board.

Finally, I am troubled by the decision by the Trump administration earlier this year to reinstitute the use of Federal private prisons. Following a critical Inspector General report documenting numerous health and public safety issues, Deputy Attorney General Sally Yates announced that the Department would end the use of these facilities in August of 2016, but Attorney General Sessions reversed this decision.

Director Inch, I look forward to hearing from you and your views on these topics and your plans for the Federal prison system. I know Chairman Gowdy shares many of these concerns, and I look forward to continuing a productive and open communication to ensure the transparency, the accountability, and the effectiveness of our Federal prisons.

And with that, Mr. Chairman, I will yield back.

Chairman GOWDY. The gentleman from Maryland yields back.

Before I introduce our distinguished panel of witnesses, I do want to acknowledge that there is precedent, and I understand the precedent and I understand the rationale behind it, for some Government witnesses, particularly in the past, have had single panels as opposed to what we have this morning. So I want to thank all of the Government witnesses that in the past may have had a single panel. I do understand the rationale behind it.

What I have fully learned in 7 years of being in Congress is that the Members benefit from single panels. The attendance is better. Therefore, the issue is more fully developed. The issues are more fully developed.

So I want to thank all the witnesses for coming and for allowing the Members to have a single panel, which is infinitely better for the issue.

With that, I will introduce you en banc from my left to right, and then I will administer an oath, and then we will recognize you individually for your opening statement. And to the extent you can, keep it within 5 minutes. Just keep in mind, we have your full opening statement. So nothing you wanted us know will not be known. It will just be communicated in writing, as opposed to orally.

We are fortunate to have the Honorable Mark Inch, Director of the Federal Bureau of Prisons. Equally fortunate to have the Honorable Michael Horowitz, Inspector General for the Department of Justice; Ms. Diana Mauer, Director of Homeland Security and Justice at the Government Accountability Office; Ms. Jennifer Doleac, assistant professor of public policy and economics at University of Virginia's Batten School and the director of Justice Tech Lab; Ms. Cynthia Roseberry, executive director of the Council for Court Excellence; and Mr. Glenn Martin, president and founder of JustLeadershipUSA.

If I could get you to all please stand and raise your right hands, I will administer the oath, as we do for all witnesses.

Do you solemnly swear or affirm that the testimony you are about to give shall be the truth, the whole truth, and nothing but the truth, so help you God?

[Response.]

Chairman GOWDY. May the record reflect the witnesses answered in the affirmative. You may take your seats.

With that, and again, with the reminder that we have a lighting system to help you—green means go, yellow means speed up. Try to get under the light before it turns red.

With that, we would recognize Director Inch.

STATEMENT OF HON. MARK S. INCH

Mr. INCH. Good morning, Chairman Gowdy, Ranking Member Cummings, and members of the committee.

I appreciate the opportunity to appear before you today and to discuss the mission and the operation of the Federal Bureau of Prisons. I am humbled to serve as the agency's ninth director, and I look forward to being part of what the Bureau does for our Nation and for the corrections profession.

I'm also honored to speak on behalf of the nearly 39,000 Bureau staff, corrections professionals who support the agency's law enforcement mission. These dedicated public servants are on the job 24 hours a day, 7 days a week, operating Federal prisons that are safe, cost-effective, and humane.

It is through their hard work and dedication that the Bureau has earned its excellent reputation. This is an agency I have admired for years from the other side of the Potomac.

Chairman Gowdy and Ranking Member Cummings, I want to thank you for your support of the Bureau. Our mission is challenging—protecting the safety of the public, our staff, and inmates, while also providing inmates with skills needed to successfully return to the communities.

Our prisons hold tens of thousands of drug traffickers, many weapons offenders, and other dangerous individuals. We house nearly 23,000 gang-affiliated inmates who pose a threat in and outside our facilities. More than 40 percent of our inmates classify as high and medium security, due in large part to extensive criminal histories, severity of the current offense, and the histories of violence. Yet and still, our staff answer the call to duty every day.

I also wish to thank the Office of the Inspector General in the Government Accountability Office for their hard work. Their audits, along with the Bureau's own internal auditing process and the regular accreditation audits by the American Correctional Association, are critical to ensuring that we remain focused on performing corrections to nationally recognized standards.

I come to the Bureau with a great appreciation for our mission. I have a well-developed set of principles about our individual responsibilities as corrections professionals. I applaud the Bureau's philosophy that all staff are correctional workers first. I am convinced that this philosophy is a critical element in the long-term effectiveness and success of the agency.

One of the things I love about the corrections profession is the selfless service demonstrated by those who choose this career. They dedicate their lives to helping and protecting others, yet receive little recognition and even less praise. Every day, Bureau staff run into situations from which others would run away so that they can ensure the safety of the public, the staff, and the inmates for whom they are responsible.

As the leader of the country's premier department of corrections, I am committed to ensuring the Bureau of Prisons staff exhibit the highest ideals of our corrections profession through the shared values, established standards of individual and institutional performance, and commitment to the character and competence of our profession. And we've put those qualities to the service of our stakeholders, the public, victims, and inmates.

I've spent these first 90 days on the job learning as much as possible about the Bureau. Although I'm not new to the corrections profession, I am impressed that all of the prisons I now oversee today are accredited by the American Correctional Association, as were the prisons I oversaw in the military. And all of our prisons are PREA compliant as well.

I've already begun reviewing our major policies and procedures, and I'm poised to start identifying both strengths and weaknesses. My initial focus is on public safety and inmate reentry and also overall agency efficiency and effectiveness. The thorough work by and of the OIG and the GAO is certainly an important guidepost to me in this process.

The Bureau looks forward to continuing to support the law enforcement efforts of the Department of Justice and the administration and fulfilling our critical role in the broader public safety efforts of the Federal, State, and local law enforcement professionals.

Chairman Gowdy, Ranking Member Cummings, and members of the committee, this concludes my formal statement. I'd be happy to answer any questions you may have.

[Prepared statement of Mr. Inch follows:]

Statement of Mark S. Inch Director, Federal Bureau of Prisons, U.S. Department of Justice, Committee on Oversight and Government Reform, U.S. House of Representatives, December 13, 2017

Good morning, Chairman Gowdy, Ranking Member Cummings, and Members of the Committee. I appreciate the opportunity to appear before you today to discuss the mission and operation of the Federal Bureau of Prisons (Bureau). I was sworn in as the Bureau's ninth Director just three months ago, and I am honored to speak on behalf of all Bureau staff-corrections professionals who support the agency's law enforcement mission. I have spent my first 90 days on the job learning as much as possible about the agency, and I am committed to reviewing all of our major policies and procedures to identify both strengths and weaknesses. I am compiling prioritized lists of areas for improvement with respect to public safety and inmate reentry and also overall agency efficiency and effectiveness.

To that end, I wish to thank the Office of the Inspector General (OIG) and the Government Accountability Office (GAO) for their hard work. Their audits on a variety of program areas, supported by the Bureau's own internal auditing process, are critical to ensuring that we remain focused on adhering to the highest standards for safety of staff, inmates, and the public. These audits will provide an important guidepost to me as I undertake my review of Bureau systems and operations.

As the leader of the country's premier department of corrections, I am committed to ensuring that Bureau staff are guided by the fundamental principles of Character, Competence, Commitment and Courage. And we put those qualities into the service of our stakeholders: the public; victims; and inmates.

Our staff carry out the agency's mission by running into situations from which others run away. Their first thought when breaking up inmate fights is the safety of others, not themselves. When a body alarm sounds, they rush to the side of their colleague. They perform CPR for inmates in distress, hoping to make the critical difference that saves a life. And as we saw over the past few months, our staff respond to crises brought on by weather and flooding, volunteering both in our institutions and in those affected communities. The work our staff do is truly inspiring. And they are quiet heroes–most people don't think about what goes on behind the walls and fences of prisons until something terrible happens to make them consider our worth.

Our Mission - A History of Public Safety and Reentry

The Bureau is the Nation's largest correctional agency; we house approximately 185,000 inmates in 122 federal prisons, 11 private prisons, and more than 200 community-based facilities nationwide. Incarceration of criminals is a valuable crime-reduction strategy and an important law enforcement tool that holds individuals responsible for their actions and deters others from committing similar crimes. As the committee recognizes, it is imperative that we effectively reintegrate individuals back into the community following release from prison to reduce the likelihood of future criminal behavior and associated victimization. To that end, the mission of the Bureau, which dates back to 1930, is to confine offenders in prisons and community-based facilities that are safe, humane, cost-efficient, and secure, and to assist inmates in becoming law- abiding citizens when they return to our communities.

The Bureau has had great success with respect to both parts of our mission: we have low rates of assaults, disturbances, and escapes, and our recidivism rate is half the states' average.[1]

These results are a testament to the hard work of our dedicated professional staff who support public safety and promote reentry.

Our Population

During the first five decades of the Bureau's existence, the number and type of inmates we housed remained fairly stable. Beginning in the 1980s, however, federal law enforcement efforts and legislative changes led to a significant increase in the federal prison population; the Bureau inmate population doubled in the 1980s and doubled again in the 1990s. Between 1980 and 2013 the population grew by approximately 800%, topping out at nearly 220,000. Despite our reliance on private corrections to house

[1] In 2016, the U.S. Sentencing Commission found that only 34% of the inmates released from the Bureau of Prisons in 2005 were re-arrested or had their supervision revoked over a three-year period.

thousands of low security criminal aliens, crowding in federal prisons reached 36% in 2013, and our inmate to staff ratio stretched to 5:1, up from historic levels of 3:1.

Over the past few years the inmate population has decreased significantly, such that today our crowding and staffing levels are much more manageable. But, we continue to face challenges that threaten the safety and security of our institutions and the community, including synthetic drugs, contraband cell phones, drones, and gang influence and activity, to name a few.

Almost half of the Bureau's inmate population is serving sentences for drug offenses, nearly 20% are convicted of weapons offenses, almost 10% are sex offenses and slightly fewer are immigration offenses. Violent offenders and property offenders, including white collar offenders, make up the balance. Sentence length varies greatly by offense type, but the overall average is 131 months-more than ten years, with half the inmates serving more than 105 months. The particular offense for which inmates are sentenced is of less importance to us in corrections than other factors such as gang affiliation, criminal history, propensity for violence and other serious misconduct, etc. More than 40% of our inmates classify as high and medium security, requiring close staff supervision and myriad safety and security precautions. We have nearly 23,000 gang-affiliated inmates.

Our Programs - Reentry Begins on Day One

Reentry is a critical component of public safety. Public safety is enhanced when individuals leaving prisons have job training, treatment for mental illness and/or substance use disorder, an education, and a general understanding of what it means to be a productive law abiding citizen. The Bureau must help the nearly 44,000 inmates who are released back into our communities each year to not repeat their past mistakes.

The Bureau uses an individualized risk assessment process to develop a reentry plan for each inmate to ensure the inmate participates in appropriate programs and treatment, in the appropriate order, during the term of incarceration. Institution staff reassess inmates every six months to determine if the individuals are making progress consistent with the plan or whether adjustments are needed. We recently completed and deployed a fully integrated online information system Insight - to record these ongoing, multidisciplinary reviews of each inmate. Insight allows for establishment of goals and monitoring progress towards these goals through user-friendly reports provided to the inmates as well as staff. Final reports regarding inmates' reentry efforts while in prison are provided to our criminal justice system partners, including United States Probation Officers and Residential Reentry Center (RRC) providers. This system has been implemented in 55 institutions thus far, and we anticipate rolling it out nationwide by late spring, 2018.

Bureau inmate programs include work, education (including literacy), vocational training, substance use disorder treatment, psychological services and counseling, observance of faith and religion, and other programs that impart essential life skills. Federal Prison Industries (FPI), Residential Drug Abuse Programming (RDAP), education, and vocational and occupational training, are particularly effective in reducing recidivism. Inmates who participate in FPI are 24 percent less likely to recidivate than similar non-participating inmates; they are also significantly less likely to engage in misconduct while in prison. FPI provides the greatest benefit to minorities, who are often at the greatest statistical risk for recidivism. Inmates who participate in vocational or occupational training are 33 percent less likely to recidivate, and inmates who participate in education programs are 16 percent less likely to recidivate. RDAP participants are 16 percent less likely to recidivate and 15 percent less likely to have a relapse in their substance use disorder within three years after release. These programs are a critical part of the Bureau of Prisons mission to keep our communities safe.

Our Goal-Effective Transition to the Community

The Bureau relies on RRCs (also known as halfway houses), and home confinement to assist inmates reintegrate into their home communities just prior to completing their prison terms. RRCs provide inmates (referred to as "residents") with a structured, supervised environment, and assistance in finding employment and housing, completing necessary programming (e.g., community based treatment services), participating in counseling, and strengthening ties to family and friends. Many inmates who transfer to RRCs spend the final few weeks of their term of imprisonment in home confinement, to which inmates may be assigned for the last 10% of their sentence, not to exceed 6 months.[2] These inmates reside in their homes but are subject to strict schedules, curfews, in-person check-ins, telephonic monitoring, and sometimes electronic monitoring.

RRC placement decisions are individualized and based on each inmate's need for reentry services. For example, inmates serving long sentences and/or having limited employment skills, little family support, no established home to which they can return, and limited financial resources have a much greater need for RRC placement than do inmates serving short sentences and those having positive family support, a home, and job skills.

RRC bed space is limited so we are judicious with our use of this resource. We balance the available capacity with the needs of releasing inmates so that all appropriate inmates have the opportunity to participate in the program. Maximizing the length of RRC placement for low-risk offenders, as some have recommended, would quickly absorb RRC capacity, thereby preventing high risk releasing inmates from having access to some period of pre-release transition through this program. Despite our continued efforts to seek additional RRC capacity in new and existing locations, there remains strong community resistance to RRCs and few vendors compete for such solicitations.

---

[2] Title 18 United States Code Section 3624(c)(2).

Our Challenges

The Bureau has little control over the number of offenders in our population. We have no role in determining which offenders are prosecuted, which offenders are convicted, and which offenders are sentenced to prison. Moreover, the Bureau has no role in determining the length of sentence imposed and only very limited impact on the amount of time served. We are responsible for ensuring that the term of imprisonment is served in facilities that are safe, secure and humane, and that offenders are provided ample opportunities for self-improvement.

The Bureau houses significant numbers of very dangerous and disruptive inmates who engage in disruptive and dangerous misconduct, including assaultive behavior toward staff and other inmates. We have had success·in managing these individuals through a variety of means, including our Special Management Unit (SMU), where disruptive inmates are removed from the general population and provided programs designed to prepare them to return to an open prison population.

As I noted previously, we have approximately 23,000 inmates affiliated with gangs in our institutions. Management of these groups requires a lot of attention and resources. Over the past few years we created institutions exclusive for inmates who have dropped out of gangs, or are in "bad standing" with gangs, or who have never had a gang affiliation. Many of the drops outs have provided valuable assistance to law enforcement in disrupting gang-related criminal activity in the community and even solving some big "cold cases." We now have seven such facilities for medium and high security inmates at various geographic locations across the country.

We house several hundred international and domestic terrorists in our institutions. While the Bureau has always held some terrorists, after 9/ll the number of these inmates increased substantially. The Bureau works closely with the National Joint Terrorism Task Force, the Federal Bureau of Investigation, and other law enforcement partners to ensure we are doing everything possible to limit opportunities for inmates to be radicalized in our institution. We remain vigilant of security risks this population may potentially pose to our prisons and our Nation.

The Bureau continues to face threats posed by dangerous contraband and their methods of introduction into our institutions; cellular phones, illicit narcotics (including the emerging threat of synthetic drugs), and drones remain chief among those. The Bureau is working closely with the Department of Justice's Unmarmed Aircraft System (UAS) Workgroup on strategies to detect and mitigate drones that pose a security threat. We have deployed new contraband-detecting technologies, including thermal fences, walk-through metal detectors, and whole-body imaging devices, and have piloted wireless interdiction technologies that show promise for countering the contraband cell phone threat. And we have plans to conduct a test of micro jamming technology later this winter. Synthetic drugs, such as fentanyl and fentanyl analogues, MDMA (ecstasy), K2 (Spice) and bath salts, are introduced into our prisons through various means, such as the mail, where they are very difficult to detect. The Bureau is leading a work group in collaboration with the U.S. Department of Homeland Security, the Postal Inspection Service, and national testing laboratories to test new security technologies to address this problem.

Inmate health care remains a challenge for us. With increasing numbers of older inmates in our institutions, many of whom have complicated and chronic medical needs, we face rising costs of health care and pharmaceuticals. At the same time, recruitment and retention of qualified medical professionals to staff our prisons - many of which are somewhat remotely located is hampered by incentives offered by the private sector. The Public Health Service is a strong partner with us, helping to fill critical positions, but shortfalls remain. Based in part on the important work conducted by the OIG and GAO, we are pursuing opportunities to develop a data analytics strategy to improve executive health care decision-making and thereby improve health and financial outcomes.

Inmates with serious mental illness pose particular difficulties in prison. We now have two secure mental health units for individuals who have a history of violent behavior and suffer from serious mental health issues - one in Atlanta, Georgia and the second in Allenwood, Pennsylvania. These units allow us to safely provide treatment and avoid placing individuals in restrictive housing, with the goal of facilitating their return to general population in prison and ultimately to their community, following completion of their prison term.

Finally, we now have three Reintegration Housing Units to allow greater opportunities for inmates who request protective custody. We are finalizing a new policy regarding these units to ensure we provide treatment and programming aimed at preparing inmates to leave these units and enter general population at another institution.

Conclusion

I look forward to continuing to support the law enforcement efforts of the Department of Justice. Chairman Gowdy, Ranking Member Cummings, and Members of the Committee, this concludes my formal statement. I appreciate the opportunity to provide the Committee with my formal statement, and would be happy to answer any questions.

Chairman GOWDY. Thank you, Director.

Inspector General Horowitz?

STATEMENT OF HON. MICHAEL E. HOROWITZ

Mr. HOROWITZ. Thank you, Mr. Chairman, Ranking Member Cummings, members of the committee. Thank you for inviting me to testify at today's important hearing.

The BOP is the largest Department of Justice component by number of employees, even larger than the FBI, and has the second-largest budget at the DOJ. Moreover, it now consumes 25 percent of the Department of Justice's budget compared to 18 percent 20 years ago. Yet despite the budget growth, the Federal prison system remains over capacity, particularly at its high-security institutions.

Given the BOP's size and its critically important responsibilities, the OIG has conducted and continues to conduct substantial over-sight of the BOP and its programs. For example, we've recently issued reviews and audits of the BOP's management of its aging inmate population, the monitoring of Federal contract prisons, efforts to interdict contraband, implementation of the Prison Rape Elimination Act, efforts to address the increasing costs of Federal inmate healthcare, use of the compassionate release program, and management of Federal Prison Industries, just to name a few. And throughout our work, the BOP has taken our reports seriously and has been responsive to our findings.

Let me briefly discuss our oversight of BOP programs that are intended to prepare inmates for release from prison and back into the community. Whatever one's view is of the Federal sentencing laws, whether you think they're fair, too harsh, or too lenient, there should be agreement that it is critical for the BOP to have effective programs for transitioning Federal inmates back into society.

The reality is that once an inmate completes their sentence, absent unusual or unique circumstances, the BOP must release that person from prison so they can return to our communities. That's true whether—whether they've committed a violent crime or a white collar crime, whether they were sentenced to a long prison sentence or a short prison sentence, and whether they acted dangerously in jail or received good time credit.

The need for effective transition and reentry programs is demonstrated by a recent U.S. Sentencing Commission report, which determined that nearly half of the Federal inmates released in 2005 were rearrested within 8 years of their release for committing a new crime or for violating their supervising conditions—their supervision conditions.

The OIG has conducted several reviews that identify ways the BOP can improve the management and administration of its reentry programs. The OIG's recent review of the BOP's release preparation program found significant deficiencies that the BOP needed to address and which the BOP has told us since our report that it has, in fact, undertaken.

Another BOP reentry program involves the placement of inmates in residential reentry centers, RRCs, also known as halfway houses, and in home confinement while serving the remainder of their sentence. Pursuant to the Second Chance Act, all Federal inmates are eligible for RRC and home confinement placement. RRCs provide a supervised environment that supports inmates in finding employment and housing; completing necessary programming, such as drug abuse treatment; participating in counseling; and strengthening ties to family, friends, and community.

The BOP spends about $360 million each year on RRCs and home confinement costs, yet a recent OIG review found significant issues with how the BOP was managing its RRC program. Once again, the BOP has been responsive to the recommendations we made and has reported to us on the steps it is currently taking to address them.

Another area where we recently reviewed—that we recently reviewed involved BOP's management of inmates with mental health issues. Our review identified several issues of concern, including that BOP mental health staff did not always document inmates' mental health disorders, and therefore, the BOP was unable to accurately determine the number of inmates with mental health issues.

In addition, we were concerned that BOP was using restrictive housing to house inmates with mental health conditions because those—that housing could negatively impact further their mental health treatment and, research shows, come out of those units further disabled and further ill-equipped to return to their communities.

We also were concerned because we identified several instances where the BOP released inmates directly from restrictive housing units into communities, and we were particularly concerned about that.

Again, the BOP is responding to our recommendations, and we look forward to reviewing them as we hear about them.

That concludes my prepared statement. I'd be happy to answer any questions the committee may have.

[Prepared statement of Mr. Horowitz follows:]

Statement of Michael E. Horowitz, Inspector General, U.S. Department of Justice, Before the U.S. House of Representatives, Committee on Oversight and Government Reform, Concerning "Oversight of the Bureau of Prisons and Inmate Reentry," December 13, 2017

Mr. Chairman, Ranking Member Cummings, and Members of the Committee:

Thank you for inviting me to testify at today's hearing examining the Office of the Inspector General's (OIG) oversight of the Federal Bureau of Prisons (BOP), including the BOP's policies and programs to help incarcerated inmates successfully transition back into society. The BOP is the largest Department of Justice (DOJ) component by number of employees, with over 37,000 staff. And its fiscal year (FY) 2017 budget of $7.1billion is the second largest budget of any DOJ component, after only the Federal Bureau of Investigation. Indeed, the BOP's budget has grown substantially over the past 20 years, from approximately $3.2 billion in FY 1997 to about $7.1billion in FY 2017, and it now consumes a significant percentage of the DOJ's budget, having increased from 18 percent of the DOJ's budget in FY 1997 to 25 percent of the DOJ's budget in FY 2017. Yet, despite this budget growth, the federal prison system remains over capacity: overall, it was 14 percent above its rated capacity at the end of FY 2017, with high security institutions operating at 25 percent over rated capacity. While these over-capacity figures have decreased significantly since 2013, when the BOP's population peaked at just under 220,000 inmates (its current population is about 184,000 inmates), the BOP is estimating that its inmate population will increase by about 2 percent in FY 2018.

Given this size and growth, it is particularly important that the OIG conduct effective oversight of the BOP and its programs, which we have done and continue to do. For example, we have issued reviews and audits of the BOP's management of its aging inmate population, monitoring of federal contract prisons, efforts to interdict contraband, implementation of the Prison Rape Elimination Act, efforts to address the increasing costs of inmate healthcare, use of the compassionate release program, and management of Federal Prison Industries, just to name a few. All of these reports and others concerning the BOP can be found on our website.

Complementing the OIG's oversight of the BOP through our audits and reviews are the OIG's investigations of criminal and administrative allegations involving BOP staff and contractors. From FY 2013 to FY 2017, the OIG's Investigations Division opened more than 1,000 cases involving BOP staff or contractors, made more than 340 arrests, had more than 280 convictions and pre- trial diversions, and investigated allegations that resulted in more than 700 administrative actions. Through these efforts, the OIG enhances the safety and security of the over 38,000 BOP staff who perform their jobs with great skill and who help keep their institutions and the community safe.

Let me turn to recent OIG reviews of BOP programs that affect the BOP's efforts to prepare inmates for release from prison and back into the community. Whatever one's view is of the federal sentencing laws - whether you think they are fair, too harsh, or too lenient - there should be agreement that it is critical for the BOP to have effective programs for transitioning federal inmates back into society. Every federal inmate, other than those who received a life sentence (which is rare for federal inmates), will be released from prison to return to their communities upon the expiration of the judge's sentence. That is true whether they received a short prison sentence or a long prison sentence, whether they committed a violent crime or a white collar crime, whether they were in a maximum security prison or a federal prison camp, and whether they acted dangerously in jail or received good time credit. From 2013 to 2015, the BOP released approximately 125,000 inmates from its custody into Residential Reentry Centers (RRC), into home confinement, or directly into communities in the United States. The need for effective BOP transition and reentry programs that reduce recidivism rates is demonstrated by a recent report from the U.S. Sentencing Commission which determined that nearly half of the federal inmates released in 2005 were re-arrested within 8 years of their release for committing a new crime or for violating their supervision conditions.

BOP Reentry Programs

The OIG has conducted several reviews that identify ways the BOP can improve the management and administration of its reentry programs.

Every BOP institution offers, and most inmates are required to participate in, a Release Preparation Program (RPP), which includes courses for inmates in the categories of health and nutrition, employment, personal finance and consumer skills, information and community resources, release requirements and procedures, and personal growth and development. At the time of our review, the BOP's objectives for the RPP were to enhance inmates' successful reintegration into the community through RPP participation; to enter into partnerships with various groups to provide information, programs, and services to releasing inmates; and to reduce inmate recidivism. However, we found that less than a third of the inmates required to participate in the RPP actually completed the entire program. Moreover, we determined that because of inconsistencies in the content and quality of RPP courses, the BOP could not ensure that all inmates received the information they needed to successfully transition back into the community. In addition, we found that the BOP did not ensure that RPPs across its institutions met inmate needs. The BOP also did not adequately leverage its relationships with other federal agencies to enhance RPP efforts. Further, the BOP did not measure the effect of the RPP on recidivism, which limited our ability to assess the program's overall effectiveness. The OIG made seven recommendations to help improve the implementation of the RPP, and all but one of those recommendations remain open. The OIG report can be found at the following link: https://oig.justice.gov/reports/2016/e1607.pdf.

Another reentry program facilitated by the BOP is the placement of inmates in RRCs, also known as halfway houses, and in home confinement while serving the remainder of their sentences. Pursuant to the Second Chance Act of 2007, all federal inmates are eligible for RRC and home confinement placement. RRCs provide a supervised environment that supports inmates in finding employment and housing; completing necessary programming, such as drug abuse treatment; participating in counseling; and strengthening ties to family and friends. Home confinement provides similar opportunities, but is used for inmates BOP believes do not need the structure or level of supervision provided by RRCs. In FY 2015, the BOP spent $360 million on RRCs and home confinement costs and reported having 181 RRCs operated by 103 different contractors as of September 2016.

The BOP's RRC and home confinement placement decisions are supposed to be driven by an individual assessment weighing an inmate's need for reentry services against the risk to the community. However, our review found that contrary to BOP policy, guidance, and relevant research, the BOP's placement decisions were not based on inmates' risk for recidivism or need for transitional services. Rather, the BOP was placing the great majority of eligible inmates into RRCs regardless of whether they needed transitional services, unless the inmate was deemed not suitable for such placement because the inmate posed a significant threat to the community. As a result, high-risk inmates with a high need for transitional services were less likely to be placed in an RRC or home confinement, and were correspondingly more likely to be released back into society directly from BOP institutions without transitional programming. Moreover, low-risk, low-need inmates were being placed in RRCs even though BOP guidance, as well as the research cited in the guidance, indicates that low-risk inmates do not benefit from and may in fact be harmed by RRC placement because of, among other things, their exposure to high-risk offenders in those facilities. We also found that the BOP was underutilizing direct home confinement placement as an alternative to RRCs for low-risk, low-need inmates, which results in fewer RRC resources being available for high-risk, high-need inmates.

Further, the BOP did not have performance measures that evaluated the efficacy of its RRC and home confinement programming, or procedures that adequately assessed the quality of services provided by RRC contractors. Moreover, the relevant, albeit dated BOP recidivism and RRC research generally found that RRCs did not appear to have a significant impact on recidivism, although RRC placement generally was found to be beneficial for high-risk offenders and to facilitate an inmate's transition back into society. The OIG made five recommendations to improve the BOP's management of this program, and two remain open.

BOP's Handling of Prisoners with Mental Illness

An important part of BOP's responsibilities is to ensure that inmates with mental illness receive the necessary treatment. One of several important reasons for doing so is because those inmates will eventually be released back into their communities. A recent OIG review concerning the BOP's use of restrictive housing for inmates with mental illness identified several issues of concern, including that BOP mental health staff did not always document inmates' mental disorders and therefore the BOP was unable to accurately determine the number of inmates with mental illness. We also found that while the BOP has taken a number of steps to address the mental health concerns for inmates in restrictive housing, significant issues remain regarding the adequacy of the BOP's policies and its implementation efforts.

In addition, we are concerned that confining inmates with mental illness in restrictive housing units (RHUs) could have a negative impact on mental health of the inmates and inhibit their ability to successfully reintegrate into society. Research shows that time spent in solitary confinement contributes to elevated rates of recidivism and that many inmates released into the community from RHUs, which can be functionally equivalent to solitary confinement, come out of these units disabled and ill-equipped to reintegrate into the community. Of note, in a sample of 239 inmates with mental illness housed in Special Management Units (SMU), which are a form of RHU, we found that 31 inmates (13 percent) were released directly into the community from the SMU. We also found that, on average, these 31 inmates had spent nearly 29 months in the SMU prior to their release.

The OIG made 15 recommendations to the BOP to improve its screening, treatment, and monitoring of inmates with mental illness who are assigned to restrictive housing, and all but one of the recommendations are open.

Conclusion

The OIG will continue to conduct oversight of the BOP's programs in order to help them improve their effectiveness and efficiency, and investigate allegations of misconduct by BOP employees or contractors to ensure a safe and secure prison environment. This concludes my prepared statement, and I am pleased to answer any questions the Committee may have.

Chairman GOWDY. Thank you, Mr. Inspector General. Ms. Mauer?

STATEMENT OF DIANA MAURER

Ms. MAUER. Well, good morning, Chairman Gowdy and Ranking Member Cummings and other Members and staff. I'm pleased to be here today to discuss the findings from our oversight efforts of offender reentry programs at the Bureau of Prisons.

Every year, thousands of Federal inmates complete their sentences, leave prison, and reenter society. The hope is they will reunite with family, become employed, and rejoin their community as a peaceful, law-abiding member. And preparing people for this re-entry is one of the main goals of the Federal correctional system.

It's also one of the most difficult to accomplish. And as was already mentioned, one recent study found that nearly half of former Federal inmates were rearrested within 8 years of release, and about a quarter were reincarcerated.

Now people who have served time in Federal prison face significant challenges. They often have less education, less employment history, and less family support than the rest of society. They also have to contend with various penalties and disadvantages after completing their sentences. And as we reported in September, these collateral consequences can limit many aspects of a person's life, such as employment, education, housing, and access to Government benefits.

Our analysis found 641 Federal collateral consequences that can be triggered by a Federal nonviolent drug conviction. Over three-quarters of these consequences last a lifetime, and 80 percent lack a prescribed way for a person to obtain relief from the consequence.

Now, of course, GAO is not taking a position on whether we have the right number of collateral consequences. That's—that's not our role. But we did interview 14 stakeholders from across the criminal justice spectrum, including judges, prosecutors, and victims' rights advocates. And we heard a striking consensus. Thirteen of 14 agreed on two key points.

First, they believe the Federal Government should take action to mitigate collateral consequences and, second, doing so could reduce the likelihood that people with prior convictions reoffend. They also agreed that any review of collateral consequences should factor in the paramount goal of public safety. Many of the stakeholders we spoke to believe that reexamining the current mix of consequences, their duration, and the ability to seek relief could have a positive impact on recidivism.

And breaking the cycle of recidivism is what successful reentry programs are all about. Over the past several years, we've seen increased focus on reentry at BOP. For example, BOP created a Reentry Services Division and developed a list of reentry programs.

However, when we looked at that list, we found that BOP could not clearly demonstrate whether the reentry programs were actually working. And in response to our recommendation, BOP has developed and begun implementing a plan to evaluate these programs.

BOP has also made great strides determining the cost of home confinement. BOP used to charge a flat rate that was simply half the cost of local reentry—residential reentry centers, or RRCs. But in response to our recommendation, BOP has issued 184 solicitations with a separate service line-item for home confinement services. As a result, BOP is now better positioned to weigh the cost and benefits of home confinement.

But they still need to take action on two of our recommendations that really get to the very heart of this morning's hearing. Two years ago, we found something all too common in Federal programs. BOP was tracking program outputs, not outcomes. Specifically, they had detailed data on the number of inmates in RRCs and home confinement, but BOP was not tracking the far more important outcomes from placing people in RRCs and home confinement, and it lacked measures to know how—to know whether those outcomes indicated success. So it's still unclear how these programs affect recidivism.

BOP has recently made progress implementing our recommendations. They started taking track—steps to track how individuals do during and after their time in an RRC, including surveying residents to get their perspectives on their experiences. While these are encouraging steps, they're still in the early stages, and we'll be monitoring BOP's progress until they fully implement our recommendations.

In conclusion, we all hope the thousands of people who leave Federal prison every year are able to rejoin their families and gainfully contribute to their communities as law-abiding citizens. Continued attention and focus from the Bureau of Prisons, continued congressional oversight, and full implementation of recommendations from GAO and the Inspector General will help make that more likely.

Mr. Chairman, thank you for the opportunity to testify this morning. I look forward to your questions.

[Prepared statement of Ms. Mauer follows:]

United States Government Accountability Office

Testimony before the Committee on

Oversight and Government Reform, House of Representatives

DEPARTMENT OF JUSTICE: CONTINUED ACTION NEEDED TO ADDRESS INCARCERATION CHALLENGES AND OFFENDERS' REENTRY

Statement of Diana Maurer, Director, Homeland Security and Justice

Why GAO Did This Study

BOP's rising costs and offender recidivism present incarceration challenges to both DOJ and the nation. For example, BOP's operating costs have generally increased over time, and in fiscal year 2017 amounted to more than $6.9 billion, or 24 percent of DOJ's total discretionary budget. In addition, from 1980 through 2013, BOP's prison population increased by almost 800 percent, from 24,640 to 219,298. While the prison population began to decline in 2013, DOJ has continued to identify prison crowding as a critical issue. GAO has examined a number of DOJ efforts to slow the growth of the prison population and to reduce recidivism through the use of reentry programs to help offenders successfully return to the community.

This statement summarizes findings and recommendations from recent GAO reports that address (1) DOJ's incarceration reduction initiatives, and (2) BOP reentry programs.

This statements is based on prior GAO products issued from February 2012 through June 2016, along with updates on the status of recommendations obtained as of December 2017. For the updates on DOJ's progress in implementing recommendations, GAO analyzed information provided by DOJ officials on actions taken and planned.

What GAO Recommends

GAO has made 10 recommendations to DOJ in prior reports to help improve performance measurement and resource management. DOJ generally concurred and has addressed or taken steps to address several. GAO continues to believe all of these recommendations should be fully implemented.

What GAO Found

The Department of Justice (DOJ) Has Fully Addressed Two of Six GAO Recommendations Related to Its Incarceration Reduction Initiatives

In June 2015 and June 2016, GAO reported that to help address challenges associated with incarceration, DOJ had, among other things, taken steps to reduce the prison population by pursuing initiatives to use alternatives to incarceration for low-level nonviolent crimes. GAO made six recommendations to DOJ related to these efforts. As of December 2017, DOJ has implemented two of the six recommendations and has not fully addressed the remaining four. Specifically, to enhance efforts to measure program outcomes, OOJ issued guidance on proper data entry and began tracking data on different types of pretrial diversion programs that allow certain offenders to avoid incarceration if they satisfy program requirements. In addition, as of December 2017, DOJ has taken steps to partially implement GAO's recommendation to address unnecessary delays in reviewing inmates' petitions to commute their sentences.

DOJ has not taken action to address recommendations to better assess the results of pretrial diversion programs or another effort to prioritize prosecutions and reform sentencing to eliminate unfair disparities, among other goals. Further, in December 2017, DOJ noted there had been policy changes since GAO made a recommendation related to enhancing measures to monitor prioritizing prosecution and sentencing reform. Although DOJ reported taking some actions to implement GAO's recommendation, these actions did not include establishing measures that incorporate key elements of successful performance measurement systems.

DOJ Has Addressed Two of Four GAO Recommendations Related to Its Reentry Programs

As part of its mission to protect public safety, DOJ's Federal Bureau of Prisons (BOP) provides reentry programming that aims to facilitate offenders' successful return to the community and reduce recidivism (a return to prison or criminal behavior). These reentry efforts include programs offered in BOP facilities as well as contractor-managed residential reentry centers (RRC)- also known as halfway houses-and home confinement services that allow inmates to serve the final months of their sentences in the community. GAO issued three reports in February 2012, June 2015, and June 2016 and made four recommendations to BOP in this area.

As of December 2017, DOJ has implemented two of the four recommendations and has begun to take action to address one of the remaining two. Specifically, to implement one of GAO's recommendations, DOJ established a plan to evaluate the effectiveness of all the 18 reentry programs it offers to inmates in BOP facilities. To implement another GAO recommendation to improve cost management, DOJ began requiring contractors to submit separate prices for RRC beds and home confinement services. As of December2017, DOJ noted it has taken initial steps to address a recommendation to track outcome data for its RRC and home confinement programs; however, it has not taken action to develop measures to assess the performance of these programs.

Chairman Gowdy, Ranking Member Cummings, and Members of the Committee:

I appreciate the opportunity to participate in today's hearing to discuss our prior work on ways in which the Department of Justice (DOJ) can better assess incarceration reduction initiatives and reentry efforts. This statement reflects prior GAO products issued from February 2012 through June 2016, along with recent updates on the status of our recommendations.

As of December 2017, DOJ's Federal Bureau of Prisons (BOP) was responsible for about 184,000 federal inmates and operating 122 institutions (prisons) across the country. BOP's rising costs and offender recidivism present incarceration challenges to both DOJ and the nation. For example, BOP's operating costs have generally increased over time, and in fiscal year 2017 amounted to more than $6.9 billion, or 24 percent of DOJ's total discretionary budget In addition, from 1980 through 2013, BOP's prison population increased by almost 800 percent, from 24,640 to 219,298. While the prison population began to decline in 2013, DOJ has continued to identify prison crowding as a critical issue, particularly in high security institutions. Further, while BOP reports that recidivism rates have declined over the past two decades, the U.S. Sentencing Commission found that of federal offenders released in 2005, 49 percent were rearrested, 32 percent were reconvicted, and 25 percent were reincarcerated during the eight year follow-up period.[3]

During the course of our prior work, DOJ was taking steps to slow the growth of the federal prison population by pursuing alternatives to incarceration at various stages of the criminal justice process for nonviolent, low-level offenders, in part to help reduce the size and related costs of the federal prison population.[4] Knowing the outcomes of these efforts can help BOP adjust its policies and procedures, and ultimately optimize their benefits.

My testimony today is based on our work examining DOJ's efforts to manage the federal prison system. This statement addresses two key areas in which we have issued reports and highlights our recommendations to DOJ to enhance program performance measurement and resource management. Specifically, this statement addresses (1) DOJ: incarceration reduction initiatives and (2) BOP's reentry programs.

This statement is based on several reports we issued from February 2012 through June 2016, and includes updates on selected aspects of these reports as of December 2017.[5] For our prior work, we reviewed relevant

---

[3] United States Sentencing Commission, *Recidivism Among Federal Offenders.- A Comprehensive Overview* (Washington, D.C.: March 2016).

[4] Low level offenses include offenses below thresholds established for specific offenses, such as fraud-related offenses under a certain amount of money and drug offenses that did not involve violence, firearms, or large scale trafficking conspiracies.

[5] GAO, *Federal Prison System: Justice Has Used Alternatives to Incarceration, But Could Better Measure Program Outcomes,* GA0-16-516 (Washington, D.C.: June 23, 2016); *Federal Prison System: Justice Could Better Measure Progress Addressing Incarceration*

laws and DOJ and BOP policies, and analyzed documentation and data on the use of incarceration alternatives at or before sentencing. In addition, we interviewed DOJ and BOP headquarters and district officials, and conducted site visits to selected BOP institutions (which were chosen to cover a range of characteristics, including but not limited to inmate gender and presence of relevant BOP programs). More information about the scope and methodology of our prior work can be found in those reports.

To update the status of DOJ's efforts to address the recommendations we made in these reports, we collected and analyzed information from DOJ and BOP program officials on actions they have taken or planned in response. We conducted our work in accordance with generally accepted government auditing standards. Those standards require that we plan and perform the audit to obtain sufficient, appropriate evidence to provide a reasonable basis for our findings and conclusions based on our audit objectives. We believe the evidence obtained provides a reasonable basis for our findings and conclusions based on our audit objectives.

Background

Key Stakeholders in the Federal Criminal Justice Process

Various DOJ and federal judiciary stakeholders play key roles in the federal criminal justice process, and as such, they can also have key roles in considering whether to use incarceration alternatives for a given offender or inmate. For example, in the course of the federal criminal justice process, a U.S. attorney is involved in the process of investigating, charging and prosecuting an offender, among other responsibilities. Federal defenders are called upon to represent defendants who are unable to financially retain counsel in federal criminal proceedings. The U.S. Probation and Pretrial Services Office (PPSO), an office within the judiciary, also has responsibilities including supervising an offender

---

Challenges, GA0-15-454 (Washington, D.C.: June 19, 2015); and *Bureau of Prisons: Eligibility and Capacity Impact Use of Flexibilities to Reduce Inmates' Time in Prison,* GA0-12-320 (Washington, D.C.: Feb. 7, 2012).

pretrial or after conviction. Federal judges are responsible for determining an offender's sentence, and, in the case of incarceration, BOP is responsible for caring for the inmate while in custody.

Federal Criminal Justice Process

Federal laws and guidelines determine what, if any, incarceration is appropriate for offenders. The Sentencing Reform Act of 1984 established the independent U.S. Sentencing Commission (USSC) within the judicial branch and charged it with, among other things, developing federal sentencing guidelines.[6] The guidelines specify sentencing guideline ranges-a range of time (in months) that offenders should serve given the nature of their offense and other factors-but also permit sentences to depart upward or downward from guideline ranges because of aggravating or mitigating circumstances. In 2005, the Supreme Court found the sentencing guidelines, which had previously been binding for federal judges to follow in sentencing criminal defendants, to be advisory in nature.[7] Regardless of the guidelines' advisory nature, judges are still required to calculate sentences properly and to consider the guideline ranges as well as the nature and circumstances of the offense, the defendant's history, and the need for deterrence, among other sentencing goals.[8]

As we reported in June 2016, alternatives to incarceration were available at various steps in the federal criminal justice process from charging and prosecution through incarceration (see Figure 1).[9]

For instance, at the front-end of the criminal justice process, there are pretrial diversion programs that can provide offenders an opportunity to avoid prosecution or incarceration if they satisfy program requirements. In addition, toward the end of inmates' periods of incarceration, BOP may place inmates in residential reentry centers (RRC, also known as halfway houses), in which inmates are housed outside of a prison environment prior

---

[6] Pub. L. No. 98-473, § 217, 98 Stat. 1987, 2017.

[7] See *United States v. Booker.* 543 U.S. 220 (2005).

[8] 18 U.S.C.§ 3553(a).

[9] We scoped the review (GAO 16-516) to focus on alternatives available once the case is considered by a U.S. Attorney's Office; therefore, we did not review alternatives pre- arrest, or those used by law enforcement.

to their release in the community. During their time in RRCs, inmates are authorized to leave for approved activities, such as work; are monitored 24 hours a day, such as through sign-out procedures; are required to work or be actively seeking work; and are required to pay a percentage of their salaries as a subsistence fee to cover some of their expenses at the RRC.

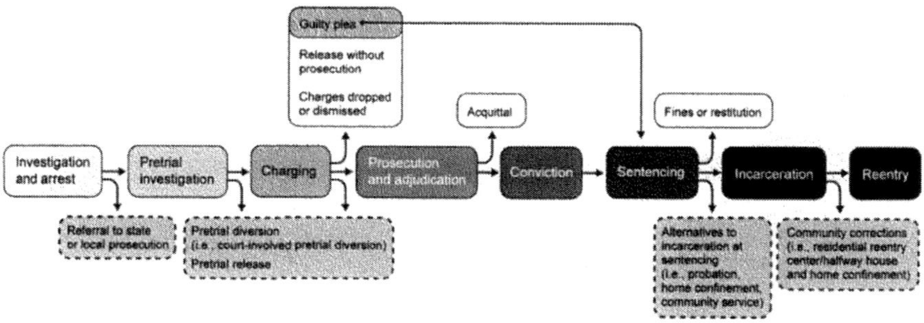

Source: GAO analysis of Department of Justice component roles and responsibilities. | GAO-18-275T.

Note: Alternatives to incarceration are shown in the bottom row. Except for the referral to state and local prosecutors, defendants can still be incarcerated federally after being provided these alternatives if they fail to meet the specific terms and conditions of the alternative.

Figure 1. Steps in the Federal Criminal Justice System Process with Alternatives to Incarceration.

In addition, BOP may place inmates in home confinement toward the end of their sentences. While in home confinement, inmates are required to remain in their homes when not involved in approved activities, such as employment, and are supervised and monitored, such as through curfews, random staff visits, or electronic monitoring.[10] RRC staff may provide the supervision of inmates in home confinement. Through an interagency agreement, BOP and the PPSO also established the Federal Location Monitoring Program, through which PPSO officers provide supervision for BOP inmates on home confinement under certain conditions. Among other

---

[10] For additional information on the technologies and systems used to track individuals through electronic monitoring, see GAO, *Electronic Monitoring: Draft National Standard for Offender Tracking Systems Addresses Common Stakeholder Needs,* GA0-1610 (Washington, D.C.: Oct. 26, 2015).

things, to qualify inmates ordinarily must be classified as minimum security level: seek and maintain employment; and pay for all or part of the costs of the Federal Location Monitoring Program.

Overview of BOP's Institutions and Role in Transitioning Offenders into Society

BOP is responsible for the custody and care of federal inmates. As of December 2017, there were a total of about 184,000 federal inmates, according to BOP. According to BOP data, 83 percent of these inmates are in the 122 institutions managed by BOP. The remainder are confined in secure privately managed or community-based facilities, local jails, or in home confinement.

BOP has a role to help ensure that offenders properly transition into society and avoid a return to prison or criminal behavior (recidivism) after they have completed their terms of incarceration. Among other activities, BOP provides reentry services to inmates within federal prisons that may include drug treatment programs, education and vocational training, and psychology services. BOP also is to facilitate the transfer of inmates into RRCs, which provide assistance as inmates transition into communities, to include home confinement RRCs provide employment counseling and job placement assistance, financial management assistance, and substance abuse treatment or counseling as well as other services, which may vary by facility. According to BOP, approximately 180 RRCs provide housing for over 7,500 federal offenders prior to release into their communities.

Federal Collateral Consequences Can Affect Reentry

As we reported in September 2017, individuals convicted of a crime may have limitations placed upon them that can affect their reentry.[11]

Individuals convicted of a crime generally face a sentence, which can include fines, probation, and incarceration in jail or prison. In addition to the sentence, individuals may also face collateral consequences- penalties and disadvantages, other than those associated with a sentence, which can

---

[11] GAO, *Nonviolent Drug Convictions: Stakeholders' Views on Potential Actions to Address Collateral Consequences,* GA0-17-691 (Washington. D.C.: Sept. 7, 2017).

be imposed upon an individual as a result of a conviction. For example, collateral consequences may prohibit people who committed crimes involving a sex offense or offense involving a child victim from working in a child care facility. Collateral consequences can be contained in federal and state laws and regulations. Notably, federal collateral consequences can serve various functions, such as enhancing public safety or protecting government interests. In 2012, the American Bar Association began compiling the first nationwide inventory of collateral consequences, known as the National Inventory of the Collateral Consequences of Conviction (NICCC). As of December 31, 2016, the NICCC contained roughly 46,000 collateral consequences established through federal and state laws and regulations.

We reported on collateral consequences contained in federal laws and regulations (i.e., federal collateral consequences) that can be imposed upon individuals with nonviolent drug convictions (NVDC).[12] Our review of the NICCC found that, as of December 31, 2016, there were 641 collateral consequences in federal laws and regulations that can be triggered by NVDC. The NICCC data indicated that these 641 collateral consequences can limit many aspects of an individual's life, such as employment, business licenses, education, and government benefits. For example, individuals may be ineligible for certain professional licenses, federal education loans, or federal food assistance. Moreover, we found that the NICCC identified that 78 percent of these 641 collateral consequences can potentially last a lifetime.

We also reported on selected stakeholders' views. We spoke to 14 individuals who were leaders of organizations representing judges, victims of crime, and states, among others-on actions the federal government could consider to mitigate these collateral consequences. Most of the stakeholders that we interviewed-13 of 14-said it was important for the

[12] For the purposes of our 2017 report, we defined NVDC as violations of laws prohibiting or regulating the possession, use, distribution, or manufacture of illegal drugs which do not include (a) offenses that have as an element the use, attempted use, or threatened use of physical force against the person or property of another, or (b) any other offense that by its nature, involves a substantial risk that physical force against the person or property of another may be used in the course of committing the offense. See GA0 17 691.

federal government to take action to mitigate federal collateral consequences for NVDC. Thirteen stakeholders said that mitigating federal collateral consequences could potentially reduce the likelihood that individuals with NVDC reoffend. Similarly, 11 stakeholders said that mitigation could potentially increase the likelihood that individuals with NVDC successfully reenter the community after jail or prison. The text box below identifies some of the statements made by stakeholders during our interviews from our prior work regarding federal collateral consequences for NVDC.

Stakeholder Perspectives on Federal Collateral Consequences for Nonviolent Drug Convictions

- The breadth of federal collateral consequences for nonviolent drug convictions is so massive and affects so many aspects of a person's life, such as family life, immigration, jury service, housing, employment, and voting, that they contribute to an underclass of people.
- "Many instances wherein the federal collateral consequences for nonviolent drug convictions end up making it hard for people to live a law abiding life. For example, they may not be able to live in public housing or may be barred from getting an occupational license or doing a particular job. This may push them to tum back to committing crimes to make some money."
- "... some federal collateral consequences for nonviolent drug convictions are sensible and appropriate. If we abolish [all that] exist you could imperil public safety..."
- "*We* can't just say we're going to err on the side of public safety and implement a wide range of collateral consequences strictly across the board. The problem is that public safety is undermined by making it impossible for individuals to move on from the criminal offense."
- "It is important not to assume that nonviolent means that there is no victim."

Source: Selected stakeholders interviewed by GAO. | GAO 18-275T.

DOJ Has Fully Addressed Two of Six GAO Recommendations Related to Its Incarceration Reduction Initiatives

Since 1980, the federal prison population increased from about 25,000 to about 184,000, as of December 2017. In June 2015 and June 2016, we reported that in part to help address challenges associated with overcrowding in certain institutions and related costs of incarceration, DOJ had taken steps to reduce the prison population by pursuing initiatives to: use alternatives to incarceration for low-level nonviolent crimes; prioritize prosecutions to focus on serious cases; and commute, or reduce, sentences of qualified federal inmates. In these reports, we highlighted potential areas for continued oversight of these initiatives and made six recommendations. DOJ concurred with five of these recommendations and partially concurred with the other. As of December 2017, DOJ has implemented two of the six recommendations and had not fully addressed the remaining four.

DOJ Could Better Measure Effectiveness of Pretrial Diversion Alternatives

In June 2016, we reported that DOJ had taken steps to pursue alternatives to incarceration for certain offenders, but could improve data collection and efforts to measure outcomes resulting from the use of pretrial diversion alternatives.[13] Our review examined two pretrial diversion programs on the front-end of the criminal justice process that provided offenders an opportunity to avoid incarceration if they satisfy program requirements. Title 9 of the U.S. Attorneys' Manual permits U.S. Attorneys' Offices to divert, at the discretion of a U.S. Attorney, certain federal offenders from prosecution into a program of supervision and services administered by the PPSO. Under the Title 9 diversion program, if the offender fulfills the terms of the program, the offender will not be prosecuted, or, if the offender has already been charged, the charges will be dismissed.

[13] GA0-16-516.

In addition to the Title 9 Pretrial Diversion Program, federal criminal justice stakeholders within some judicial districts have voluntarily established court-involved pretrial diversion practices. Court-involved pretrial diversion allows certain federal offenders the opportunity to participate in supervised programs or services, such as a drug court to address criminal behavior that may be linked to addiction to drugs or alcohol. Program participants are to meet regularly with court officials including a judge and pretrial services officer to discuss their progress in the program. If the offender satisfies program requirements, the offender may not be prosecuted, charges may be dismissed, or the participant may receive a reduced sentence.

While DOJ had collected some data on the use of pretrial diversion, we found that the data were of limited usefulness and reliability because its case management system did not distinguish between the different types of diversion and DOJ had not provided guidance to U.S. Attorneys' Offices as to when and how pretrial diversion cases are to be entered in the system. In addition, we found that DOJ had not measured the outcomes or identified the cost implications of its pretrial diversion programs. To address these deficiencies, we made four recommendations to DOJ. The first two relate to tracking and entering pretrial diversion data, while the second two relate to assessing outcomes based on the data. Specifically, we recommended that DOJ (1) separately identify and track the different types of pretrial diversion programs, (2) provide guidance to its attorneys on the appropriate way to enter data, (3) identify, obtain, and track data on the outcomes and costs of pretrial diversion programs, and (4) develop performance measures to assess diversion program outcomes. DOJ concurred with all four of our recommendations.

In October 2016, DOJ took actions to fully implement the first two recommendations. Specifically, in September 2016, DOJ provided guidance to staff in its U.S. Attorneys' Offices that outlines (1) the use of two new pretrial diversion codes-one for Title 9 pretrial diversion and another for court-involved diversion and (2) the appropriate entries to create and dispose of each type of pretrial diversion. Attorneys were instructed to use the codes starting on October 1, 2016. However, as of

December 2017, DOJ has not implemented the third and fourth recommendations. We continue to believe that by obtaining data on the costs and outcomes of pretrial diversion programs and establishing performance measures, DOJ would gain multiple advantages in its ability to manage these programs and optimize their outcomes and cost implications.

DOJ Could Better Assess Initiatives to Address Prison Overcrowding and Costs

In June 2015, we reported that DOJ could better measure the efficacy of two incarceration initiatives designed to address challenges related to overcrowding and rising costs.[14] One of these was the Smart on Crime initiative, announced in August 2013 as a comprehensive effort to:

- prioritize prosecutions to focus on the most serious cases;
- reform sentencing to eliminate unfair disparities and reduce overburdened prisons;
- pursue alternatives to incarceration for low-level nonviolent crimes;
- improve reentry to curb repeat offenses and re-victimization; and surge resources to prevent violence and protecting most vulnerable populations.

In our report, we found that DOJ had established indicators that were well-linked to these goals; however, the indicators lacked other key elements of successful performance measurement systems, such as clarity, a measurable target, or context. For example, none of the indicators had numerical targets by which to assess whether overall goals and objectives are achieved. To address this deficiency, we recommended that DOJ modify its Smart on Crime indicators to incorporate key elements of successful performance measurement systems. DOJ partially concurred with the recommendation, and agreed to continually refine and enhance the

---

[14] GAO-15-454.

indicators to improve their clarity and context. However, DOJ did not agree that establishing measurable targets for its indicators was appropriate. We recognized that it might not be appropriate to create targets for every indicator. Nevertheless, we maintained that measurable performance targets that are properly developed, communicated, and managed, can aid Department leadership in the admittedly challenging task of assessing progress in the Smart on Crime Initiative.

In March 2017, DOJ noted that, due to a change in administration, the status of the Smart on Crime Initiative was uncertain. In May 2017, the Attorney General issued a new charging and sentencing policy to all federal prosecutors that effectively rescinded any previous policy of DOJ that is inconsistent with the new charging and sentencing policy, including certain aspects of the Smart on Crime Initiative.[15] 1n December 2017, DOJ stated it would start to collect data on and monitor the implementation of this new policy. However, DOJ did not provide information on how it plans to modify its indicators to incorporate key elements of successful performance measurement systems. To the extent that DOJ continues to implement other aspects of the Smart on Crime initiative, such as improving reentry and surging resources to prevent violence we continue to believe this recommendation is valid.

The second initiative we addressed in our June 2015 report was the Clemency Initiative, which encourages nonviolent, low-level federal offenders to petition to have their sentences commuted, or reduced, by the President. Commutation of sentence, as we reported, has long been considered to be an extraordinary remedy that is rarely granted. According to DOJ, in 2013, then-President Obama expressed a desire to review more petitions, and DOJ pledged to expedite the review of such petitions in order to provide them to the President for consideration. However, we found that DOJ had not adequately assessed the extent to which the

---

[15] See Memorandum For All Federal Prosecutors, Attorney General Jefferson B. Session Ill, Department Charging and Sentencing Policy (May 10, 2017) (available as of December 1, 2017 at https:/Jwww.justice.gov/opa/press-release/file/965896/download). The new policy directed prosecutors to return to the practice of charging the "most serious readily provable offense." It also provided for exceptions under some circumstances with supervisory approval.

Clemency Initiative is expeditiously identifying meritorious petitions because it had not tracked how long it takes for petitions to clear each step in its review process or identified and addressed any processes that may contribute to unnecessary delays. We made a recommendation to DOJ to address this deficiency. DOJ concurred, but in March 2017 DOJ stated that it had no standard review process to evaluate. In December 2017, DOJ reported to us that it has taken steps to accelerate the review of commutation cases, such as assigning two attorneys to spend additional time on commutation cases. Although DOJ's actions are consistent with our recommendation, DOJ has not tracked how long it takes for petitions to clear each step in its review process. This makes it unclear whether DOJ's actions are addressing the processes that contribute to unnecessary delays.

DOJ Has Addressed Two of Four GAO Recommendations Related to its Reentry Programs

As part of its mission to protect public safety, BOP provides reentry programming that aims to facilitate offenders' successful return to the community and reduce recidivism. These reentry efforts include programs offered in BOP facilities, as well as RRC and home confinement services that allow inmates to serve the final months of their sentences in the community. In our February 2012, June 2015, and June 2016 reports we highlighted potential areas for continued oversight and made four recommendations to BOP. As of December 2017, BOP has implemented two of the four recommendations and has taken action to address one other recommendation.

BOP Has Developed a Plan to Evaluate Its Reentry Programs

In June 2015, we reported that BOP had 18 reentry programs available to inmates in BOP institutions in the areas of inmate treatment and education.[16] We found that while BOP had plans to evaluate the

---

[16] GAO-15-454.

performance of some of its reentry programs, it did not have a plan in place to prioritize evaluations across all of these programs. As a result, we recommended that BOP include, as part of its current evaluation plan, all18 of BOP's national reentry programs, and prioritize its evaluations by considering factors such as resources required for conducting evaluations. In May 2016, BOP provided to us an evaluation plan that was consistent with our recommendation. BOP has continued to update the evaluation plan to reflect changes in priority. For example, the most recent plan, updated in July 2017, lists BOP's Mental Health Step Down Unit program as its top priority, with a target evaluation date of fiscal year 2018. According to BOP, this reflects the need for analysis of services for seriously mentally ill inmates.[17]

BOP Has Taken Steps to Assess Costs of Home Confinement Services

In February 2012, we reported that BOP did not know the actual cost of home confinement services.[18] To facilitate inmates' reintegration into society, BOP may transfer eligible inmates to community corrections locations for up to the final 12 months of their sentences.[19] Inmates may spend this time in a RRC and in confinement in their homes for up to 6 months.[20] BOP contracts with private organizations to manage the RRCs and monitor inmates in home confinement.[21] At the time of our review, BOP was paying a rate of 50 percent of the overall per diem rate negotiated with the RRC for each inmate in home confinement. For example, if BOP paid a contractor the average community corrections per diem rate of $70.79 for each inmate housed in a RRC, BOP would pay $35.39 per day for that contractor's supervision of each inmate in home confinement. However, according to BOP, the agency did not require contractors to

---

[17] For additional information on BOP mental health services, see GAO, *Bureau of Prisons: Timelier Reviews, Plan for Evaluations, and Updated Policies Could Improve Mental Health Services Oversight,* GA0-13-1, (Washington, D.C,: July 17, 2013).

[18] GA0-12-320.

[19] 18 U.S.C. § 3624(c).

[20] Id.

[21] Through an interagency agreement, BOP and the PPSO also established the Federal Location Monitoring Program, through which PPSO officers provide supervision for BOP inmates in home confinement under certain conditions.

provide the actual costs for home confinement services as part of their contract and therefore did not know the cost of home confinement. To help BOP better manage its costs, we recommended that BOP establish a plan for requiring contractors to submit separate prices of RRC beds and home confinement services. BOP implemented this recommendation and determined that all new solicitations as of February 1, 2013, will have separate line items for RRC in-house beds and home confinement services. According to BOP, as of November 2017, 184 solicitations with separate RRC bed and home confinement service line items have been issued since February 2013.

BOP Could Better Measure the Outcomes of RRCs and Home Confinement

In June 2016, we reported that BOP was not positioned to track the information it would need to help measure the outcomes of inmates placed in RRCs and home confinement and did not have performance measures in place.[22] Specifically, we found that, as part of its strategic plan, BOP had two measures-one to track the number of inmates placed into RRCs, and another to track the number of inmates placed in home confinement. However, these measures did not help assess the outcomes of RRCs and home confinement, such as how these programs may or may not affect the recidivism rates of inmates. To address this deficiency, we made two recommendations to BOP to (1) identify, obtain, and track data on the outcomes of the RRC and home confinement programs; and (2) develop performance measures by which to help assess program outcomes. DOJ concurred with these recommendations.

As of December 2017, BOP has taken steps to implement our recommendation to identify, obtain, and track data on the outcomes of RRCs and home confinement. In particular, BOP reported to us that it has developed a revised Statement of Work for use with its RRC contractors that requires the contractors to track and report quarterly to BOP on,

---

[22] GAO-16-516.

among other things, the number of placements into and releases from RRCs and home confinement; revocations from RRCs or home confinement; and RRC and home confinement residents that have secured full, part-time, or temporary employment BOP plans to compile these data to track contractor performance and program outcomes. Further, BOP reported to us that it has developed a voluntary survey that asks RRC residents about their RRC experiences, including the amount of help they received in finding and keeping a job, and finding a place to live. These actions are in line with our recommendation and we will continue to monitor their implementation. However, as of December 2017, BOP has not provided evidence to us that it has developed performance measures by which to help assess program outcomes. We continue to believe BOP should do so.

Chairman Gowdy, Ranking Member Cummings, and Members of the Committee, this concludes my prepared statement. I would be pleased to respond to any questions that you may have.

STATEMENT OF JENNIFER DOLEAC

Ms. DOLEAC. Chairman Gowdy, Ranking Member Cummings, and other members of the committee, thank you for inviting me to testify in this hearing about prisoner reentry.

I'm an assistant professor of public policy and economics at the University of Virginia. I'm also the director of the Justice Tech Lab, which works to find effective, scalable solutions to criminal justice problems.

In addition to my roles at UVA, I'm a senior social scientist at the Lab at D.C., a research group in the mayor's office here in the District, and a nonresident fellow in economic studies at the Brookings Institution. I'm also a member of the Poverty, Employment, and Self-Sufficiency Network organized by the Institute for Research on Poverty at the University of Wisconsin.

To each of these roles, I bring my expertise in the economics of crime and discrimination. In recent years, I've been particularly focused on the issue of prisoner reentry. In addition to a number of ongoing studies testing the impacts of new interventions on reentry outcomes, I've studied the effects of ban-the-box policies, also called fair chance policies. This is the topic I'll focus on today, though I'll note that the views I express here are my own and don't represent those of any of the organizations I'm affiliated with.

Two-thirds of people who are released from prison will be arrested again within 3 years. This high recidivism rate signals our collective failure to help this group successfully reintegrate to civilian life. The question facing policymakers is what we can do to facilitate more successful reintegration and break that cycle of incarceration.

Those who go through the criminal justice system face a wide array of challenges that make this task difficult. Those challenges include low education, limited and interrupted work histories, lack of stable housing, and high rates of substance abuse, mental illness, and emotional trauma. All of these factors help explain why this population has trouble finding stable employment upon release from prison.

Ban-the-box aims to increase access to jobs by prohibiting employers from asking job applicants about their criminal histories until late in the hiring process. The hope is that if some people with records can get their foot in the door, those who are a good fit for the job will be able to communicate their work readiness during an interview before the employer runs a background check.

But work readiness, the ability to show up on time every day and do a good job, is difficult to discern from a job application and even from an interview. Employers clearly believe that a criminal record is a negative signal about work readiness, and they're also worried about negligent hiring lawsuits and bad press that might result from hiring someone with a record.

Unfortunately, ban-the-box does not do anything to address the reasons employers might be reluctant to hire someone with a criminal record. It just tells them they can't ask. Since many employers still don't want to hire people with criminal records, especially those with recent convictions, they may try to guess who has a record when they aren't allowed to ask up front.

In the United States, young black men without college degrees are much more likely than others to have a recent conviction that might worry an employer. And so employers who want to avoid interviewing people with recent convictions may simply avoid interviewing applicants from this group. As a result, we might see ban-the-box hurt this group more than help them. Indeed, this is what has happened.

In the written testimony I submitted to this committee, I summarized the empirical evidence from the best studies on this topic, as well as the broader literature on how information affects discrimination in the labor market. The evidence can be summarized as follows.

First, delaying information about job applicants' criminal histories leads employers to discriminate against groups that are more likely to have a recent conviction. This hurts young, low-skilled black men who don't have criminal records.

Second, the best evidence suggests that ban-the-box does not increase employment for people with criminal records and might even reduce it.

Third, these findings are consistent with empirical evidence from other contexts, such as drug testing and credit check bans. Studies consistently show that removing information about characteristics that disadvantage protected groups actually hurts those groups more than it helps them. In the absence of information, employers do not simply assume the best about people. They try to guess who has the characteristics they're trying to avoid. Rather than reducing discrimination, this approach effectively broadens it to the entire group.

Finally, effective approaches to this policy problem are likely to be policies that directly address employers' concerns, such as investing in rehabilitation, providing more information about applicants' work readiness, and clarifying employers' legal responsibilities in the hiring process.

Overall, the academic literature provides strong evidence that despite the best intentions, ban-the-box has not helped people with criminal records and has harmed young, low-skilled black men without records, who already struggle in the labor market for a variety of reasons. Based on this evidence, I urge this committee to reject the Fair Chance Act and focus on other policy options that are likely to be more successful.

Thank you, and I look forward to your questions. [Prepared statement of Ms. Doleac follows:]

Empirical Evidence on the Effects of Ban the Box Policies, Testimony before the U.S. House Committee on Oversight and Government Reform, Jennifer L. Doleac, University of Virginia, December 13, 2017

Chairman Gowdy, Ranking Member Cummings, and other members of the Committee: Thank you for inviting me to testify in this hearing about prisoner reentry. My remarks will focus on the empirical evidence on one popular approach to improving reentry outcomes: Ban the Box policies (also called Fair Chance policies). This evidence can be summarized as follows:

1) Delaying information about job applicants' criminal histories leads employers to statistically discriminate against groups that are more likely to have a recent conviction. This reduces employment for young, low-skilled, black men.
2) This negative effect is driven by a reduction in employment for young, low-skilled, black men who don't have criminal records. When these men can no longer signal their clean record on a job application, employers assume there is a high likelihood that they have a record and do not interview them.
3) The best evidence suggests that Ban the Box does not increase employment for people with criminal records, and might even reduce it.

4) Effective approaches to this policy problem are likely to be policies that directly ad- dress employers' concerns about hiring people with criminal records, such as investing in rehabilitation, providing more information about applicants' work-readiness, and clarifying employers' legal responsibilities.

Background on Ban the Box

Two-thirds of people who are released from prison will be arrested again within three years (Cooper, Durose and Snyder, 2014). This high recidivism rate signals our collective failure to help this group successfully reintegrate to civilian life. The question facing policymakers is what we can do to facilitate more successful reintegration and break this cycle of incarceration.

Those who go through the criminal justice system face a wide array of challenges that make this task difficult. These challenges include low education, limited and interrupted work histories, lack of stable housing, and high rates of substance abuse, mental illness, and emotional trauma (see Raphael, 2010, and Doleac, 2016, for more complete discussions; Appendix figures A.1 through A.3 show the most recent statistics on mental health and substance abuse for jail and prison inmates). All of these challenges can be made worse by the experience of incarceration. People with criminal records also have a history of illegal behavior, and to the extent that past behavior predicts future behavior this could be worrisome to potential employers. All of these factors help explain why this population has trouble finding stable employment upon release from prison. A lack of stable employment may be one reason we sec such high recidivism rates.

There is surely heterogeneity within this population: some people with records are more work-ready[23] than others. Why don't employers hire at least those who are work-ready? Unfortunately, work-readiness is difficult

[23] I will use the term "work-ready" to refer to a combination of soft skills and job-specific skills that make someone a reliable and productive employee.

to discern from a job application, so employers are forced to infer it based on the information they can observe, such as education and work history. Many also view a criminal record as valuable information of work-readiness. Anecdotally, some employers are so reluctant to hire people with criminal records that they immediately discard applications from anyone who checks the box on the application saying they've been convicted of a crime. This limits opportunities for people with criminal records who are work-ready, and imposes large costs on society if it contributes to the high recidivism rates mentioned above.

Ban the Box (BTB) aims to increase access to jobs by prohibiting employers from asking job applicants about their criminal histories until late in the hiring process. The hope is that if some people with records can get their foot in the door, those who are a good fit for the job will be able to build rapport with the employer and communicate their work-readiness during an interview, before the employer runs a background check. This gives the employer a chance to decide if the person is qualified before knowing about their record, and this could increase the likelihood that the employer hires the applicant. BTB could also bring more people with records into the labor force, if the question on applications about past convictions had previously discouraged them from applying for jobs. Both effects could lead to an increase in employment for people with criminal records. Because people with records are disproportionately African-American, this could also reduce racial disparities in employment.

Unfortunately, BTB does not do anything to address the many reasons employers might be reluctant to hire someone with a record: the challenges I listed above likely make the average person with a record less work-ready than the average person without a record. On top of concerns about productivity, employers may worry that hiring someone with a criminal record puts them at risk of a negligent hiring lawsuit or negative media attention that could put them out of business. EEOC guidance instructs employers to use reasonable judgment in considering whether a prior conviction is relevant given the responsibilities of the job being considered. But if an employee commits a violent offense on the job, any previous conviction could look like a red flag, and the employer could be held liable in a court of law or the court of public opinion; either result could be catastrophic for a business owner. In this context, it makes sense that employers would avoid hiring people with records when they have qualified people without records to choose from.

Since employers still don't want to hire people with criminal records - especially those with recent convictions - they may try to guess who has a record when they aren't allowed to ask. In the United States, observable characteristics such as race, age, gender, and education level are highly correlated with the likelihood of having a recent criminal conviction. Young black men who don't have a college degree arc much more likely than others to have a recent conviction that might worry an employer, and so employers who want to avoid interviewing people with recent convictions may avoid interviewing applicants from this group.[24] As a result, we might see BTB hurt this group more than it helps them.

The direction and magnitude of the effects of BTB are empirical questions, and a number of recent studies shed light on what these effects have been.[25] Overall, they provide strong evidence that BTB has not helped people with criminal records, and has harmed young, low-skilled black men without records, who already struggle in the labor market for a variety of reasons. Based on this evidence, I urge this Committee to reject the Fair Chance Act and focus on other policy options that are likely to be more successful.

---

[24] Discrimination based on race is, of course, illegal in the United States. If one could prove that a particular applicant was not hired for a particular job because of his race, that would be grounds for a lawsuit. Unfortunately, such a thing is difficult to prove. Because of this our anti-discrimination laws are difficult to enforce in practice. Reasonable people can differ in their belief about how much we might be able to reduce racial discrimination if we increased enforcement efforts. Given this, readers should think of the results I will present as the effects of BTB and other policy interventions in the context of the level of anti-discrimination enforcement in effect during the past decade.

[25] It is important to distinguish between BTB the policy and BTB the social movement. "Ban the Box" has become the slogan of a social movement in favor of second chances and against stigmatizing those with a criminal past. The social movement has humanized the formerly incarcerated, and led to a cultural change and greater political will to improve reentry outcomes. These are, without a doubt, positive developments. The issue I will address in my testimony is not the effects of BTB the social movement, but the effects of BTB the policy, which delays when employers are allowed to ask about an applicant's criminal record. Disentangling these effects is difficult but has been the goal of economists studying this topic in recent years.

The Effects of Ban the Box on Employment

The Research Challenge

Measuring the effect of BTB policies on employment is not a straightforward exercise. To measure the effect of BTB in a particular place, we need to know what would have happened if that place had not adopted BTB. That is, what is the counterfactual? The problem, of course, is that we do not simultaneously observe both events either a place adopts the policy or not. So, when considering the impact of BTB in particular places, we need to find a good control group that can serve as the counterfactual.

Ban the Box policies are not implemented at random, so places that adopt them are likely to be different from places that do not. Indeed, they tend to be more urban, and have larger black populations (Doleac and Hansen, 2016). Such differences are easily observed, but others are not. For instance, places that adopt Ban the Box are likely to be those where residents are more motivated to help people with criminal records, and to reduce racial disparities in employment. A simple pre-post comparison of employment for people with criminal records, or even a basic comparison of employment trends in places that do and do not adopt the policy, could therefore be misleading.

For instance, a frequently cited report on BTB in Durham, NC, shows that the share of people hired by the city government who had criminal records increased after BTB was implemented in 2011 (Atkinson and Lockwood, 2014). What the report does not say is that the unemployment rate fell dramatically in Durham during that period (2011-2014), which coincided with a national economic recovery. Employment of people with criminal records surely would have increased even if BTB had not been implemented, because the tighter labor market meant employers had to dig deeper into their applicant pools to fill open positions. Without a control group people who would be subject to the same employment trends as those with criminal records, but who wouldn't be affected by BTB we can't tell whether BTB had any effect on employment in Durham.

Another challenge in studying policies aimed at helping people with criminal records is that high-quality data on this group do not exist at the national level. There is no national dataset that links administrative data on criminal histories with employment outcomes. Our major national surveys, such as the American Community Survey and the Current Population Survey (CPS), do not ask about criminal records.[26]

The studies I'll describe below are thus forced to take other approaches to measuring the effects of BTB laws. Agan and Starr (2016) conduct a field experiment that generates new data. Doleac and Hansen (2016) use the CPS to study the effects of BTB on demographic groups likely to have a recent conviction, to consider net effects indicative of statistical discrimination, but we cannot separate effects on people with and without criminal records. Rose (2017) and Jackson and Zhao (2017) both link administrative data on criminal histories and employment at the state level, to measure the effect of BTB on people with criminal records. The lack of similar administrative data at the national level means that these state-level analyses are the best available for understanding policy effects on people with criminal records.

Recent Research: Overview

The following four papers represent the best evidence so far on the employment impacts of BTB. Two consider the unintended consequences of BTB for young black men without records. Both find evidence of statistical discrimination that is consistent with economic theory and with other work on the role of information in labor markets. Two other papers measure the effect of BTB on people with criminal records. Table 1 summarizes the findings of these four BTB studies.

---

[26] National Longitudinal Survey of Youth (NLSY) is often used to study the relationship between criminal history and outcomes like employment, but there are two important drawbacks to using this dataset: (1) it's a relatively small sample, so statistical power to detect effects is limited, and (2) criminal history information is self-reported. Researchers have shown that such self-reports are often wildly inaccurate, and that inaccuracy may vary with race (Kirk and Wakefield, 2018). The accuracy of reporting might also change as the perception of stigma changes for instance, after BTB policies are passed, respondents might be less hesitant to admit their criminal records to interviewers. This makes the NLSY problematic for studying the effects of BTB.

Since places that adopt BTB are probably more motivated to help people with criminal records than places that do not, all of the estimates below are likely biased toward finding a beneficial effect of the policy. The fact that all find negative or zero results suggests the actual effects are even more negative than the estimates I will present.

The studies described below represent the most rigorous evidence available on BTB. Other studies exist, and some find beneficial effects of BTB, but they do not meet the rigorous standards of the literature. More specifically, in their current form they do not credibly control for other factors that might affect employment outcomes, and so do not isolate the effect of BTB on employment. (All are currently working papers and so may change in response to suggestions from colleagues and peer reviewers.) Since the evidence specific to BTB is relatively new, and not all of the studies have been peer-reviewed, it will be helpful to consider the findings in the context of other work on statistical discrimination in labor markets. Together, this literature tells a consistent story.

Recent Research: Unintended Consequences of BTB

Agan and Starr (2016) ran a field experiment where they sent thousands of job applications from fake applicants, all of whom were young men without college degrees. They randomized whether the applicant was black or white, and whether or not they had a non-violent felony conviction. They submitted these applications before and after Ban the Box laws targeting private employers went into effect in New York City and New Jersey, and then observed which applicants received a call for an interview (a "callback"). Before Ban the Box, individuals with records were called back at lower rates than those without records. The racial gap was small: white applicants were only 7% more likely than black applicants to receive a callback. After BTB, that racial gap widened to 43%. (See Figure 1.) While white applicants were called back at nearly the same rate as before, black applicants were called back at a rate in between the rates at which those with and without records were called before BTB. This may help black men with records, but it hurts black men without records; this tradeoff is consistent with the hypothesis that in the absence of information about a criminal record, employers statistically discriminate based on race and are less likely to interview applicants from groups that include lots of people with recent convictions.

The advantage of this randomized experiment is that Agan and Starr were able to isolate the effects of race and criminal history from other factors that might affect callbacks for real applicants. The disadvantage is that they don't see who actually gets a job. That is especially important in this context, as some (perhaps many) applicants with criminal records who are now getting callbacks might ultimately be rejected when their criminal history is revealed.

My own work with Benjamin Hansen (Doleac and Hansen, 2016) uses a different approach. We use data from the CPS and the timing of BTB policies across the country as a natural experiment to measure the effects of BTB on actual employment.[27]

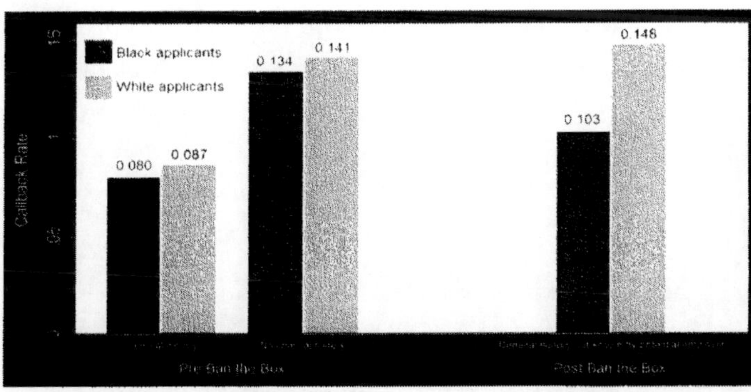

Notes: Figure source: Agan and Doleac (2017), based on results from Agan and Starr (2016).

Figure 1. Callback Rates by Race and Criminal Record Before and After Ban the Box.

This is a less clean experiment than the Agan and Starr study, as the timing of these policies is not random, but the advantage is that we are able to see actual employment outcomes (instead of just callbacks). We show that, after controlling for observable differences between places, as well as

[27] The CPS does not include information about respondents' criminal records, so we cannot separately measure effects on those with and without records.

regional employment shocks such as the Great Recession, places with and without BTB exhibit "parallel trends" in employment outcomes that is, the pre-policy trends in employment look very similar. This is the empirical standard for arguing that the places without the policy are a good counterfactual for the treatment group: since employment trends were similar across the two groups before the policy change, we can reasonably assume that the trends would have continued to be similar if the policy change had not occurred.

Having established a good control group, we then measure the effect of BTB on employment for young men without college degrees the group most likely to be helped by the policy if it helps people with recent convictions get jobs, or hurt by the policy if it leads employers to statistically discriminate. We find that BTB *reduces* employment by 5% for black men in this group (See Figure 2). This estimate is robust to a large number of additional checks: for instance, restricting the sample to only cities, or to places that eventually adopt BTB. We even find the same effect after controlling for monthly unemployment rates at the local level evidence that our results are not driven by local employment shocks that our controls might have missed.

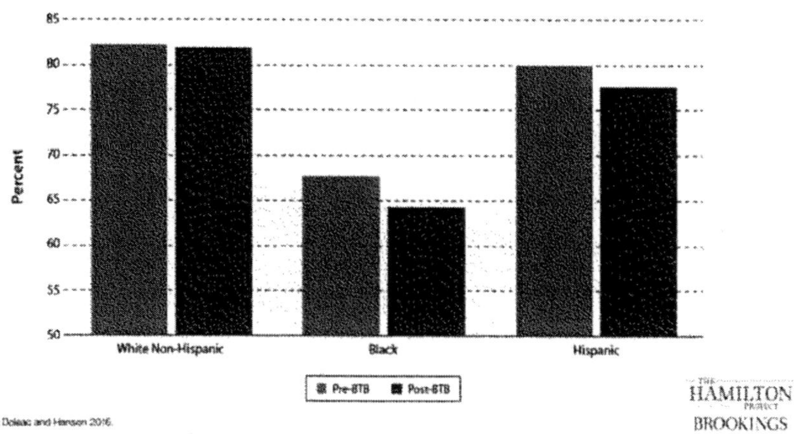

Notes: Figure source: Doleac (2016), based on results from Doleac and Hansen (2016).

Figure 2. Effect of Ban the Box on Employment for Young, Low-Skilled Men, by Race.

During the period we studied, 2004-2014, the majority of BTB policies were targeted at the public sector. However, since human capital is mobile across sectors, it is not obvious where we would expect to see effects on employment. People who might have found jobs in the private sector and now spend their time searching (unproductively) for government jobs might now remain unemployed; that would result in a drop in private sector employment. We test the effects of the policy by sector and find that about half of the negative result for young black men is driven by a loss of private sector jobs, and the other half is driven by a loss of public sector jobs. This is evidence against the hypothesis posed by some that the government is somehow different and immune to discrimination concerns.

Who do employers hire instead when they do not hire young black men without college degrees? If they want to avoid hiring someone with a recent conviction who is at risk for future criminal activity, they may statistically discriminate in favor of white applicants, older applicants, and/or women. It appears that when BTB targets public employers, those employers shift from hiring young black men to older black men. When BTB targets private employers, they shift from hiring young black men to young white men (consistent with Agan and Starr, 2016, who found that white men were helped by the private BTB laws in NYC and NJ). We cannot tell from our data whether the older black men and young white men who are now being hired at higher rates have criminal records themselves, or if they are simply individuals without records who are less qualified than the young black men without records who are no longer being hired.

Recent Research: Effects on People with Criminal Records

Some might be willing to tolerate large negative effects for people without records if we see benefits for at least some people with records. But the two best studies on this topic find no such benefits. Both studies link criminal history records with employment data the ideal administrative data for this exercise. One study, Rose (2017), compares individuals with criminal records in Seattle, where BTB was implemented, with similar people in other parts of the state. The pre-period trends for these two groups are nearly identical, so it seems like the people from outside Seattle are a good control group in this context. When Rose compares employment trends after BTB went into effect in Seattle, he finds the policy had no effect on employment for people with records. (See Figure 3).

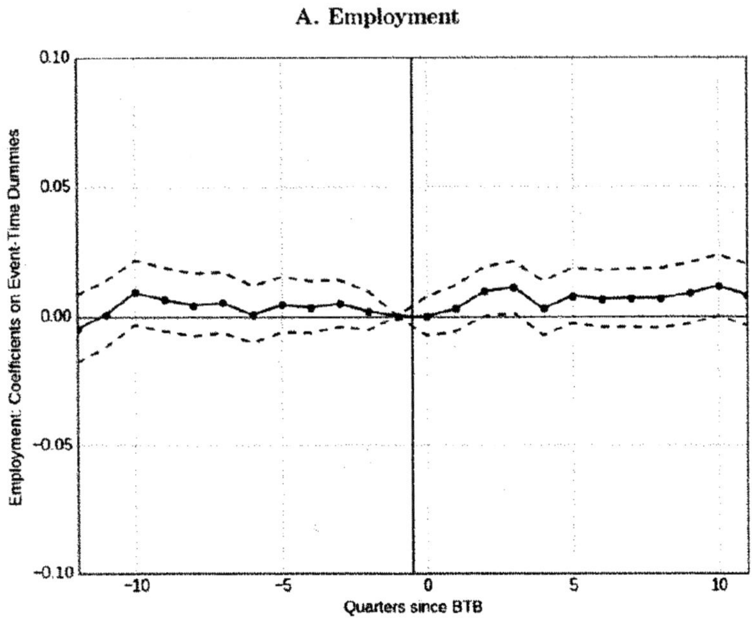

Notes: Figure source: Rose (2017). Figure plots the estimated coefficients on the interaction of event time and treatment indicators and 95% confidence intervals. See source for more information.

Figure 3. Effect of Ban the Box on recently-released offenders in Seattle.

Table 1. Summary of main results from studies on Ban the Box

	Employers covered (public/private)	Empirical strategy	Sample	Outcome measure	Main result
Agan and Starr (2016)	Private	Audit study	NYC and NJ, young men without a college degree	Callbacks	BTB increased the racial gap in callbacks (favoring white applicants) from 7% to 43%
Doleac and Hansen (2016)	Both	Difference-in-difference	National, young men without a college degree	Employment	BTB reduced employment by 5% for young, low-skilled black men
Jackson and Zhao (2017)	Both	Difference-in-difference	People with criminal records in MA	Employment	BTB reduced employment for people with criminal records by 5%
Rose (2017)	Both	Difference-in-difference	People with criminal records in WA	Employment	Seattle's BTB policy had no effect on employment for people with criminal records

Another study, Jackson and Zhao (2017), compares people with criminal records in Massachusetts at the time BTB was implemented (the treatment group) with people who did not have records yet but would be convicted later (the control group). The motivation for this strategy is that both groups should be similar in terms of education, behavior, and other disadvantages that might result in a criminal conviction, but only the treatment group is immediately affected by BTB. Because these different populations have different age profiles those with records are older than those without - they weight individuals in each group so that the pre-BTB trends look similar. They then measure changes in employment for the treatment group relative to the control group. They find that BTB *reduced* employment for people with criminal records in Massachusetts, by about 5% (See Figure 4).

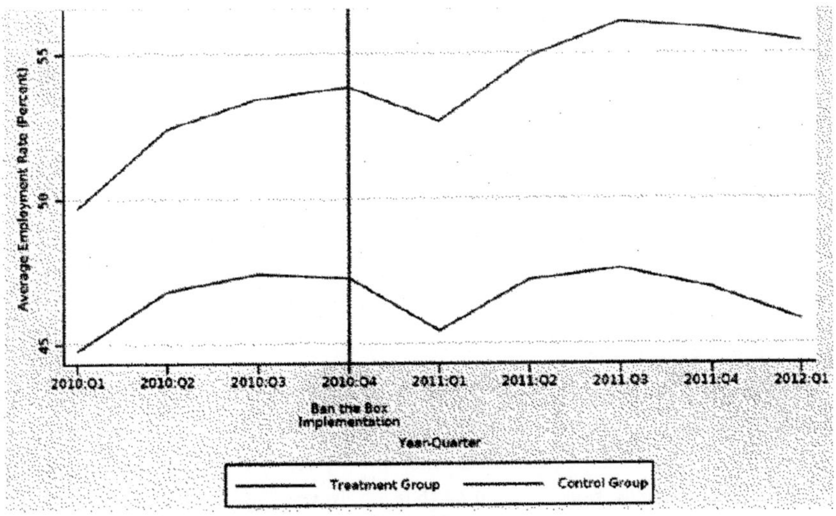

Notes: Figure source: Jackson and Zhao (2017).

Figure 4. Effect of Ban the Box on people with criminal records in Massachusetts.

This is consistent with qualitative work showing that people with criminal records become discouraged when interviewing for jobs that they eventually do not get because of their records sometimes even after working for a probationary period (Augustine, 2017). Removing or delaying information that employers find valuable makes it harder to identify good matches early, and so risks wasting everyone's time and giving job applicants false hope. This is costly to job-seekers as well as to employers.

Other Evidence on Statistical Discrimination in Labor Markets

(This section is drawn heavily from the text of Doleac and Hansen, 2016)

Ban the box policies seek to limit employers' access to criminal histories. This access itself is relatively new. Before the internet and inexpensive computer storage became available in the 1990s, it was not easy to check job applicants' criminal histories. A number of studies consider how employment outcomes changed as criminal records became more widely available during the 1990s and early 2000s, and their findings foreshadow those described above: when information on criminal records is easily available, firms are more likely to hire low-skilled black men (Bushway, 2004; Holzer, Raphael and Stoll, 2006; Finlay, 2009; Stoll, 2009). In fact, many of those studies explicitly predicted that limiting information on criminal records, via BTB or similar policies, would negatively affect low- skilled black men as a group. For example:

> [S]ome advocates seek to suppress the information to which employers have access regarding criminal records. But it is possible that the provision of more information to these firms will increase their general willingness to hire young black men, as we show here and since we have previously found evidence that employers who do not have such information often engage in statistical dis- crimination against this demographic group. (Holzer, Raphael and Stoll, 2004)

> Employers have imperfect information about the criminal records of applicants, so rational employers may use observable correlates of criminality as proxies for criminality and statistically discriminate against groups with high rates of criminal activity or incarceration. (Finlay, 2009)

> [Ban the box] may in fact have limited positive impacts on the employment of ex-offenders....More worrisome is the likelihood that these bans will have large negative impacts on the employment of those whom we should also be concerned about in the labor market, namely minority especially black - men without criminal records, whose employment prospects are already poor for a variety of other reasons. (Stoll, 2009)

There is also evidence from other contexts that statistical discrimination increases when information about employees is less precise. Autor and Scarborough (2008) measure the effects of personality testing by employers on hiring outcomes. Conditioning hiring on good performance on personality tests (such as popular Myers-Briggs tests) was generally viewed as disadvantaging minority job candidates because minorities tend to score worse on these tests. However, the authors note that this will only happen if employers' assumptions about applicants in the absence of information about test scores are more positive than the information that test scores provide. If, in contrast, minorities score better on these tests than employers would have thought, adding accurate information about a job applicant's abilities will help minority applicants. They find that in a national firm that was rolling out personality testing, the use of these tests had no effect on the racial composition of employees, though they did allow the firm to choose employees who were more productive.

Wozniak (2015) found that when employers required drug tests for employees, black employment rates increased by 7-30%, with the largest effects on low-skilled black men. As in the personality test context, the popular assumption was that if black men are more likely to fail a drug test, then employers' use of drug tests when making hiring decisions would disproportionately hurt this group. It turned out that a drug test requirement allowed non-using black men to prove their status when employers would otherwise have used race as a proxy for drug use.

In another related paper, Bartik and Nelson (2016) hypothesize that banning employers from checking job applicants' credit histories will negatively affect employment outcomes for groups that have lower credit scores on average (particularly black individuals). The reasoning is as above: in the absence of information about credit histories, employers will use race as a proxy for credit scores. They find that, consistent with statistical discrimination, credit check bans reduce job-finding rates by 7-16% for black job-seekers. As with BTB policies, one goal of banning credit checks was to reduce racial disparities in employment, so this policy was counterproductive.

The recent studies on BTB therefore contribute to a growing literature showing that well-intentioned policies that remove information about racially-imbalanced characteristics from job applications can do more harm than good for minority job-seekers. Advocates for these policies seem to think that in the absence of information, employers will assume the best about all job applicants. This is often not the case. In the above examples, pro- viding information about characteristics that are less favorable, on average, among black job-seekers criminal records, drug tests, and credit histories-actually helped black men and black women find jobs. These outcomes are what we would expect from standard statistical discrimination models. More information helps the best job candidates avoid discrimination.

This growing literature has important implications for anti-discrimination policy in the United States: When we discover that employers' use of particular information has a disparate impact on a protected group, we often tell them they can't use that information anymore. But it turns out that in all of these settings, removing that information simply leads employers to statistically discriminate instead. (Indeed, the statistical correlation that causes the disparate impact makes statistical discrimination more effective.) That is, rather than reducing discrimination, this approach effectively broadens the discrimination to the entire group.

Alternatives to Ban the Box

There are other policy options that are likely to have larger benefits for people with records, without unintentionally harming young black men without records. The key is figuring out what employers are worried about, and then finding a way to directly address those concerns.

Most employers simply want to find applicants who will show up on time every day and do a good job. They appear to view a criminal record as a negative signal about that, and in the absence of better information they screen those applicants out. If we could give them better information, or address the problems that make this population less work-ready, employers will care less about the criminal record.

Effective policies will likely do one or more of the following:[28]

1) Improve the average work-readiness of people with criminal records.
2) Provide more information to employers about the work-readiness of job applicants with criminal records.
3) Clarify employers' legal responsibilities in hiring to make clear which applicants do and which do not pose an undue risk.

Improving the Average Work Readiness of People with Criminal Records

This strategy could involve investment on several fronts, including education, job training, mental health treatment, and substance abuse treatment. Recent work by Wen, Hockenberry and Cummings (2017) shows that increasing access to substance abuse treatment through expansions of Medicaid reduced both violent and property crime rates. While this does not speak directly to the effects of substance abuse treatment on employment, it suggests that access to treatment has a meaningful effect on a driver of criminal behavior, which is also likely to affect work-readiness.

---

[28] See Doleac (2016) for a longer discussion of principles to guide policy in this area.

Providing More Information About Work-Readiness

Fully rehabilitating everyone who goes through the criminal justice system will take time. In the meantime, providing more information about applicants' work-readiness will help employers identify those applicants who would make good employees despite their criminal record. One type of information that many employers find valuable is successful completion of a challenging rehabilitation or job training program, or even active participation in such a program. See Piehl (2009) for a description of a reentry program that employers trust to send them work-ready employees.

Court-issued certificates of qualification for employment (also called employability or rehabilitation certificates) provide another example of how to provide valuable information to employers. In a growing number of jurisdictions, individuals with criminal records can go before a judge and present evidence of their rehabilitation and work-readiness. If the judge is convinced, he or she can issue a certificate of qualification. The recipient can then show that certificate to employers when applying for jobs. To the extent that employers view the judge as a credible evaluator of work-readiness, this could outweigh the effect of a criminal record.

Clarify Employers' Legal Responsibilities

Certificates of qualification could address liability concerns as well. For employers who worry about the legal liability or negative press associated with hiring someone with a record, finding a way to shift the risk involved from the employer to someone else can address this concern. Employers likely view certificates of qualification as insurance against negligent hiring lawsuits and negative press. If someone with a certificate of qualification later commits a crime on the job, the employer can credibly argue that there's no way they could have predicted such an event and deflect any blame to the court system. After all, a judge certified the applicant as being work-ready.

There is empirical evidence that certificates of qualification are effective. Leasure and Andersen (2016) ran an audit study to test the effect of these certificates on callbacks for a job. They randomized whether a job applicant had a felony conviction, a felony conviction and a certificate of qualification, or no conviction at all. They found that applicants with a certificate were called back just as often as those with no conviction at all, suggesting that this type of intervention provides valuable information to employers that allays concerns about an applicant's criminal record. (See Figure 5). Since this intervention provides more information about the applicant, rather than taking information away, there is no reason to expect unintended consequences of the sort caused by BTB it should lead to less guessing about applicants' work-readiness, not more.

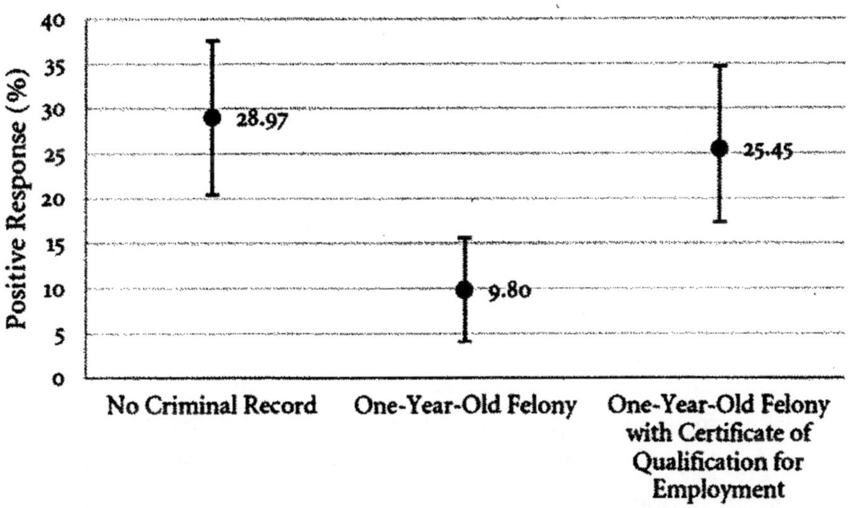

Notes: Figure source: Leasure and Andersen (2016). Overall Likelihood Ratio x_2 = 14.114, $p < 0.001$. No criminal record vs. One-year-old felony Likelihood Ratio x_2 = 12.691, $p < 0.001$. One year old felony vs. Certificate of Qualification for Employment Likelihood Ratio x_2 = 9.151, $p < 0.01$. No criminal record vs. CQE Likelihood Ratio x_2 = 0.339, n.s. "Positive response" refers to interview invitations or job offers. Circles indicate point estimates of percentages. Error bars indicate 95% confidence interval.

Figure 5. The Effect of Certificates of Qualification for Employment on Positive Employer Responses.

Given the growing evidence that BTB is not having the benefits we'd hoped for people with criminal records, and is actually harming disadvantaged groups without records, it would be helpful to shift our policy focus to creative solutions like these that take employers' concerns seriously and find ways to address them.

REFERENCES

Agan, Amanda, and Jennifer Doleac. 2017. "The Effects of 'Ban the Box on the Employment of Black Men." *Econofact*, available at http://econofact.org/the-effects-of-ban-the-box-on-the-employment-of-black-men.

Agan, Amanda, and Sonja Starr. 2016. "Ban the Box, Criminal Records, and Statistical Discrimination: A Field Experiment." *Quarterly Journal of Economics,* forthcoming.

Atkinson, Daryl V., and Kathleen Lockwood. 2014. "The benefits of Ban the Box: A case study of Durham, NC." *The Southern Coalition for Social Justice*, available at https://www.southerncoalition.org/wp-content/uploads/2014/10/BantheBox_WhitePaper-2.pdf.

Augustine, Dallas. 2017. "Working Around the Law: Navigating Legal Barriers to Good Work During Reentry." *Working paper.*

Autor, David H., and David Scarborough. 2008. "Does Job Testing Harm Minority Workers? Evidence from Retail Establishments." *Quarterly Journal of Economics,* 123(1): 219–277.

Bartik, Alexander W., and Scott T. Nelson. 2016. "Credit Reports *as* Resumes: The Incidence of Pre-Employment Credit Screening." *MIT Economics Working Paper Number 16-01.*

Bronson, Jennifer, and Marcus Berzofsky. 2017. "Indicators of Mental Health Problems Reported by Prisoners and Jail Inmates, 2011-12." *Bureau of Justice Statistics Special Report,* NCJ 250612.

Bronson, Jennifer, Jessica Stroop, Stephanie Zimmer, and Marcus Berzofsky. 2017. "Drug Use, Dependence, and Abuse Among State Prisoners and Jail Inmates, 2007-2009." *Bureau of Justice Statistics Special Report,* NCJ 250546.

Bushway, Shawn D. 2004. "Labor Market Effects of Permitting Employer Access to Criminal History Records." *Journal of Contemporary Criminal Justice,* 20: 276-291.

Cooper, Alexia D., Matthew R. Durose, and Howard N. Snyder. 2014. "Recidivism of Prisoners Released in 30 States in 2005: Patterns From 2005 to 2010." *Bureau of Justice Statistics, NCJ 244205,* Available at http:/ /www.bjs.gov/indcx.cfm?ty=pbdetail&iid=4986.

Doleac, Jennifer L. 2016. "Increasing employment for individuals with criminal records." *The Hamilton Project*, available at http:// www.hamiltonproject.org/papers/increasing_employment-for_ individuals_with_criminal_records.

Doleac, Jennifer L, and Benjamin Hansen. 2016. "Does "ban the box help or hurt low- skilled workers? Statistical discrimination and employment outcomes when criminal histories are hidden." *NBER Working Paper No. 22469.*

Finlay, Keith. 2009. "Effect of Employer Access to Criminal History Data on the Labor Market Outcomes of Ex-Offenders and Non-Offenders." In *Studies of Labor Market Intermediation.* ed. David H. Autor, 89-125.

Holzer, Harry J., Steven Raphael, and Michael A. Stoll. 2004. "The Effect of an Applicant's Criminal History on Employer Hiring Decisions and Screening Practices: Evidence from Los Angeles." *National Poverty Center Working Paper Number 04-15, University of Michigan.*

Holzer, Harry J., Steven Raphael, and Michael A. Stoll. 2006. "Perceived Criminality, Criminal Background Checks, and the Racial Hiring Practices of Employers." *Journal of Law and Economics,* 49: 451-480.

Jackson, Osborne, and Bo Zhao. 2017. "The effect of changing employers' access to criminal histories on ex-offenders' labor market outcomes: Evidence from the 2010-2012 Massachusetts CORI reform." *Federal Reserve of Boston Research Department Working Paper 16-30.*

Kirk, David S, and Sara Wakefield. 2018. "Collateral Consequences of Punishment: A Critical Review and Path Forward." *Annual Review of Criminology,* 1(1).

Leasure, Peter, and Tia Stevens Andersen. 2016. "The Effectiveness of Certificates of Relief as Collateral Consequence Relief Mechanisms: An Experimental Study." *Yale Law and Policy Review Inter Alia,* 35(11): 11-22.

Piehl, Anne Morrison. 2009. "Preparing Prisoners for Employment: The Power of Small Rewards." *Manhattan Institute for Policy Research, Civic Report no. 57.*

Raphael, Steven. 2010. "Improving Employment Prospects for Former Prison Inmates: Challenges and Policy." *NBER Working Paper 15874.*

Rose, Evan. 2017. "Does banning the box help ex-offenders get jobs? Evaluating the effects of a prominent example." *Working paper·,* available at https:llekrose.github.iolfiles lbtb _seattle_ ekr.pdf.

Stoll, Michael A. 2009. "Ex-Offenders, Criminal Background Checks, and Racial Consequences in the Labor Market." *University of Chicago Legal Forum,* 381-419.

Wen, Hefei, Jason M Hockenberry, and Janet R Cummings. 2017. "The effect of Medicaid expansion on crime reduction: Evidence from HIFA-waiver expansions." *Journal of Public Economics,* 154: 67-94.

Wozniak, Abigail. 2015. "Discrimination and the Effects of Drug Testing on Black Employment." *Review of Economics and Statistics,* 97(3): 548·566.

APPENDIX

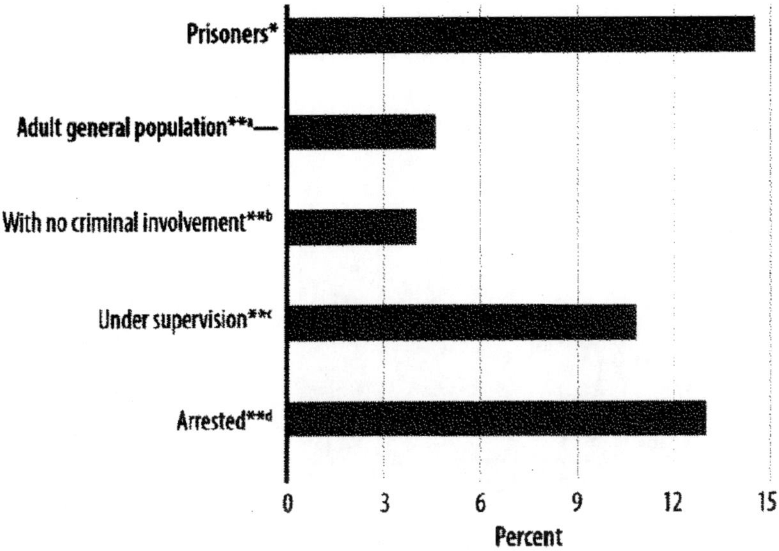

Notes: Figure source: Bronson and Berzofsky (2017). Includes persons with a score of 13 or more on the K6 scale. (See source for definitions.)

* Comparison group.

** Difference with the comparison group is significant at the 95% confidence level.

[a]General population estimates were standardized to the prison population based on sex, race, Hispanic origin, and age.

[b]Includes respondents from the 2009-2012 NSDUH who indicated they had not been arrested or on probation or parole in the past 12 months.

[c]includes respondents from the 2009-2012 NSDUH who indicated they had been on probation or parole in the past 12 months.

[d]Includes respondents from the 2009-2012 NSDUH who indicated they had been arrested in the past 12 months.

Data source: Bureau of Justice Statistics, National Inmate Survey, 20112012; and Substance Abuse and Mental Health Services Administration, National Survey on Drug Use and Health (NSDUH), 2009-2012.

Figure A.l. Prisoners and adult general population who met the threshold for serious psychological distress, 2009-2012.

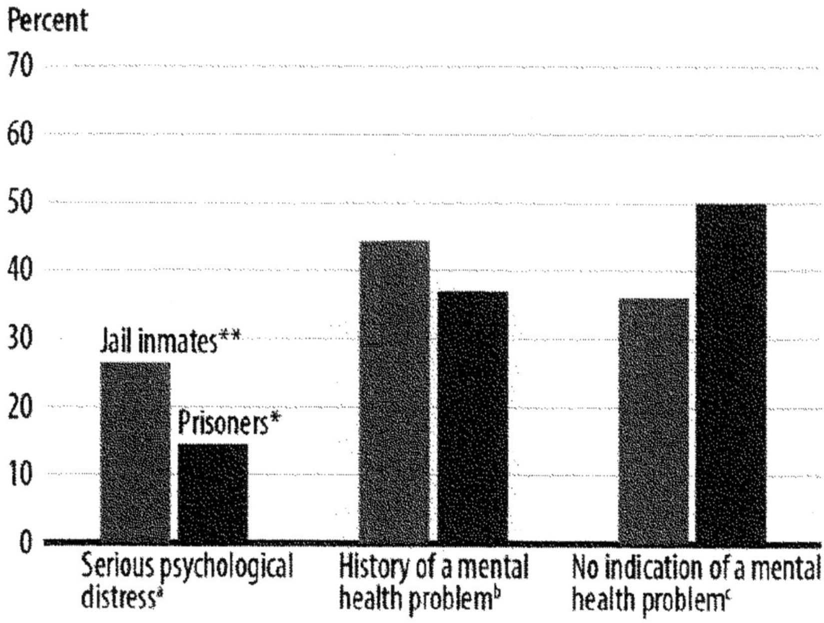

Notes: Figure source: Bronson and Berzofsky (2017).

* Comparison group.

** Difference with the comparison group is significant at the 95% confidence level.

[a]Includes persons with a score of 13 or more on the K6 scale. (See source for definitions.)

[b]Includes inmates who reported they had ever been told by a mental health professional they had a mental disorder.

[c]Includes inmates with a score of 7 or less on the *K6* and who had never been told by a mental health professional they had a mental disorder.

Data source: Bureau of Justice Statistics, National Inmate Survey, 2011-2012.

Figure A.2. Mental health status of prisoners and jail inmates, by type of mental health indicator, 2011-2012.

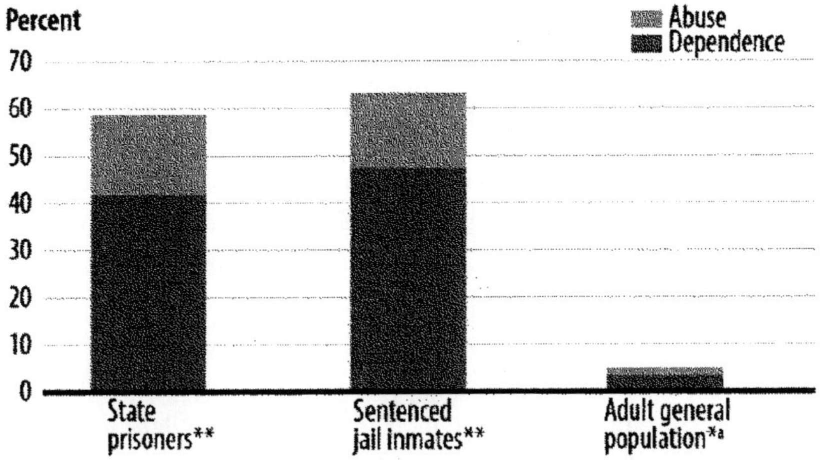

Notes: Figure source: Bronson et al. (2017). (See source for definition of dependence and abuse based on the Diagnostic and Statistical Manual of Mental Disorders, Fourth Edition).

* Comparison group.

** Difference with the comparison group is significant at the 95% confidence level.

[a]General population estimates have been standardized to the state prisoner population by sex, race, Hispanic origin, and age.

Data source: Bureau of Justice Statistics, National Inmate Surveys, 2007 and 2008-00; and Substance Abuse and Mental Health Services Administration, National Survey on Drug Use and Health, 2007-2000.

Figure A.3. Inmates and adult general population who met the criteria for drug dependence or abuse, 2007—2009.

Chairman GOWDY. Thank you, Professor.

Ms. Roseberry?

STATEMENT OF CYNTHIA W. ROSEBERRY

Ms. ROSEBERRY. Chairman Gowdy, Ranking Member Cummings, and members of the committee and staff, thank you for inviting me to participate in today's oversight hearing on the Federal Bureau of Prisons and reentry.

My perspective and understanding of the Bureau of Prisons comes from my experience as a Federal public defender, private criminal defense attorney in Atlanta and Chicago, as project manager of Clemency Project 2014, as executive director of the Council for Court Excellence, and as a member of the Charles Colson Task Force on Federal Corrections, a nine-person, bipartisan, congressional blue ribbon panel led by former Congressman J.C. Watts Jr. and former Congressman Alan Mollohan and supported ably by the Urban Institute.

My comments are my own and not as a representative of any entity about which I speak.

Since the sevenfold increase in its population in the 1980s, the Bureau of Prisons has been operating at crisis levels for decades. People of color and people from poor communities, not unlike the one in which I was reared, Mr. Cummings, are largely part of the population in the world's largest incarcerated population.

Despite recent reductions in population, overcrowding continues, spreading the staff thin, with staff members performing duties outside of their expertise. As a result, the Bureau of Prisons has not lived up to its goal of rehabilitation, missing the opportunity to improve public safety.

As my former fellow Colson task force member John Wetzel, the Secretary of the Pennsylvania Department of Corrections, would say, public safety is a logical consequence of good corrections policy. Returning citizens need effective reentry programming, but BOP policies and practices have not kept up with best practices in the field. "One size fits all" does not work. Efforts must be, one, data driven; two, evidence-based and individualized with measurable outcomes; and three, transparent.

Data-driven efforts. Coordinated consistency in standards, practice, and data collection are essential to BOP's success. Crafting goals and measuring outcomes are accomplished by the collection of data. The Federal corrections system must also standardize assessment protocols and case management practices.

As project manager of Clemency Project 2014, I witnessed the havoc wreaked by inconsistency throughout the system in something as simple as the coding of the statutes of conviction. As a practitioner, I have experienced firsthand how inconsistency in policies such as those where access to programming and client visitation and correspondence negatively impact reentry.

It is critical that agencies within the Federal corrections systems work collaboratively to facilitate smooth transition home. The BOP must consistently coordinate with RRCs. Recently, one young woman who was scheduled for release to a halfway house had secured employment, only to be told that there was an error in her release date for several months. And other families report extended stays because of errors in release dates.

The current system lacks the highly coordinated cross-agency data-sharing platform and procedures that can improve the transition process. Critical information like completion of mental health evaluations is not always passed from the BOP to halfway houses through the supervision, leading to less effective reentry planning and support. D.C. Code offenders experience more difficulty because they are not housed close to D.C. before their reentry.

Evidence-based. Although the evidence shows that individualized treatment and programs can improve outcomes, BOP's own study shows that out of its approximately 16,000 available programs, only a handful are evidence-based. Evidence-based individualized programming would allow the BOP to establish priorities and make data-driven decisions like resource allocations and ways to maximize time outside of facilities for successful reentry. Educational, occupational, and other programs can respond to changes in demand through proper allocation.

Recent reports of videoconferencing only has daunted some of the hopes of those who are incarcerated and their families. If BOP were to focus on the evidence that connections with families increases successful reentry, BOP could ease visitation difficulties without compromising security and expand programs designed to enhance family bonds, including those between incarcerated parents and children.

As a 20-year defense lawyer, you might find it surprising to hear me say that I'm concerned about the safety of the staff at the BOP as well. They want to engage in professional corrections efforts. Evidence-based individualized program benefits BOP staff. If public safety is a natural outcome of good corrections policy, then safe working conditions result from the proper resource allocation that evidence-based individualized programming provides.

Evidence-based program must begin at day one. The BOP mantra "reentry begins at one—at day one" is belied by the fact that the effects of incarceration are not measured. Through CP 2014, I came to understand that returning people to society after long incarceration without evidence-based individualized programming is like sending someone to an alien planet.

One gentleman who was released reported being confused when someone told him they would call him on their BlackBerry. Another woman reported that she experience indignity because she didn't know how to wash her hands. When she was first incarcerated, sinks were not automatic.

At most, we should send people home better. At least we should not make them worse. We also owe it to the victims of crime to make the people who committed crimes and served their sentences better before we send them home. If we take the extreme measure of removing someone from society because of their crimes, we should also take on the responsibility to first do no harm, especially since most hail from and return to marginalized communities.

Far too often, measures like the mechanism to ensure effective implementation and assessment, it's not clear, for example, that all individuals are receiving the appropriate support and treatment consistent with best evidence on what works to reduce recidivism.

For example, studies have shown that under certain circumstances, halfway houses can be ineffective or even harmful to a person's prospects for reentry. The right individuals, those who stand to gain from halfway houses, should matriculate through them.

The Colson task force has recommended two oversight bodies. One would provide advice on the best corrections practice to ensure accountability and compliance, and the other would be a high-level working group to oversee and coordinate implementation of the reforms.

The task force also recommended developing better system-wide performance measures that would be shared with the public. We need to know what's going on inside our prisons.

And lastly, as reentry must start on day one, reentry doesn't end on the last day of custody. The myriad of collateral consequences that NACDL has counted, more than 5,000, must relate—most relate neither to the conduct for which people were convicted, nor to public safety. Looking through the lens of public safety, a working group could identify those found to unnecessarily impede successful reentry as candidates work for appeal. Once we send a person to prison and they come out, we should stamp their receipt paid-in-full.

This concludes my remarks. I look forward to your questions. [Prepared statement of Ms. Roseberry follows:]

WRITTEN TESTIMONY OF CYNTHIA W. ROSEBERRY, EXECUTIVE DIRECTOR, COUNCIL FOR COURT EXCELLENCE, BEFORE THE UNITED STATES HOUSE OF REPRESENTATIVES, COMMITTEE ON OVERSIGHT AND GOVERNMENT REFORM, OVERSIGHT OF THE BUREAU OF PRISONS AND INMATE REENTRY, DECEMBER 13, 2017

Chairman Gowdy, Ranking Member Cummings, and members of the Committee, thank you for inviting me to participate in today's oversight hearing on the Bureau of Prisons (BOP) and reentry. This hearing provides a timely opportunity to 1) discuss how the BOP can most effectively promote successful reentry and 2) encourage more transparency and accountability regarding BOP's current efforts to implement the many recommendations that have previously been made to improve reentry.

My perspective and understanding of the BOP comes from my experience as a federal defender and criminal defense attorney in Atlanta, the project manager of Clemency Project 2014, and a member of the Charles Colson Task Force on Federal Corrections. The testimony I provide here is my own and not as a representative of any of these entities.

For those who may not know, the Colson Task Force was established by Congressional mandate in 2014 as a nine person, bipartisan panel charged with developing practical, data-driven recommendations to enhance public safety by creating a more just and efficient federal corrections system. Led by its chair, former Congressman J.C. Watts, Jr., and vice-chair, former Congressman Alan B. Mollohan, the Task Force conducted over a year of fact-finding, rigorous data analysis, and discussions with key experts and stakeholders. The Urban Institute provided valuable research, analysis, and strategic support. The Task Force endorsed a broad set of reforms affecting all stages of the federal criminal justice system.

The work of the Task Force was grounded in several principles, two of which are especially pertinent here: 1) correctional policy should improve public safety and 2) correctional interventions and programming should be individualized. This means that federal corrections policies should be designed to ensure that people involved in the federal criminal justice system are provided the tools for successful release and reentry, which will improve safety in our nation's communities.

Based on its fact-finding, and consistent with these principles, the Task Force made a series of recommendations directed to BOP, which I'd like to discuss today:

1) promote a culture of safety and rehabilitation in the BOP
2) incentivize participation in risk-reduction programming
3) ensure successful reintegration by using evidence-based practices, and
4) enhance system performance and accountability through increased transparency.

Promote a Culture of Safety and Rehabilitation in the BOP

The BOP needs to create a culture of both safety and rehabilitation inside its facilities. Federal prisons have been operating at crisis levels of overcrowding for decades. Despite recent reductions, overcrowding remains high at medium and high security facilities to the detriment of BOP staff and those incarcerated. It is challenging to operate safe, rehabilitative environments with that level of crowding.

Nonetheless, population reduction in recent years - from a peak of almost 220,000 in 2013 to about 185,000 in 2017- should enable BOP to reexamine its staffing levels and housing assignments. Making sure that individuals are housed in accordance with rated cell capacity and maintaining appropriate inmate-to-staff ratios are prerequisites to operating safe facilities. Reduced overcrowding should also enable staff to focus on rehabilitation. The Task Force learned, for example, that federal corrections staff were often pulled away from their professional positions to provide basic safety and security functions in facilities.

In response to these findings, the Task Force encouraged BOP to implement new ways of doing business. Our assessment found that BOP's policies and practices had not kept up with best practices in the field and that much work needed to be done to create a culture of rehabilitation inside federal prisons. And let's be clear: public safety is a logical consequence of good corrections policy. A wealth of evidence is now available to identify correctional practices that lead to the best outcomes.

Evidence shows that using actuarial risk and needs assessments to guide correctional treatment and programs can improve outcomes.[29] It allows practitioners to individualize treatment and services, an evidence-based practice that is essential to improving public safety. However, the Task Force found that the BOP did not adequately account for risk of recidivism or capture individual needs for treatment Because a validated risk and needs assessment is the foundation of prison-based services and treatment, the Task Force recommended the BOP adopt a similar tool.

---

[29] Aegisdottir et al. 2006; Andrews, Bonta, and Wormith 2006; Grove et al. 2000, as cited in Bonta and Andrews 2007.

Risk and needs assessments wouldn't only improve individualized treatment efforts. They would allow the BOP to analyze its program capacity and make data-driven decisions about where resources are needed. Based on the information the Task Force and others have collected about insufficient programming, BOP should expand educational programs and occupational training opportunities immediately.

The unique circumstances and attributes of each case and each person entering the BOP system should inform the rehabilitation programs, treatment, and services provided. The Task Force recommended that the BOP adopt best practices demonstrated by the states in assessing all federally incarcerated persons' risk of recidivism and programming needs. Delivering programming based on risk and needs is an evidence-based practice shown to reduce the risk of recidivism. Data and research should guide practice.

The BOP should also take steps to create conditions of confinement that support rehabilitation.

It should have housing and security procedures that consider the needs of its diverse population, including the aged, infirm and LGBT populations.

Incentivize Participation in Risk-Reduction Programming

Providing evidence-based programming based on risk and needs can only go so far in promoting public safety. The research suggests that effective treatment aimed at behavior change requires strong incentives and positive reinforcement.[30] The Task Force recommended that corrections policies incentivize participation in risk reduction programming. Evidence shows that encouraging more people to participate in programming while in prison can improve public safety and restore the lives of people returning to their communities.

---

[30] Andrews and Bonta 2010; Bonta and Andrews 2007; Cullen and Gendreau 2000; Drake and Barnoski 2008; Latessa, Cullen, and Gendreau 2002; National Research Council 2008; Petersilia 2004, 2007; Taxman, Soule, and Gelb 1999.

The Task Force recommended that people in federal prison be eligible to earn time off credits if they complete programs and treatment prescribed in their individualized case plans. Further, it recommended that those at higher risk of recidivism earn credits by completing intensive, evidence-based programs pursuant to their case plans. Lower risk individuals should be able to earn time off, but their case plans would be less onerous.

The Task Force also recommended that earned time for the intensive Residential Drug Abuse Program be expanded so that all those who have demonstrated substance abuse problems be incentivized to participate in the program. Currently, people with histories of violence are restricted from benefiting from this incentive. But, all individuals should be strongly incentivized to participate in programming that addresses their needs, regardless of the nature of their criminal histories. This would require both the BOP and Congress to expand the criteria for this incentive.

The BOP already uses some institutional incentives (such as reducing security level) to encourage program participation and completion. The Task Force recommended that the BOP review these policies and expand earned privileges further to include more recreation time, expanded visiting hours, and other institutional incentives. It further recommended that these be available to all those in federal prison, including those serving life sentences.

The BOP has the discretionary authority to recommend early release for people that BOP staff deem rehabilitated. Under a transparent system with measurable outcomes, BOP staff are in a unique position to discern rehabilitation and make recommendations for release.

Finally, the Task Force recommended that Congress establish a judicial second look function, to review and possibly reduce the sentences of people who have served at least 15 years behind bars. As the Project Manager of the Clemency Project 2014, I managed lawyers who reviewed the cases of many people who had served decades behind bars. Some had turned their lives around while in prison, contributing to the prison community by teaching classes and preparing others for reentry. The data suggests that as such individuals age, their risk of recidivism falls considerably.[31]

Ensure Successful Reintegration by Using Evidence-Based Practices

Almost everyone confined in the federal prison system will return to their home communities one day, and BOP should do all it can to ease the transition back to the community. One important way the BOP can help people prepare for their return is by facilitating relationships with family members. The Task Force learned, however, that prison visitation procedures-which can change and vary by institution- sometimes hinder regular family visits. The Task Force therefore recommended that the BOP establish a central family affairs and visitation office to oversee prison visitation procedures, with a focus on easing visitation difficulties without compromising security. The office would also work to expand programs designed to enhance family bonds, particularly between children and incarcerated parents. Consistent with the research, by implementing these programs the BOP could help reduce recidivism rates while greatly improving the lives of family members.

It's critical that all agencies within the federal corrections system- BOP facilities, federal halfway house contractors, and federal probation office-work collaboratively to facilitate a smooth transition home for people released from federal prisons. At present, the systems lack the highly coordinated, cross-agency data sharing platforms and procedures to improve the transition process. Critical information- such as case plans, program completion and mental health evaluations-is not always passed along from BOP to halfway houses to community supervision agencies, leading to less effective reentry planning and support. Improving data sharing among these agencies could improve efficiency and system-wide outcomes.

---

[31] Blumstein and Nakamura 2009; Sampson and Laub 2004.

Residential reentry centers (RRCs) could also play a pivotal role in the transition from prison to the community in the federal system, but BOP needs to ensure that the right individuals-those who stand to benefit from a federal halfway house-transition through them and receive reentry services matched to their needs. Studies have shown that under certain circumstances, stays at halfway houses can be ineffective or even harmful to a person's prospects for successful reentry.[32]

A great deal of work was done over the last few years to assess the RRCs and develop recommendations for improvement. Recommendations from the Colson Task Force, Department of Justice (DOJ) Inspector General's office, Deloitte, and others culminated in a series of action steps laid out by DOJ in late 2016.

There is a lack of transparency about the new Administration's approach to BOP and the RRCs, but some of the recent indications about the RRCs have not been positive. We have heard about modifications to the RRC contracts, including a shift away from the commitment to adopt performance based contracting, and a reduction in the number of contracts and available bed-space. DOJ and BOP committed to moving towards performance-based contracting in 2016, but we have since learned that the revised Statement of Work reflecting these changes has been revised or is not being fully implemented. For example, we understand that the provisions requiring certain types of programming (Cognitive Based Treatment) have been eliminated. If they have, in fact, backed away from this commitment, the potential improvements for those housed in RRCs will not be realized.

Enhance System Performance and Accountability through Better Coordination across Agencies and Increased Transparency

The Task Force urged more collaboration among agencies, increased transparency about agency policies and practices, and additional

[32] Lowenkamp and Latessa 2002.

mechanisms to hold agencies and the overall federal corrections system accountable for results. This starts with BOP being more transparent and accountable about its operations and programming.

Experience from state criminal justice reform efforts suggests that far too often reform measures lack the mechanisms to ensure effective implementation and assessment. To that end, the Task Force recommended two new oversight bodies to improve accountability. One would be for BOP, and would provide advice on best corrections practice, ensure accountability, and promote compliance. The other would be a high-level working group headed by the DOJ and the Judiciary (Criminal Law Committee) to oversee and coordinate implementation of the reforms. It also recommended developing better system- wide performance measures that would be shared with the public. Regular reporting of recidivism rates was at the top of our list for improved performance metrics.

Ultimately, coordinated efforts require consistency in standards, practice, and data collection. The federal corrections system must work towards standardized assessment protocols and case management practices. As the BOP develops its risk and needs assessment, it should consult with US Probation and RRC contractors to develop comparable measures. By improving the handoff across agencies, the Task Force believed the federal corrections system could further reduce recidivism rates.

Finally, the Task Force expressed concern about the adverse impact of collateral consequences and recommended that the new Joint Working Group review them through the lens of public safety.

Moving Ahead

The roadmap for BOP reform is straightforward. I have attached a list of the recommendations from the Colson Task Force as well as references to other suggestions regarding RRCs. Given the size and complexity of the BOP, however, implementation will be difficult under the best of circumstances. The key question is whether BOP, working with its partners, is committed to adopting and implementing the changes. Last year, there seemed to be momentum to reform the BOP, including the RRCs, but it is unclear what is currently underway. Requiring BOP to be more transparent about its ongoing operations by issuing regular reports with agreed upon performance measures, would support effective oversight, improve accountability, and promote successful reentry.

References

Aegisdottir, Stefania, Michael J. White, Paul M. Spengler, Alan S. Maugherman, Linda A. Anderson, RobertS. Cook, Cassandra N. Nichols, Georgios K. Lampropoulos, Blain S. Walker, Genna Cohen, and Jeffrey D. Rush. 2006. "The Meta-Analysis of Clinical Judgment Project: Fifty-Six Years of Accumulated Research on Clinical Versus Statistical Prediction." *Counseling Psychologist* 34: 341-82.

Andrews, D. A., James Bonta, and J. Stephen Wormith. 2006. "Recent Past and Near Future of Risk and/or Need Assessment." *Crime and Delinquency* 52 (1): 7-27.

Andrews, D. A., and James Bonta. 2010. *The Psychology of Criminal Conduct*. 5th ed. Newark, NJ: Anderson.

Blumstein, Alfred, and Kiminori Nakamura. 2009. "Redemption in the Presence of Widespread Criminal Background Checks." *Criminology* 47 (2): 327-59.

Bonta, James L, and D. A. Andrews. 2007. *Risk-Need-Responsivity Model for Offender Assessment and Rehabilitation 2007–D6*. Ottawa: Public Safety Canada. http://www.pbpp.pa.gov/lnformation/Documents/Research/EBP7.pdf.

Bonta, James L, and D. A. Andrews. 2007. *Risk-Need-Responsivity Model for Offender Assessment and Rehabilitation 2007–Q6*. Ottawa: Public Safety Canada. http://www.pbpp.pa.gov/lnformation/Documents/Research/ EBP7.pdf.

Charles Colson Task Force on Federal Corrections. 2016. *Transforming Prisons, Restoring Lives: Final Recommendations of the Charles Colson Task Force and Federal Corrections*. Washington, DC: Urban Institute. https://www.urban.org/research/publication/transforming-prisons-restoring-lives/view/full report.

Cullen, Francis T., and Paul Gendreau. 2000. "Assessing Correctional Rehabilitation: Policy, Practice, and Prospects." In *NIJ Criminal Justice 2000: Policies, Process, and Decisions of the Criminal Justice System*, edited by Julie Horney, 109–76. Washington, DC: National Institute of Justice, US Department of Justice.

Deloitte. 2016. *U.S. Department of Justice Bureau of Prisons Residential Reentry Centers Assessment: Recommendations Report*. Washington, DC: Deloitte Development, LLC. https://www.justice.gov/archives/dag/page/file/914006/download.

Drake, Elizabeth K., and Robert Barnoski. 2008. *Increasing Earned Release from Prison: Impacts of 2003*. Law on Recidivism and Criminal Justice Costs. Olympia: Washington State Institute for Public Policy. http:/fwww.wsipp.wa.gov/ReportFile/1039/WsippIncreased-Earned-Release-From-Prison-Impacts-of-a-2003-Law-on-Recidivism-and-Crime-Costs-Revised Fuii-Report.pdf.

Grove, William M., David H. Zald, Boyd S. Lebow, Beth E. Snitz, and Chad Nelson. 2000. "Clinical versus Mechanical Prediction: A Meta-Analysis." *Psychological Assessment* 12 (1): 19-30.

Latessa, Edward J., Francis T. Cullen, and Paul Gendreau. 2002. "Beyond Professional Quackery: Professionalism and the Possibility of Effective Treatment." *Federal Probation* 66 (2): 43-49.

Lowenkamp, Christopher T., and Edward J. Latessa. 2002. *Evaluation of Ohio's Community Based Correctional Facilities and Halfway House Programs Final Report*. Cincinnati, OH: University of Cincinnati. https://www.uc.edu/content/dam/uc/ccjr/docs/reports/project reports/HH CBCF Reportl.pdf.

National Research Council. 2008. *Parole, Desistence from Crime, and Community Integration*. Washington, DC: National Academies Press.

Petersilia, Joan. 2004. "What Works in Prisoner Reentry? Reviewing and Questioning the Evidence." *Federal Probation* 68 (2): 3-9.

___. 2007. "Employ Behavioral Contracting for 'Earned Discharge' Parole." *Criminology and Public Policy* 6 (4):807-14.

Sampson, Robert J., and John H. Laub. 2004. "Life-Course Disasters? Trajectories of Crime among Delinquent Boys Followed to Age 70." *Criminology* 41(3): 301-40.

Taxman, Faye S., David Soule, and Adam Gelb. 1999. "Graduated Sanctions: Stepping into Accountable Systems and Offenders." *Prison Journal* 79 (2): 182-204.

US Department of Justice, Office of the Inspector General. 2016. *Audit of the Federal Bureau of Prisons' Management of Inmate Placements in Residential Reentry Centers and Home Confinement, Audit Report 17-01.* Washington, DC: US Department of Justice. https://oig.justice.gov/reports/2016/a1701.pdf#page=l.

RECOMMENDATIONS BY AUTHORITY

Recommendation 1: Reserve Prison for Those Convicted of the Most Serious Federal Crimes

	Recommendation	Congress	Executive Branch	Judiciary
1.1	**Mandatory minimums for drug offenses**	✓		✓
1.1.a	Repeal drug mandatory minimum penalties, except for drug kingpins; apply Fair Sentencing Act retroactively	Congress		
1.1.b	Revise Sentencing Guidelines to reflect role and culpability; prescribe alternatives to prison for lower-level drug trafficking offenses			USSC
1.2	**Mandatory minimums for weapon possession**	✓		✓
1.2.a	Enable judges to sentence below the mandatory minimum weapon enhancement for possession associated with nonviolent offense	Congress		
1.2.b	Monitor impact of change and consider similar departure mechanisms for other mandatory minimums	Congress		USSC
1.3	**Mandatory minimum research and sunset provisions**	✓	✓	✓
1.3.a	Update report on mandatory minimum penalties re: unwarranted disparities or disproportionately severe sentences			USSC
1.3.b	Apply sunset provision to any future mandatory minimum penalties	Congress		
1.3.c	Prepare prison, fiscal, and racial impact assessments for proposed legislative and Sentencing Guidelines changes		DOJ, other agencies	US Courts, USSC

1.4	**Alternatives to incarceration**	✓	✓	✓
1.4.a	Prescribe probation for lower-level drug trafficking offenses and consider doing so for other offense types			USSC
1.4.b	Promulgate information regarding alternatives to incarceration			USSC
1.4.c	Increase use of alternatives to incarceration including front-end diversion courts, problem-solving courts, and evidence-based probation		US Attorneys	Judges
1.4.d	Authorize and fund front-end diversion programs and problem-solving courts, evaluating alternatives	Congress		OJP
1.5	**Federal prosecution**		✓	
1.5.a	Review case selection and charging practices regarding federal interest and jurisdiction		US Attorneys	
1.5.b	Analyze data from all US Attorneys' offices to determine application of Smart on Crime		US Attorneys	

Recommendation 2: Promote a Culture of Safety and Rehabilitation in Federal Facilities

	Recommendation	Congress	Executive Branch	Judiciary
2.1	**Safety and security in BOP**	✓	✓	
2.1.a	Assess and reallocate staffing to ensure appropriate inmate-to-staff ratios		BOP	
2.1.b	Ensure individuals are housed in accordance with rated cell capacity		BOP	
2.1.c	Enable individuals to earn up to 15 percent off sentence to incentivize good conduct	Congress		
2.2	**Risk and needs**		✓	
2.2.a	Develop and implement an actuarial risk and needs assessment tool		BOP	
2.2.b	Develop case plans and deliver programming based on individual risk and needs		BOP	
2.3	**Programming**		✓	
2.3.a	Develop aggregate criminogenic risk and needs profile of its population		BOP	
2.3.b	Conduct a systemwide assessment of facility-specific programming needs		BOP	
2.3.c	Allocate programs and treatment offerings in accordance with facility risk and need		BOP	
2.3.d	Expand educational and occupational opportunities in accordance with facility need		BOP	
2.4	**Conditions of confinement and rehabilitative culture**		✓	
2.4.a	Train all staff on communication, problem solving, and procedurally just resolution practices		BOP	
2.4.b	Use segregated housing as punitive measure only in extraordinary circumstances		BOP	
2.4.c	Ensure housing and security procedures respond to specific needs of diverse population		BOP	
2.4.d	Develop appropriate and nonrestrictive housing options for those in need of protective custody		BOP	
2.5	**Family engagement**		✓	
2.5.a	House people close to home communities		BOP	
2.5.b	Establish visitation and family affairs office to oversee and ease visitation procedures		BOP	
2.5.c	Expand video conferencing and other visitation programs		BOP	
2.5.d	Enhance support for families of people in prison		BOP	

Recommendation 3: Incentivize Participation in Risk- Reduction Programming

	Recommendation	Congress	Executive Branch	Judiciary
3.1	**Risk-reduction programming**	✓	✓	
3.1.a	Enable individuals not serving life sentences to earn up to 20 percent off time served by complying with individualized case plans	Congress		
3.1.b	Enable individuals, including those serving life sentences, to earn facility-based privileges		BOP	
3.1.c	Enable all Residential Drug Abuse Program participants not serving life sentences to earn up to one year off time served	Congress	BOP	
3.2	**Second Look provision**	✓		✓
3.2.a	Enable resentencing for anyone who has served more than 15 years of their sentence	Congress		
3.2.b	Develop guidelines for Second Look reviews and sentence modifications			USSC

Recommendation 4: Ensure Successful Reintegration by Using Evidence-Based Practices in Supervision and Support

	Recommendation	Congress	Executive Branch	Judiciary
4.1	**Prerelease custody and Residential Reentry Centers (RRCs)**		✓	
4.1.a	Make recommendations regarding allocation of RRC beds, alternatives to RRC placement, and performance-based RRC contracts		BOP Performance, Accountability, and Oversight Board (Board)	
4.2	**Safe and seamless reintegration**		✓	✓
4.2.a	Improve coordination by establishing a shared information system		BOP	Probation
4.2.b	Share information on risk and needs assessment, program participation, medical and mental health status, and aftercare information		BOP	Probation
4.3	**Supervised release and early termination**			✓ **Probation Judges**

Recommendation 5: Enhance System Performance and Accountability through Better Coordination across Agencies and Increased Transparency

	Recommendation	Congress	Executive Branch	Judiciary
5.1	**Establish joint Department of Justice/ Judiciary working group (Joint Working Group) to oversee reforms**		✓	✓
5.1.a	Monitor implementation of recommended legislative and policy changes		Joint Working Group	Joint Working Group
5.1.b	Submit an annual report on reform progress and performance metrics		Joint Working Group	Joint Working Group
5.2	**Caseload reporting and performance metrics**		✓	✓
5.2.a	Review and expand annual reporting of caseload data for the corrections and supervision population		Joint Working Group	Joint Working Group
5.2.b	Develop metrics and an ongoing review for performance measurement; disseminate recidivism data annually		Joint Working Group	Joint Working Group USSC
5.3	**Establish BOP Office of Victim Services**		✓	
5.4	**Membership, role, and capacity of the USSC**	✓		✓
5.4.a	Expand voting membership of USSC to include representation of victims, formerly incarcerated individuals, defense attorneys, and experts in sentencing and corrections	Congress		USSC
5.4.b	Routinely monitor and report on the impact of sentencing changes			USSC
5.4.c	Revise 2011 mandatory minimum report			USSC
5.5	**Permanent BOP Performance, Accountability, and Oversight Board (Board)**		✓	
5.5.a	Work with BOP to develop and promulgate performance metrics		BOP Board	
5.5.b	Monitor development of new risk and needs assessment and implementation of new earned time credits		Board	
5.5.c	Review BOP data on internal performance, safety, and security metrics for external consumption		Board	
5.5.d	Oversee development and implementation of comprehensive 10-year plan to restructure federal prison system		Board	
5.5.e	Review BOP oversight, accreditation, auditing, and compliance mechanisms		Board	
5.5.f	Conduct special studies such as review of prerelease custody practices and procedures, focused on RRCs		Board	
5.6	**Collateral consequences and barriers to reintegration**	✓	✓	✓
5.6.a	Review federal collateral consequence laws		Joint Working Group	Joint Working Group
5.6.b	Allow Pell grants for incarcerated persons	Congress		
5.6.c	Eliminate executive branch criminal history disclosure on employment applications for federal contractors		President	
5.6.d	Codify criminal history disclosure changes for federal employees and contractors	Congress		

Recommendation 6: Reinvest Savings to Support the Expansion of Necessary Programs, Supervision, and Treatment

	Recommendation	Congress	Executive Branch	Judiciary
6.1	**Resources for reform**	✓	✓	✓
6.1.a	Fund BOP to implement validated risk and needs assessment tool, catalog current program offerings and capacity, and expand necessary programs and treatment	Congress	BOP	
6.1.b	Fund US Probation to increase staffing, programs, and services	Congress		Probation
6.1.c	Fund Courts to establish the Second Look function	Congress		US Courts
6.1.d	Fund USSC to expand capacity and training	Congress		USSC
6.1.e	Fund DOJ Office of Justice Programs (OJP) to incentivize front-end diversion programs, problem-solving courts, and other alternatives to incarceration	Congress	OJP	
6.2	**Develop recommendations for reinvesting savings from the reduced BOP population**	**Congress**	**Joint Working Group**	**Joint Working Group**

Note: For the following recommendations, congressional action, funding, or approval may be required before they can be fully implemented by the identified agencies: 1.1.b, 1.4.a, 2.1.a, 2.1.b, 2.3.d, 3.2.b, 6.1, and 6.2.

Chairman GOWDY. Thank you, Ms. Roseberry.

Mr. Martin?

STATEMENT OF GLENN E. MARTIN

Mr. MARTIN. Thank you. Good morning.

Thank you, Chairman Gowdy, Ranking Member Cummings, and members of the committee and staff.

I'd like for you to describe in one word the last person who sold you a pair of sunglasses or a pair of glasses. You might say "man."

You might say "woman." You might say "young." You might say "old," "funny," "enthusiastic."

Seventeen years ago, I left prison after serving 6 years, and I searched for a job. I visited 50 different employers. When I exited prison, I left with a quality liberal arts degree and about $100,000 in fines, fees, restitution, and child support.

The third employer I visited, his name was Michael. And after two interviews, he said to me, "You're the perfect fit. You're very articulate. I think you'll be able to sell sunglasses and glasses better than anyone else I've interviewed. I'm going to offer you the job."

Within 2 hours I arrived at home after the second interview to a voice message saying that he hadn't noticed that I put that I had a felony conviction on my application and that he was rescinding the job offer based solely on the criminal conviction. I should have applied for that job as a father, a brother, a son, a qualified job seeker. But those identities were taken from me because in America, everyone who stands at sentencing in a criminal court is sentenced to a lifetime of punishment.

The fact of the matter is that we have a ceremony that brings people down in that moment, and we have no equal ceremony to bring people back up. We have left 70 million Americans in that moment.

When I was released, policies like ban-the-box, policies like the ones the Fair Chance Act would promote did not exist. Today, I run an organization with over 50 staff positions and over 370 formerly incarcerated alums of our training seminars. Not once have I asked staff or trainees about their criminal history during the initial application process. I never needed to.

I assess someone's preparedness based on their experience and on something far more meaningful and powerful, their humanity. But I am the exception, and because of that, because most employers cannot or will not see past a person's worst moment, the 6-plus million people who are currently under correctional control in this country will face the same barriers to reentry that I faced.

One in three black men will relive the setbacks I was forced to endure, despite their best efforts at building towards redemption. We know reducing recidivism means eradicating these barriers, something that ban-the-box and the Fair Chance Act can help us to achieve.

But Jennifer Doleac, despite lacking lived experience and the cultural competency needed to design and interpret her own research, wants to tell you what you should do to help us. In her research, Ms. Doleac says that the ban-the-box policy increases discrimination in employment. She blames these policies for creating what we've known to exist in our country since its founding, racism.

Ms. Doleac argues that casting aside the scarlet letter of criminality hurts black people because then employers will just assume that all of us have something to hide. Her argument seems to rest on the idea that killing ban-the-box policies will help the few black men who have not been branded, shackled, and caged in our justice system because their comparative goodness will allow them to stand out.

This argument against ban-the-box and the Fair Chance Act urges you to set aside these ideas—set these ideas aside so that the "good and well-behaved black men" might succeed, while the millions of us who have been marginalized by decades of tough on crime policies are discarded like trash. Well, the piece of trash you see sitting in front of you now helps 50 people build families, strengthen communities, and contribute to our tax base in America.

Discarding qualified and motivated job seekers is not justice. That's not how to make America great again. This exclusion fundamentally contradicts the values enshrined in the document you are sworn to defend and uphold.

The Fair Chance Act and ban-the-box policies work. They are part of the solution that will help all of us. They are crucial pieces of holistic reform needed to reduce recidivism and to start undoing decades of bad policy that have led to our current state of mass incarceration. They are the first steps in building a smarter and safer justice system.

More importantly, to me and millions of others, ban-the-box was started by formerly incarcerated people in a storefront in Oakland, California, and made it all the way to the halls of power. The power of this policy as a tool to educate and inspire employers and policymakers is immeasurable. I urge this Congress to consider the Fair Chance Act before you adjourn and to hear and elevate the often-ignored voices of the people who have been most impacted by that law in your guiding deliberations.

I'm happy to answer questions. Thank you for the opportunity. [Prepared statement of Mr. Martin follows:]

JLUSA: Glenn E. Martin: Testimony on Policies Relating to Bureau of Prisons Reentry, Fair Chance Act, and Ban the Box

Delivered to the Committee on Government and Oversight Reform: Wednesday, December 13, 2017

To Chairman Gowdy, Ranking Member Cummings, and the Committee:

Today I respectfully submit testimony regarding the significant barriers to reentry faced by millions of formerly incarcerated individuals; the need to eliminate these counterproductive barriers; the policies you can implement to achieve that goal, including passage of H.R. 1905 - the *Fair Chance Act;* and how my personal experience as a formerly incarcerated American and the experience of other formerly incarcerated men and women can inform your actions. There are four key points I hope to convey in my testimony:

1) Reducing recidivism requires successful reentry.
   In their 2016 report, the Federal Interagency Reentry Council reminded us that holistic reentry, which includes access to stable housing, education, and employment, reduces recidivism, and a period of stability that lasts just a few years can have significant, positive consequences on ensuring the long-term success of an individual's reentry.[33]
2) Successful reentry requires access to meaningful employment opportunities.
   Transitioning out of and away from the criminal justice system necessitates the ability to transition into more stable opportunities in our community. As the *Council of State Governments* notes, research indicates that holding a job reduces one's chances to

[33] Lynch, L. and Munoz. C. (Eds.) (2016). *The Federal Interagency Reentry Council: A Record of Progress and Roadmap for the Future.* Washington. D.C.: United States Department of justice.

recidivate, and job stability over an extended period of time can reduce the likelihood that an individual will reoffend.[34]

3) Access to meaningful employment opportunities requires implementation or expansion of *Ban the Box* policies and the passage of the *Fair Chance Act.* Approximately seventy million people in America have a criminal record, and there are over one-hundred million criminal records at the state level.[35] The insidious stigma of criminality disproportionately impacts black men, as one-in-three of us will be incarcerated in our lifetime.[36] Employers have a demonstrable and well-recognized reluctance to offer opportunities to the men and women with these records,[37] so a nationwide policy that both highlights how employers are systematically ignoring qualified jobseekers and simultaneously levels the playing field is a key step in achieving equity of opportunity.
4) Understanding the lived experience of formerly incarcerated people is vital for successful reform.

The data, the analysis, and the academic research are compelling and should help guide your actions as elected leaders in our country. However,

---

[34] Duran, L., Plotkin, M., and Potter, P. (2013). *Integrated Reentry and Employment Strategies: Reducing Recidivism and Promoting job Readiness.* New York, NY: Council of State Governments justice Center; Visher, C., Debus, S., and Yahner, j. (2008). *Employment After Prison: A Longitudinal Study of Releases* in *Three States.* Washington, D.C.: Urban Institute; Sampson, R. and Laub, J. (1993). *Crime in the Making: Pathways and Turning Points Through Life.* Cambridge, MA: Harvard University Press.

[35] Friedman, M. (2015).just *Facts: As Many Americans Have Criminal Records as College Diplomas.* New York, NY: Brennan Center for justice at the New York University School of Law.

[36] Lyons, C., Pettit, B. (2011). *Compounded Disadvantage: Race, Incarceration, and Wage Growth.* Oxford, U.K.: Oxford University Press on behalf of The Society for the Study of Social Problems.

[37] Lynch, L. and Munoz. C. (Eds.) (2016). *The Federal Interagency Reentry Council: A Record of Progress and Roadmap for the Future.* Washington. D.C.: United States Department of justice. Citing: Albright, S. and Denq. F. (1996). *Employer Attitudes Toward Hiring Ex-Offenders;* Giguere, R. and Dundes, L. (2002). *Help Wanted: A Survey of Employer Concerns about Hiring Ex-Convicts;* Holzer, H., Raphael, S., and Stoll, M. (2004). *The Effect of an Applicant's Criminal History on Employer Hiring Decisions and Screening Practices: Evidence from Los Angeles;* and Pager, D. (2007). *Marked: Race, Crime, and Finding Work in an Era of Mass Incarceration.*

the lived experiences of those millions of men and women who will be directly impacted by the decisions you make should also inform those actions and should empower your understanding of these issues by offering a vital and often ignored perspective.

I offer this testimony as a national advocate for criminal justice reform and as President of just Leadership USA, a national advocacy organization, and also as someone whose personal experiences have shaped and defined my views of practices and solutions in this field.

I have not only studied, analyzed and debated the policies that you are considering. I have also lived with the consequences of the decisions local and national policymakers have made over the past five decades - decisions that have led to mass incarceration, the unjustifiable and unrelenting consequences of that incarceration, and the creation of a new underclass of citizenship in America. Six years in prison and, to date, seventeen years of post-incarceration reentry have taught me that those closest to the problem are closest to the solution, but often farthest from the power and resources needed to drive necessary change. I have experienced the problem of government-sanctioned discrimination from our nation's employers, and know what can and must be achieved so that the people who are returning from our prisons and jails do not face these same, unjustifiable challenges. Today, I am speaking with the people who have the power and resources needed to bring proposed solutions to fruition immediately. I ask that you continue to hear my voice and the voices of the millions of others under correctional supervision in this country as you discuss, debate, and determine your next steps after today's hearing.

Reducing Recidivism Requires Successful Reentry

There is a strong bipartisan consensus at all levels of our government that we must make a concerted effort to reduce recidivism.[38] The question is not *if* we should achieve this goal, but *how.*

---

[38] Khan, S. (2016). *Criminal justice Reform: A Rare Area of Bipartisan Consensus.* Berkeley, CA: Berkeley Political Review.

Simply put, successful holistic reentry- a reentry process that prioritizes access to stable housing, healthcare, education, and employment- is the key factor in reducing recidivism.[39]

There is an unmistakable urgency to addressing this issue. Today, two-plus million Americans are incarcerated in our country. Another four-plus million men and women are under some form of correctional supervision. Over six million Americans will have their ability to reenter into their communities determined, in part, by the decisions you make today.[40] And while there has been a lot of emphasis on what we can do to prevent incarceration moving forward, we have not done enough to deal with the fact that millions of people presently suffer the injustices related to incarceration.[41]

This lack of concrete action is especially alarming considering that at least 8% of working-age people in our country are labeled by others as "ex-felons," meaning that nearly one-in-ten of the people who are in our workforce have their access to employment impeded by the stigma of justice involvement.[42] This stigma disproportionately impacts people who look like me. Young black men are ten times more likely than their white counterparts to have been incarcerated, and black men who do not have a high school education have a 50% chance of being incarcerated in their lifetime.[43]

---

[39] Bowman, S. and Travis, R. (2012). *Prisoner Reentry and Recidivism According to the Formerly Incarcerated and Reentry Service Providers: A Verbal Behavior Approach.* San Marcos, TX: *School* of Criminal justice at Texas State University; Bouffard, J. and Bergseth, K. (2008). *The Impact of Reentry Services on juvenile Offenders' Recidivism.* Greenbelt, MD: Youth Violence and juvenile justice.

[40]. Jacobson, M. and Schiraldi, V. (2017). *Less* is *More: How Reducing Probation Populations can Improve Outcomes.* Cambridge, MA: john F. Kennedy School of Government at Harvard University.

[41] Pager, D. (2003). *The Mark of a Criminal Record.* Chicago, lL: Northwestern University.

[42] Pager, D. (2003). *The Mark of a Criminal Record.* Chicago, IL: Northwestern University; Jacobson, M. and Schiraldi, V. (2017). *Less is More: How Reducing Probation Populations can Improve Outcomes.* Cambridge, MA: john F. Kennedy School of Government at Harvard University.

[43] Pager, D. (2003). *The Mark of a Criminal Record.* Chicago, IL: Northwestern University; Pettit, B. and Western, B. (2001)."Inequality in Lifetime Risks of Imprisonment." Paper presented at the *annual meetings of the American Sociological Association*. Anaheim, August.

But this problem is not limited to black America. Our nation has 5% of the world's population and over 20% of the world's incarcerated population. Our prison population grew by 408% between 1978 and 2014.[44] All of us are disproportionately impacted by the policies that drive mass incarceration. Moreover, the fastest growing prison populations today are in rural areas, a surge fueled by a large increase in the number of incarcerated white women.[45]

Our widening state of mass incarceration has created a second class of citizens. We have already built the world in which millions suffer at the hands of discriminatory polices and practices. It is up to you to decide whether or not we are going to take steps to undo these policies and dismantle an infrastructure that has created unbearable, untenable, and unjustifiable obstacles for too many of us.

Anything short of fully and forcefully removing the barriers that exist in the reentry journeys of these Americans will result in your tacit approval of the fact that we, as a nation, believe that there are some people who are worthy of opportunities for growth and transformation, and many who are not.

This Congress must enact laws and promote policies that eliminate the barriers to successful reentry. From my own experience and from the experience of the hundreds of formerly- and currently- incarcerated men and women that just Leadership USA works with and learns from every day, I know that there are several components required to build a comprehensive reentry process. One of the most vital of those components is the one we're discussing today: employment.

Successful reentry requires access to meaningful employment opportunities. Employment is more than a piece of the reentry puzzle.

---

[44] ACLU. (2017). *The Prison Crisis.* Online: https:/fwww.aclu.orgfprison-crisis; Liptak, A. (2008). *U.S. Prison Population Dwarfs that of Other Nations.* New York, NY: New York Times.

[45] Huling, T. (2002). *Building a Prison Economy* in *Rural America.* New York, NY: The New Press; Yurkanin, A. (2017). *Poor, Rural, and Addicted: Drugs Drive Surge* in *White Women* in *Prison.* Birmingham, AL: AL.com.

Employment is, in many instances, the primary determinant of whether or not a person's reentry will be successful.[46] Access to employment is the bridge to other aspects of holistic reentry and reintegration, including the ability to afford housing, pay for medical and family needs, pay child support, and care for our loved ones, who- due to our own involvement in the criminal justice system and the similarity in circumstances between their lives and ours - are especially susceptible to being intercepted and entrapped by the justice system.[47] Furthermore, maintaining employment is the only way that the millions of men and women who are on probation or parole can pay the burdensome fees associated with that supervision - payments that are crucial since missing one payment could send someone back to jail or prison for a sentence that's even longer than the one associated with their underlying charge.[48] Simply put, employment can and in many cases does empower and accelerate successful, permanent reentry.[49]

While people who do not have lived experience with these issues will say that self-motivation is required on our part before you fulfill your responsibilities in easing reentry, those of us who have had to endure the painful branding of the criminal justice system and the stigma associated with it will all tell you: we will seize any opportunities we can to ensure the cessation of our involvement with the justice system. But, far too often, our motivations to succeed are overshadowed by the lack of motivation

---

[46] Laub, J. and Sampson, R.. (2001). *Understanding Desistance from* Crime. Cambridge, MA: Crime and justice.

[47] Duran, L., Plotkin, M., and Potter, P. (2013). *Integrated Reentry and Employment Strategies: Reducing Recidivism and Promoting job Readiness.* New York, NY: Council of State Governments justice Center; Rose., D. and Clear, T. (2001). *Incarceration, Reentry, and Social Capital: Social Networks* in *the Balance.* Washington, D.C.: United States Department of Health and Human Services.

[48] Jacobson, M. and Schiraldi, V. (2017). *Less is More: How Reducing Probation Populations can Improve Outcomes.* Cambridge, MA: john F. Kennedy School of Government at Harvard University.

[49] Duran, L., Plotkin, M., and Potter, P. *(2013).Integrated Reentry and Employment Strategies: Reducing Recidivism and Promoting job Readiness.* New York, NY: Council of State Governments justice Center.

from elected officials and employers to eradicate the barriers that prevent that success.

We can and do apply to jobs as soon as we are able to. But 56% of employers will not consider any applicant with a criminal record.[50] Consider that while remembering the statistics cited above about how many people who, like me, must carry a criminal record with them throughout their life. Yet, even when we do not have a criminal record, black applicants receive callbacks in the job application process at a rate that is 20% less than our white counterparts.[51] In fact, a white man with a criminal record actually has a better chance of landing gainful employment than a black man without any record at all. And for the millions of black men and women who do have a criminal record, positive outcomes in the job process for are reduced by 57%.[52] We have less than 5% chance at earning a callback in an interview.[53] Motivation is not the problem. Opportunity is, and until you take meaningful action to eliminate that gap between us and the jobs we are trying to fill, these disparities and the related consequences will worsen.[54] A key step in that action is implementation of the *Fair Chance Act* and promotion of *Ban the Box* policies for public and private employers in this country.

---

[50] Pager, D. (2003). *The Mark of a Criminal Record.* Chicago, IL: Northwestern University.

[51] Pager, D. (2003). *The Mark of a Criminal Record.* Chicago, IL: Northwestern University; Bendick, M., Jackson, C., and Reinoso, V. (1994). *Measuring Employment Discrimination through Controlled Experiments.* Review of Black Political Economy.

[52] Pager, D., Western, B., and Bonikoswki, B. (2009). *Discrimination in a Low Wage Labor Market: A Field Experiment* Thousand Oaks, CA: American Sociological Review.

[53] Pager, D. (2003). *The Mark of a Criminal Record.* Chicago, IL: Northwestern University; Bendick, M., Jackson, C., and Reinoso, V. (1994). *Measuring Employment Discrimination through Controlled Experiments.* Review of Black Political Economy; Pager, D., Western, B., and Bonikoswki, B. (2009). *Discrimination in a Low Wage Labor Market: A Field Experiment.* Thousand Oaks, CA: American Sociological Review.

[54]. Hetey, R. and Eberhardt, J. (2014). *Racial Disparities in Incarceration Increase Acceptance of Punitive Policies.* Washington, D.C.: Association of Psychological Science; Lyons, C., Pettit, B. (2011). *Compounded Disadvantage: Race, Incarceration, and Wage Growth.* Oxford, U.K.: Oxford University Press on behalf of The Society for the Study of Social Problems.

Access to Meaningful Employment Opportunities Requires Implementation of Ban the Box Policies and the Passage of the Fair Chance Act

In my ardent support for *Ban the Box* policies and the passage of the *Fair Chance Act,* let me be unmistakably clear on this point: these measures will not on their own eliminate the challenges faced by formerly incarcerated men and women who are seeking access to employment upon their release. More specifically, these measures will not erase the racism in our employment systems that is a direct consequence and carry-over from the structural, entrenched, and - in some cases - deepening racism of our criminal justice system.[55]

In light of my first point, I refer you to an oft-circulated graphic that depicts three young children standing behind a fence attempting to watch a baseball game on the other side of the fence. One child is tall and can see over the fence; one is of medium height and can barely see over the fence; and one is the shortest of the three and cannot see over the fence. That small child represents the millions of formerly incarcerated individuals, and the game the children are watching represents what would be considered a successful reentry back into the community for those millions of Americans.

On one panel of this graphic, each child is standing on a box that is the same size, and the caption says, "Equality." However, with each child having the same sized box upon which to stand, the tallest child has a better view, the middle child has a good view, but the smallest child still cannot see. The second panel of this graphic depicts the tall child having no boxes to stand on, the middle child standing on one box, and the small child standing on two boxes. The caption here is "Equity," with the idea being that equity - our ultimate goal - is not achieved by one-sized-fits-all solutions. Those solutions tend to benefit the people who do not need the extra support at the expense of people who are already most harmed by our current policies.

---

[55] Hetey, R. and Eberhardt, J. (2014). *Racial Disparities in Incarceration Increase Acceptance of Punitive Policies.* Washington, D.C.: Association of Psychological Science.

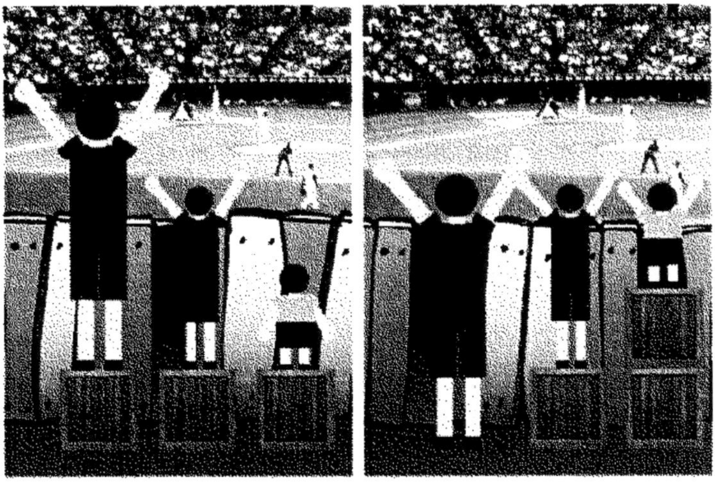

Jennifer Doleac and a small number of others[56] without lived experience with these issues will argue that *Ban the Box* and the *Fair Chance Act* are these 'one-sized-fits-all' solutions that we acknowledge will not, on their own, be sufficient. They will argue that these policies will result in what the first panel on that graphic represents: worsening systematic racism and discrimination. Their argument rests on findings showing that when employers cannot inquire into criminal history, they will make discriminatory decisions based on the perceived race of an applicant, instead. In other words, giving everyone one box just sets us back further- it hurts the people that you're trying to help the most.

What Doleac and others miss, however, is this: we cannot give the smallest child -that black man or woman who has been released from incarceration - two boxes to stand on unless and until we give him one box to stand on, first. *Ban the Box* and the *Fair Chance Act* are that one box.

---

[56] La Gorce, T. (2017). *As 'Ban the Box' Spreads, Private Employers Still have Questions.* New York, NY: New York Times; Semuels, A. (2016). *When Banning One Kind of Discrimination Results in Another.* Washington, D.C. The Atlantic. Agan, A. and Starr, S. (2016). *Ban the Box, Criminal Records, and Statistical Discrimination: A Field Experiment.* Ann Arbor, MI: University of Michigan Law School.

These are the policies that can lay the foundation to do what must be done. They are a first step in the process.

More work will be required to achieve true racial equity in post-incarceration employment and reduce the barriers that black and brown men face in attempting a successful reentry process, but the need for future steps cannot and should not obviate your willingness to take step one.

As United States Representatives, understanding this means understanding the moral obligations of the positions that you hold, and not allowing the power of those positions to be curtailed by misguided and limited empirical analysis that sets out not to derive a conclusion but to prove a conclusion that has already been formed. So, while I acknowledge that *Ban the Box* is not a cure-all solution, I also urge you to recognize that the work being done to undermine its value is flawed.

In some sense, Doleac's conclusions are predictable. They are the result of allowing preconceived notions of blackness and criminality to define an outlook on reality, and they are the product of an analysis totally lacking in the cultural competency that is required for accurate data interpretation.

But when that cultural awareness is factored in and when a study is conducted with an open mind, the results are startling: we have seen, in some areas of this country, a nearly 300% increase in the amount of applicants with criminal records who receive a call-back interview when *Ban the Box* policies were implemented.[57]

Moreover, while the impact of these policies is most readily felt in the early stages of a job application process, several other studies have shown that moving past those stages and actually gaining personal interaction with an employer has a significantly positive impact on determining whether or not someone will ultimately land the job.[58] Again- *Ban the Box* and the *Fair Chance Act* are not sufficient, but their necessity is obvious and cannot be overstated.

---

[57] Atkinson, D. and Lockwood, K., (2014). The Benefits of Ban the Box: A Case Study of Durham, NC," The Southern Coalition for Social justice.

[58] Pager, D. (2003). *The Mark of a Criminal Record.* Chicago, IL: Northwestern University; Fahey, J., Roberts, C., and Engel, L. (2006). *Employment of Ex-Offenders: Employer Perspectives.* Boston, MA: Crime & justice Institute.

Beyond this data-driven refutability of its central findings, Doleac's argument is fundamentally flawed in two important respects. First, it attempts to reverse causality and allege that *Ban the Box* policies are creating something that has existed in our national hiring practices for centuries: racism,[59] *Ban the Box* does not create racism in hiring practices. If anything, it exposes how deeply that racism is entrenched.[60] Second, Doleac relies on this erroneous causal reversal to claim that *Ban the Box* is detrimental to the cause and that we, as black job applicants actually fare better when the stigma of our criminal justice involvement can be brought front-and-center in the job application process, because we are assumed to have that involvement, anyway.

What is truly stunning about this half of Doleac's argument is the inference contained therein: for the few black men who have not been wrongfully arrested, tried without due process, convicted to an overly harsh sentence, or mired in the unnecessarily burdensome traps that are our probation and parole systems, doing away with *Ban the Box* will help them because it will allow them to promote their comparative 'goodness' over the criminality that, for researchers like Doleac, defines everything about us, our potential, and our commitment to an employment opportunity.[61]

Doleac's argument seems premised on the idea that you should only seek to help the 'good', 'well- behaved' black men, and that trying to help the others -us - hurts our brothers and sisters who, for reasons that go far beyond the scope of today's hearing, are not victimized by our justice system. Not only is this demonstrably untrue, as most black applicants fare worse than our white counterparts, but also it speaks to an ignorance of the scope of our incarceration problem.[62] The problem is too big for marginal,

---

[59] Hernandez, P. (2017). *Ban-the-Box "Statistical Discrimination" Studies Draw the Wrong Conclusion.* New York, NY: National Employment Law Project.

[60] Hernandez, P. (2017). *Ban-the-Box "Statistical Discrimination" Studies Draw the Wrong Conclusion.* New York, NY: National Employment Law Project; Emsellem, M. and Avery, B. (2016). *Racial Profiling in Hiring: A Critique of New "Ban the Box" Studies.* New York, NY: National Employment Law Project.

[61] Emsellem, M. and Avery, B. (2016). *Racial Profiling in Hiring: A Critique of New "Ban the Box" Studies.* New York, NY: National Employment Law Project.

[62] Pager, D., Western, B., and Bonikoswki, B.. (2009). *Discrimination in a Low Wage Labor Market: A Field Experiment.* Thousand Oaks, CA: American Sociological Review; jacobson, M. and Schiraldi, V. (2017). *Less is More: How Reducing Probation Populations*

cultural reforms to serve as our go-to solutions. Bold policy transformation is vital.

Ban the Box and the *Fair Chance Act* are crucial components of creating a racially just and equitable employment situation for the millions of black and brown men who have a criminal record. These policies are an integral part of comprehensive and unapologetically bold criminal justice reform that will be necessary to undo the decades of racist, myopic, and erroneous policies that were enacted through this body. The *Fair Chance Act* and a requirement for all employers to *Ban the Box* in their application processes will open up job opportunities for formerly incarcerated individuals who might otherwise steer clear of potential opportunity for fear of how the stigma of justice involvement will set them back not just in that application, but in their overall reentry.[63]

Additionally, as this hearing seeks to understand what the United States Government and the Bureau of Prisons can do to lower the barriers to successful reentry, l urge each of you to understand that the *Fair Chance Act* and the message its passage would promote are essential not just in removing those barriers, but also in preventing those barriers from reemerging as future reforms take hold. There are myriad reasons that black and brown men face unique challenges in seeking gainful employment, and these challenges are only increased when we have been deemed by the systems you put in place to be criminals, or- worse yet- irredeemable and unemployable. The *Fair Chance Act,* while not sufficient to undo the cumulative effects of your collective inaction on this front, would be a crucial step forward in increasing access to employment for formerly incarcerated individuals, which- along with other vital reforms -

can Improve Outcomes. Cambridge, MA: john F. Kennedy School of Government at Harvard University.

[63] Hernandez, P. (2017). *Ban-the-Box "Statistical Discrimination" Studies Draw the Wrong Conclusion.* New York, NY: National Employment Law Project; Emsellem, M. and Avery, B. (2016). *Racial Profiling in Hiring: A Critique of New "Ban the Box" Studies.* New York, NY: National Employment Law Project Rainsford, W. (2016). *No, 'Ban-the-Box' Does Not Worsen Racial Inequality.*

will reduce recidivism and result in a safer, fairer, more cost-efficient criminal justice system.[64]

And to speak to Doleac's central thesis one last time, I would urge you to leverage her misguided conclusion to improve your work: if *Ban the Box* policies do expose the deep-seated nature of racism in our nation's employers, use the knowledge gained from their implementation to develop other tools that can be used in collaboration with the *Fair Chance Act* to end these abhorrent practices for good. Use the power and resources at your disposal to do what you know must be done based on the experiences of people like me- people who have been closest to the problems we must solve.

Understanding the Lived Experience of Formerly Incarcerated People Is Vital for Successful Reform

If you want to step in my shoes and walk on the paths that led me here, I ask each of you to think back to the last time you brought a pair of sunglasses. I ask each of you to go back to that moment when the salesperson showed you the latest styles and rang you up after you chose a pair that you liked. And I ask you, now: describe that salesperson in one word.

Most of you would probably say they were a "person," or perhaps a "man" or "woman." Some of you might say "old" or "young." I am willing to bet, though, that none of you would say "criminal." And that's ironic, because my being branded a criminal by a system that Congress helped to build is the reason that I could not get a job selling sunglasses after serving six years in New York State Prison.

---

[64] Hernandez, P. (2017). *Ban-the-Box "Statistical Discrimination" Studies Draw the Wrong Conclusion.* New York, NY: National Employment Law Project; Emsellem, M. and Avery, B. (2016). *Racial Profiling in Hiring: A Critique of New "Ban the Box" Studies.* New York, NY: National Employment Law Project. Rainsford, W. (2016). *No, 'Ban-the-Box' Does Not Worsen Racial Inequality;* Stapleton, M. (2016). *Ban the Box Laws Are Working.* Chicago, IL: Sargent Shriver National Center on Poverty Law.

That was the first job for which I applied as I was coming out of prison. I walked into the shop in downtown New York and applied to be a salesperson. I was excited just to be out of prison and to be this close, so quickly, to what felt like a first step toward home and away from the cages, walls, and barbed wire fences that had been my existence for most of the previous ten years.

The manager at the store said he'd be excited to hire me, and that he would call me the next day with more details. I could not have been prouder- I was going to be one of the lucky ones who got a job. Having a job meant everything. I was going to be one of the guys who never went back.

That feeling came crashing down later that night when the manager called me and told me that he ran a background check and found a felony conviction on my record. There was no point denying it. He was right I'd lost an opportunity because of something that I did six years ago-something that I thought I'd been punished for, already. Isn't that why I was incarcerated - to punish me and to teach me a lesson? It turns out that my sentence did not end when I stepped beyond the prison walls. In many ways, the second half of my sentence was just beginning.

I applied to fifty jobs in thirty days. None was willing to hire a convict or a felon or an inmate. They may have been willing to hire a son or a brother, but those were identities that were taken from me by the stigma of conviction and incarceration. Those were identities that I was forced to set aside because *Ban the Box* was not something I could benefit from. It did not exist then. So, instead, I was forced to confront the identity that had been given to me by a system designed to keep me trapped.

The setbacks were more than an immediate problem. They were an agonizing reminder that six years of planning may have been fruitless. They were the crushing body-blows that force young black men like me to reconcile with the fact that our incarceration is not limited to the physical boundaries of our cages. The setbacks proved that preparedness was pointless -that in the face of the hurdles I was forced to confront, years of learning, healing, and transformation meant nothing when all the labor market cared about was the fact that I bore a scarlet letter alerting them to my status as a criminal. Our government is complicit in this. Unless our government takes meaningful action, including passage of the *Fair Chance Act,* our government will continue to protect and promote the re-victimization of men and women - especially of men and women of color- who have already fallen prey to a justice system that does less to restore our humanity than it does to repackage and perpetuate past forms of racial discrimination and segregation.

When you are sentenced in a court of law, there is a ceremony involved. The other men and women from throughout the community get to come watch as another young black man is shackled and taken away, his voice drowned out by the chorus of his oppressors. But when you are released from that sentence, you find yourself looking up at towering cement wall and looking back through the doors at the only friends and family you've known for the past several years. There is no ceremony to welcome you back. There is only the constant reminder that too many people in the community did not want you back in the first place.

There is a moment where the world sits us down.

There is not a moment where the world helps us stand back up.

While passage of the *Fair Chance Act* will not be tantamount to having a ceremony for someone's return, and while it will not, on its own, be the hand that reaches out to us to get us back on our feet, it will be a meaningful step in that direction.

It would be, for many of us, the first time that the very same systems that held us back are now going to be the systems that help propel us forward. It would signal to us that you recognize the challenges we face and that you intend to do something about those challenges. It would make clear to the six- plus million Americans who must endure the collateral consequences of our criminal justice system that you still represent them and are willing to fight for and protect their best interests.

I know how meaningful your action could be because I work with the men and women whom your decisions will most directly affect. I am the founder and President of just Leadership USA, a national advocacy organization that seeks to cut the correctional population in the United States in half by 2030 by empowering the people most impacted by the criminal justice system to drive criminal justice reform. In an organization with over 50 staff positions and that runs leadership trainings that now have over 370 graduates, I have never once asked any applicant about a criminal conviction. I have never needed to, because I am able to assess their preparedness by seeing something much more powerful and meaningful: their humanity.

I have often said that the hardest day in prison is the last because you know you're leaving behind some of the best and the brightest that this nation has to offer. Fortunately, today, I'am able to work with and help elevate the voices of many of these men and women. But there are millions of people who my work will not reach - millions of people whose hope for redemption rests in your hands.

I urge you, as members of this Committee and your colleagues, as our elected Representatives in Congress, to Pass the *Fair Chance Act* and do everything in your power to promote *Ban the Box* policies. I, and millions of others, are counting on you.

Glenn E. Martin
Founder and President of Just Leadership USA

Chairman GOWDY. Thank you, Mr. Martin.

I usually ask my questions last. So I would ask the indulgence of my colleagues on this side. There is another hearing next door that I am expected at.

Professor Doleac, I received a phone call over the weekend from Cory Booker, who is very interested in this bill. He took a little different approach than one of your former panelists—or one of your current panelists in critiquing your research, but I think the underlying questions are the same.

So why don't you take a minute and explain to us why you think what is being proposed has the opposite impact?

Ms. DOLEAC. So there have now been two very good studies looking at the impacts of the unintended consequences of ban-the-box and two studies looking at the impacts of ban-the-box on people with criminal records. Both meet the very high, rigorous standards of the academic literature here where the primary concern is isolating the effect of the policy from underlying and completely separate economic trends and other factors that might be driving employment outcomes.

The main concern about ban-the-box is that if employers don't want to hire people with criminal records and we tell them they can't ask, then they are going to try to guess. And because having a criminal record is so highly correlated with race and, especially a recent conviction, with age and having—whether you have a college degree, in the United States, it's pretty easy to statistically discriminate against young black men who don't have college degrees.

And you know, with all due respect to Mr. Martin, the evidence simply contradicts what he thinks is going on. The idea that—that our research is simply revealing that racial discrimination is a problem, of course, racial discrimination is a problem. But before ban-the-box, more young black men were getting jobs than were after ban-the-box. This seems to have reduced—reduced employment for this group and not helped them.

Chairman GOWDY. All right. Well, I am in a very unusual spot among Members of Congress, which is I am open-minded. I haven't made up my mind. I have watched men leave State and Federal prison and desperately try to get a job, and the only job they could get in my hometown was washing other people's cars.

And thank God for William Hunt and other people who took a chance on these guys that have already paid their debts to society. I am not talking about people convicted of violent offenses. I am not talking about people being convicted of crimes against children. I am not even talking about bad check writers and others who have a hard time rehabilitating themselves. I am talking about non-violent drug offenses.

And we say, okay, you have served your sentence. You have got to go get a job. You have got to meet your societal and familial obligations. And they can't.

So let us assume your research is correct. Let us assume there is a reason you are a professor and I am not. That you are smarter and that you know how to do studies and interpret other people's studies. Let us just assume that. I don't think there will be any contradiction on any of that.

What do you propose? What would work? For those of us who don't want—we just passed a bill on evidence-based rulemaking not a month ago. Congress, I think almost unanimously, passed a— passed a bill that we are going to use evidence and facts upon which to base our policies. And what you are arguing is if you do that, you won't take this approach.

Let us assume for the sake of argument that you are right. What approach works?

Ms. DOLEAC. Great question. So, so what this policy is hoping to achieve is that we're hoping that by preventing employers from asking about a criminal record, they won't care about the criminal record anymore. That's really the goal of, I think, everyone in this room. We want employers to be willing to hire people with criminal records, and the question is how do we—how do we help them do that?

So, so the real goal is to try to figure out what employers actually care about, what they're worried about when they see the box checked on a job application, and then find policy interventions that can directly address those concerns. If employers are worried about work readiness, if they're worried that—that, you know, the average person coming out of prison has much higher rates of substance abuse and mental illness and is very likely to be rearrested in the near future, finding ways to—to really invest in rehabilitation so that they don't have those associations with a criminal record anymore.

That's going to take time. That's the longer-term goal of, I think, everyone here, and it's going to take investment of real resources. In the shorter term, I think the best way to reach the goal that ban-the-box and the Fair Chance Act would have reached in helping those who are qualified for jobs get jobs is finding ways to provide additional information about their work readiness to employers.

One—one policy intervention that's been tried in a few different places, and it seems very promising, and research evidence is supporting that it's having the effects we hoped for, is employability or rehabilitation certificates. So if you have a criminal record and you can go in front of a judge and argue that you've been rehabilitated, there have been very nice audit studies showing that if you send out job applications randomizing if you have a felony conviction or a certificate of rehabilitation or no conviction at all, those with the certificate are called back at equal rates as those without any conviction.

I've heard that those are extremely difficult to get. That can be changed. That's obviously something that is adjustable. But the very—the basic idea of providing more information rather than taking information away seems far more promising.

Chairman GOWDY. Well, I am out of time. I hope you will continue to do your research. You know, most of us live in a world of anecdote. We don't have the luxury of doing studies.

I can tell you in my own life, including with one of your panelists, the very first time I met Inspector Horowitz, he told me something that I otherwise never would have known. Never would have known. It wasn't an important thing.

But the fact that he was willing to tell me something that I really wasn't entitled to know, he went up 10 stages in my mind just because he was willing to tell me something. It actually had the opposite—it made me trust him, like him, want him to get the job even more.

Has there been any research into that? Into people who say, you know what, you are going to find this out at some point, let me be the one to tell you. Because I can imagine employers, even if it is the law, human nature being what it is, may wonder at the end, why didn't you tell me this up front?

Is there any—is there any—and I know you are not a psychologist, but is there any research into how the listener hears information volunteered from the very person that it could hurt being the one who volunteers it?

Ms. DOLEAC. I don't know of any research on that. Anecdotally, I've heard that the guidance that individuals coming out of prison are given is generally to be upfront. When they get the interview, to be upfront about their criminal history and to explain, you know, what happened and what they've learned from it and the steps they've taken to change. But I don't—I don't know of any research on that. So ——

Chairman GOWDY. All right.

Ms. DOLEAC.—at this point, just anecdotal.

Chairman GOWDY. I really mean it when I say this is my last question, all right? Negligent hiring is a civil cause of action in some States. So for employers who don't want to wait on the Government, who want to do it themselves, what protections are afforded them when plaintiff's attorneys, as they do from time to time, find even an isolated incident where an employer didn't ask and something—something bad happened, and they are confronted with a negligent hiring case?

How do we protect those employers that want to—that want to do what Mr. Martin and Ms. Roseberry are advocating for? With or without us doing it, they want to do it. How do you protect them from civil causes of action?

Ms. DOLEAC. I don't think we have a really clear answer to that yet. It's another area where these employability or rehabilitation certificates seem very promising. You know, these are court-issued certificates that say this person has been rehabilitated and is no longer a risk. And so to the extent that a negligent hiring lawsuit is accusing an employer for putting their customers and other employees at undue risk, if the worst happens and someone that they hire who has a criminal record commits a violent crime on the job—I think that's the worst nightmare of any employer—then they can take that certificate and say, look, I did everything I was supposed to do. This judge said that this person wasn't a risk. There is no way I could have known.

So thinking of creative solutions that, in effect, shift the risk from employers to the courts or to government I think is probably the best way to deal with this negligent hiring concern. And it's not just the legal liability, but it's also worries about bad press. Even if they know that they wouldn't actually lose a lawsuit, they could face very negative media attention that could put them out of business, and that—that's the catastrophic risk that employers are worried about.

Chairman GOWDY. The gentleman from Maryland?

Mr. CUMMINGS. Thank you very much, Mr. Chairman.

Now come on, let us not kid ourselves. The elephant in the room is racism, and it is a big elephant. Now, Mr. Martin, I don't have it at my hand—I wish I did. But I have read studies where it showed that a white person with a record had a better chance of getting a job than a black man without a record. Are you familiar with that?

Mr. MARTIN. I'm not only familiar with that study, I ——

Mr. CUMMINGS. Can you keep your voice up, please?

Mr. MARTIN. Sorry. I'm not only familiar with the study, I served as the project manager on the study. It was the audit—the largest audit study ever conducted in America to date, when that research happened. The principal researchers were Bruce Western and Devah Pager of Princeton at the time.

And we visited 3,500 different employers in the entry-level labor market. We actually hired young men—white, black, Hispanic—to serve as job seekers. And so we sent them out into the labor market with resumes that were manufactured by us that showed some evidence of them having involvement in the criminal justice system.

And after visiting 3,500 different employers and doing thousands of audits, yes, the finding was that a white person with a criminal record has a better chance of getting employed than a black person without a criminal record who is similarly situated with respect to their employment history. And you know, the question by Chairman Gowdy about how do we respond to employer concerns about liability? Those concerns are legitimate. I've done many focus groups to really dig in on what employer concerns are, and liability ranks number one.

But for instance, the New York City Bar Association was able to draft a piece of legislation that gives employers rebuttable presumption when they consider the EEOC guidance and New York State's anti-discrimination law, which somewhat mirrors each other, essentially saying that you should be giving qualified job applicants a chance to explain evidence rehabilitation, how long since the criminal conviction, what have they done since the criminal conviction to rehabilitate themselves, and so on. So there are other policy prescriptions that we can have in place to respond to employer concerns.

Certificates of relief I would totally discount, particularly because they are so difficult to get, and to suggest that we can sort of easily change that, I've doing this work for 17 years, much of it legislative reform, many bills that I have drafted and advanced in legislatures myself, it is not easy to change those pieces of legislation. I have not been successful with one in my 17-year career, to be quite frank.

Mr. CUMMINGS. You know, as you were talking, I couldn't help but think about years ago, when I—maybe about 3, maybe 4 years ago, I visited Johns Hopkins Hospital in Baltimore. And so I drove up, and I noticed they had this security firm checking everybody out. They were better—to me, they were just as good as the Secret Service.

And so I asked the guy, I said, "Is this a new firm?" And it was a firm which was established by former inmates, and all the employees were former inmates, and they were doing a hell of a job.

You know, Mr. Martin, how important is it to be free of the stigma of a criminal record when applying for a job? How important is that?

Mr. MARTIN. Thank you for that question.

Thirteen years after exiting prison, I was invited to the White House to meet with senior policy advisers to the then-President.

And after 2 months of background checks and everything else it takes to get into the White House, when I got to the White House, I find out that my 21-year-old conviction meant I couldn't enter the White House.

And while most formerly incarcerated people may not ever get invited to the White House, I was struck that day by what the implications were for a person who is 21 years away from his conviction, invited to the White House, has done work to help so many people at places like the Fortune Society supported by Member Maloney and others, couldn't get access to that place. And I wondered what it meant for the men and women who were exiting prison that day who were trying to get a job at the local Starbucks or McDonald's or somewhere else.

The fact of the matter is that we have created an entire underclass of citizenship in this country, and this Government has a responsibility to respond to that.

Mr. CUMMINGS. And how important is ban-the-box policies in reducing recidivism? You know, I heard Ms. Doleac, and she doesn't seem to feel, based on her research, that this is—that it helps. She says it hurts. I mean, I just want to know your response to that.

Mr. MARTIN. Sure. Well, first of all, we need to parse her research because if I give her research credit, then it's only one small section of job seekers with criminal records where she found evidence that they're being hurt by this. There are many other categories where she actually admits that those folks did better as a result of the policy.

But I don't want to lose the fact that we would not be having this discussion again today if formerly incarcerated people did not create this ban-the-box policy in Oakland, California, as a way to educate policymakers about the importance of creating job opportunities for people with criminal records. I cannot understate what it means to want to apply for a job, to know that you're qualified, and to have the chilling effect of the question about the criminal record on the application.

Remember, we—there are things that we actually cannot measure, and it doesn't mean that they're not important. But you cannot measure the job seeker who has a quality 2-year liberal arts degree that he or she learned—or earned in prison as a result of Pell Grants, when they were eligible actually not applying for a job because of the fact that we live in a country where the labor market doesn't create access for job seekers who have a criminal conviction.

We can't measure that, but it should be important to this country. The chilling effect alone of the criminal record would be removed if we had this ban-the-box policy in place.

Mr. CUMMINGS. In 2015, I first introduced the Fair Chance Act with then-Chairman Issa and Senator Booker and Senator Ron Johnson. This bill would codify the existing OPM rule that prohibits Federal agencies from requesting criminal histories for certain nonsensitive jobs until after conditional offer of employment.

Mr. Martin, do you think that OPM's current guidance has had a positive impact on ex-offenders?

Mr. MARTIN. I think it's had a positive impact. You know, granted, my response here is anecdotal. I've spoken to people who have found the courage to apply for jobs based on the fact that this policy is in place. I also recognize that efforts made by the Federal Government, the Federal Government speaks with a megaphone and sends a very strong message to States and cities, where the majority of people in this country are actually incarcerated and under correctional supervision.

And so if for no other reason alone, a message from the Federal Government about the importance of qualified job seekers having a chance to compete for employment, I think it was President Bush that said it well during the 2004 State of the Union address that this is the land of second chances, and we should give an opportunity for people to turn their lives around and be contributing members of society.

Mr. CUMMINGS. It would be—it would be political or legislative malpractice if I didn't ask this question. In the African-American community, there is a term that I hear over and over again, "the prison industrial complex." There is a belief that there are folks who are making money and trying to create private prisons or whatever in their neck of the woods so that they can keep the economy going.

And we have, of course, seen some 60 Minutes stories that bear some of that out. But I just want your comment and then yours, Mr. Inch, on that.

Mr. MARTIN. You know, prisons throughout the '80s, '90s, and early 2000s were the most effective stimulus program for rural communities that lost industries. The fact of the matter is that many governors across the country promised prisons to communities that were losing other industries.

I have a brother—I grew up in poverty. I grew up on public assistance, single mother, two brothers. My older brother fought in four tours of duty, active, in war. Ultimately became a correction officer for 10 years and is now a U.S. Marshal. My brother is one of the 3 million people who benefit from the criminal justice system that we've currently created because it propelled him from poverty into upper middle class.

I think that, yes, there are private prisons that exist that benefit from the incarceration particularly of people of color and who have—in the past, there is much evidence of them promoting policies that have led to increased incarceration and mass incarceration. But I don't want to lose sight of the fact that the perverse incentives that have led to that commercialization of punishment exists and started in our Government-run prisons and jails.

And so everything has grown alongside each other. While we have said we are working to end mass incarceration, the fact of the matter is that we have grown everything—probation, parole, electronic monitoring, you name it. And so the footprint of the criminal justice system has disproportionately impacted people of color, yes. But it also disproportionately impacts particularly poor white Americans.

When you compare us to any other country in the world, white Americans are equally disproportionately impacted by mass incarceration in the criminal justice industrial complex.

Mr. CUMMINGS. Mr. Inch, and then I thank you very much. I appreciate it.

Mr. INCH. Ranking Member Cummings, just so I can have clarification, are we talking the private prison industry or the array of our Federal prison system?

Mr. CUMMINGS. Both.

Mr. INCH. Both. Okay, thank you, sir.

One can certainly look—and I'll focus really on those private prisons we use and then the array of 122 Federal installations. One can look over time and location and see that the placement of the facilities was based on a variety of reasons that may have been above and beyond the most effective and efficient use of that particular facility.

If I were speaking only as a practitioner, only as a practitioner, which, you know, would be inappropriate for all the decisions that go into the placement of Federal installations, we certainly look at the population base of the location to ensure large enough population base to hire not only the correctional officers, which would be an entry level to the facility, but also the technical psychologists and the like of the facility. That's a consideration.

There's a consideration of placement. Certainly, it's already been mentioned here and was mentioned in opening comments, the aspect of connection with families, the importance of that. In my opening comments, I talked about victims. There's victims of crime.

There's victims among us, staff, and there's the forgotten victims, which are the families of the offenders.

So the placement where visitation can be facilitated with the inmate population, certainly that's an aspect, too. There's even logistics reasons.

All that has to be balanced with other considerations that are placed at least in the Federal system in which then the money is certainly authorized and the placement decided. So I can only speak then from the practitioner.

Chairman GOWDY. The gentleman yields back. The chair will now recognize the gentleman from Alabama, Mr. Palmer.

Mr. PALMER. Thank you, Mr. Chairman. I really appreciate all of you being here, sincerely, and the topic of this hearing.

Prior to Congress, I ran a think tank for 25 years, and this is one of the areas that the last 2 or 3 years that I was there we were focused on. And looking at the material and particularly the release preparation program, one of the things that I didn't see was a concerted effort to help inmates achieve either a high school diploma or a vocational degree or an associate's degree that would really—it would do two things, Mr. Martin. It would prepare people to enter the workforce, but it also gives them that ceremony.

I mean, it is—I really appreciate what the chairman has said about, you know, you don't want to be soft on crime. But at the same time, when someone has paid their debt, that debt is paid, and they ought to be able to reenter society.

Ms. Roseberry, I was looking at the information in the Colson task force report, and the thing that I didn't see in it was recommendations for a program to help inmates achieve a high school diploma or another degree. And when you look at who is in prison—again, back to what Mr. Martin said—it is disproportionately poor people, regardless of color. And it is disproportionately people who are high school dropouts.

And one of the reports shows that 68 percent of State inmates are high school dropouts. And that is regardless of race, gender. This is something I am more focused on finding solutions, and I think the solution is before they go in the prison door, and then unfortunately, we have got to focus on how we get them out the prison door.

And looking at the Colson task force, one of the things that I was looking for is one of the things that we have suggested in Alabama, to this point to no avail, was to utilize online learning programs. I mean, there are excellent opportunities for people to achieve a high school diploma, to get an associate or vocational degree, networking with businesses who are prepared to hire these people when they come out.

We are at a point in our economy right now where there is competition for workers and particularly workers with certain skills. But also—and going back to the Colson task force, I had the great privilege to know Chuck Colson, a godly, wonderful man—to integrate into that these faith-based groups that can help prepare them for reentry. Do you want to comment on that?

Ms. ROSEBERRY. Yes. First of all, I'd like to say with respect to your comment about the front end, you're absolutely right. If we're talking about, for example, ban-the-box creating the presumption that African-American men have more connections with the criminal justice system, perhaps the solution is to stop overpolicing those communities and incarcerating those individuals to begin with.

But the Colson task force did look at the fact that the Bureau of Prisons staff were spread thin by virtue of overcrowding, and we made the recommendation that because we found waiting lists, for example, for GEDs to be years long and the opportunity to be eligible for programs to be put on the back end of the serving of a sentence, and also for lifers, there was no eligibility. We made the recommendation that the Bureau of Prisons incentivize participation in these programs—of course, after reallocating resources—so that those programs could be provided to everyone.

Also in our recommendation that programming be individualized, be evidence-based, data-driven, and individualized, you would see that folks who needed educational programming would have an opportunity to get it by virtue of it having been identified for them.

Mr. PALMER. Let me address that. There was a report from the Alliance for Excellence in Education that reported on underserved students. They are disproportionately poor, regardless of race. There is over 1,200 of those schools. In New York, there were 199 of them. These are schools that have very high dropout rates.

And again, going back to the dropout rate and then the information from the Bureau of Prisons, it shows that inmates who leave prison who do not have a high school diploma, their recidivism rate is 60.4 percent. So when I talk about on the front end, this is outside of the purview of the Bureau of Prisons, obviously. It is all about how do we put more emphasis on helping particularly young African-American males stay in school? That is a pathway to a better future.

But for those who are incarcerated, I really believe we ought to look at a way to incentivize. If I may, Mr. Chairman? Mr. Horowitz, you were talking about there is no incentive for them to enter the program. To incentivize by looking at if these inmates who have not committed violent felonies who are going to be paroled, that if they achieve a high school diploma, they are eligible for an earlier release. If they achieve an associate or vocational degree.

That creates an incentive, Mr. Martin. It gives them a goal. It gives them a vision for a future that, frankly, I don't think exists right now in our prisons. Would you like to comment on that, anybody?

Ms. ROSEBERRY. I'd just like to reiterate that the task force did recommend incentivizing these programs, even for those who are serving life, and suggested that the reward for them could be better confinement conditions, et cetera. And for others who have a release date, that the release date would be moved back with good time.

Mr. MARTIN. Just briefly, two things. One, it was a correctional counselor who said to me I should go to college after I got my GED.

Mr. PALMER. You were a high school dropout?

Mr. MARTIN. Yes. And so I earned that GED. And while he was looking at those test scores, said to me, "You should go to college."

So as important as the degree was, you're right. There was a bit of a moment where another human being in a position of authority who was seeing hundreds of people that day saw something in me that I might not have even seen in myself in that moment. So there is the value of that and everything else that comes from education.

There's also the piece about the conditions of confinement. The fact of the matter is that facilities that have more programs do better with respect to safety of correction officers. Why? Because the people who are serving time there want to take advantage of those opportunities, and also the folks who may not yet be college ready or even ready to get their GEDs have something to look forward to and to look up to. I can't tell you how many people I helped to actually get their own GED after being in college while I was incarcerated.

Mr. PALMER. Mr. Chairman, there is a report—and I am sure Mr. Martin and Ms. Roseberry, maybe everyone on the panel is familiar with—from Pew, the Collateral Costs: Incarceration's Effect on Economic Mobility. It is the very thing that Mr. Martin has been talking about.

There is also an article that young black men without a high school diploma are more likely to be found in a cell than in a workplace. And I just want to emphasize that I think we want to make sure that our society is safe, that law enforcement is able to do its job. But at the same time, there is a reality that we have got to recognize that most of these people are going to reenter society, and I don't think we are doing enough to prepare them for that.

And I yield back.

Mr. RUSSELL. [Presiding] The gentleman yields back.

And the chair now recognizes the gentlelady from the District of Columbia, Ms. Holmes Norton.

Ms. NORTON. Thank you very much. I very much appreciate this hearing from the ranking member and the chairman.

I have a question for Mr. Inch, but I really also want to get to these, what I see are some competing studies here because I very much respect scholarship. I was a tenured professor of law, and so I have got to somehow reconcile with them.

Mr. Inch, the Bureau of Prisons is considered the best prison in the world, and there are many thoughtful programs. You hire people in the

Bureau of Prisons who have advanced degrees. In light of the quality of personnel at the Bureau of Prisons, and I know I will be seeing you about D.C. inmates shortly, until recently—this is before you came, people on home confinement even were charged 25 percent of anything they happened to make, imagine people who have just gotten out of prison, to pay back to the Bureau of Prisons.

Some of that was gotten rid of before you came. But now if you are in a halfway house, which is, of course, imprisonment, you are still not released from prison, you are still charged 25 percent. I don't know why you don't just charge them 25 percent for being in jail.

How can you possibly reconcile charging people who happen to get a job 25 percent of anything they make to give back to you, the Bureau of Prisons, rather than to their children, rather than to their families, and rather than to keeping themselves out of jail?

Mr. INCH. Thank you, Congresswoman Holmes Norton, and I'm sorry we had to delay our meeting.

Ms. NORTON. That is quite all right. It was my fault.

Mr. INCH. It actually was a loss in my family.

So the use of RRCs, actually, this is something new I'm learning.

In the military corrections, we did not avail ourselves of the Federal program, and I need to bound my comments by of our 223 facilities, I've been to one during this first 90 days. It was actually in Baltimore and really appreciated the reception I received there, the insights, and the contract provider that actually runs quite a few of our residential reentry centers, they were kind enough to come up as well.

The aspect specifically that you asked for in terms of ——

Ms. NORTON. Paying 25 percent of it, if you happen to get a job, which most people don't get one.

Mr. INCH.—25 percent if ——

Ms. NORTON. What is the rationale, given how research-based most of your policies are? What is the rationale? Because I got to get to this —

Mr. INCH. Yes. So the rationale—I'm sorry. Then the rationale is real-life budgeting. The aspect that ——

Ms. NORTON. Is what?

Mr. INCH. Real-life budgeting. That with employment —— Ms. NORTON. I see.

Mr. INCH.—that a portion of that employment actually has to go to living expenses and all that. So, say, at the end of the 4-month period ——

Ms. NORTON. But he doesn't give 25 percent of his—25 percent of his salary to an outside party. So if he has got to budget, wouldn't you rather him budget for his family?

Mr. INCH. Well, the aspect is—I would argue the aspect is that real aspect of our budgeting upon then release from the residential reentry center is, in fact, going to be for housing and for food. And so building that into the budget during the period of transition seems appropriate to me.

Ms. NORTON. I don't understand that you have answered my question, but I am going to see you shortly.

Look, there are—Ms. Doleac, I respect your study, and I particularly respect studies that contradict one another in the academic environment. And there is a study by Terry-Ann Craigie for ban-the-box even with what are some of the findings you have made. Now, for me, I am going to need more rationale than I thought I would need for ban-the-box.

You say the best evidence—this is your testimony—suggests that ban-the-box does not increase employment for people with criminal records and might reduce it. I got to take that seriously.

You also say, and again, I am reading from your testimony, "While white applicants were called back at nearly the same rate as before, black applicants were called back at a rate in between the rates at which those with and without records were called back before ban-the-box. This may help black men with records, but it hurts black men without records."

So my question for you is, do you believe your sample was broad enough? And with the Craigie study, the study that I just indicated, essentially her response was, look—I would agree with her.

Look, racial discrimination is even worse. So you got to deal with racial discrimination. But as I see it, both forms of discrimination are captured in your study, and you don't find that anybody gets helped with ban-the-box.

Would you somehow reconcile what you are saying with what she is saying?

Ms. DOLEAC. Sure. So just to clarify, the studies that I'm talking about in my written testimony, there are actually four different studies. So I'm not finding all of those things in my own study.

The—the evidence that ban-the-box reduces employment or reduces employment for black men or, at the very least, doesn't help them comes from two very nice studies now that link criminal history records with employment records, one in Massachusetts and one in Seattle.

The study in Massachusetts compares people who are affected by ban-the-box when Massachusetts implemented the policy with folks who—with a very similar control group that is not affected by ban-the-box, and they find that employment falls for individuals with criminal records after ban-the-box goes into effect.

This is consistent with new qualitative evidence from a graduate student at UC–Irvine, Dallas Augustine. She's been spending the last couple of years talking to people coming out of jail and prison and finding that, you know, what I think a lot of us would know anecdotally. It's extremely frustrating to go through a job process and build rapport with an employer and get a conditional offer, maybe even work for a probationary period, and then not get the job when they finally check your criminal record.

And ban-the-box increases the likelihood that that happens for anyone who actually does get their foot in the door. And so to the extent that that discourages people and they just give up and stop looking, you know, I think a lot of people would rather know up front if they're not going to get the job because they have a criminal record.

The study by Terry-Ann Craigie I know well. It's a working paper. I think it at this point does not credibly isolate the effect of ban-the-box from other employment factors. There is—this is the main challenge that economists work very hard to—to overcome is figuring out what the impact of a policy is separate from the impact of just underlying economic trends and other factors that might drive employment.

At this point, she has a treatment and control group, and I think, to get a little bit wonky, the challenge is to show that your treatment and control group look very similar before the policy is passed so that you know you have a good counterfactual. So you know you have a good idea of what would have happened in a place that passes ban-the-box if the place hadn't passed that policy.

At this point, her study is not able to show that. You know, it's a working paper, still a work in progress. I'm sure she'll figure that out.

Ms. NORTON. Mr. Chairman, I would like to have that study introduced into the record, and I would like to say that the notion has to be taken very seriously that ban-the-box ends up with race being used as a proxy for discrimination. So I am very interested in the kinds of research that your hearing has uncovered and in further research into this area.

Thank you very much.

Mr. RUSSELL. The gentlelady yields back, and without objection.

Mr. RUSSELL. The chair now recognizes the gentleman from Kentucky, Mr. Comer.

Mr. COMER. Thank you, Mr. Chairman.

My questions are going to be directed toward Director Inch. Recently, there have been closures of some reentry centers and a significant number of inmates whose referral dates to the reentry centers have been shortened or canceled. What is administration's commitment to reentry services going forward?

Mr. INCH. Thank you, Congressman Comer, for that question.

Of course, as I came on 3 months ago, it was at this time where certainly in media and in the framework or what was being presented was a perception of changing administration focus. I can assure you that's not the case, certainly not in my first 3 months of experience.

We had a lot of learning in the RRC administration, actually with the help of OIG and, of course, the good look, the good recommendations that we received. The closing of the 16 facilities, which really the correct way to say it is the not executing option years of contracts, or not renewing contracts, really was dealing with the efficiency of the system. Underused facilities or facilities that were of a contracting type that it really wasn't the optimal.

We've done a lot of work to create a standard statement of work in contracting. So we are looking to the efficiency of the system. Those 16 facilities accounted for about 1 percent of the bed space. Coupled with that perceptions that come was bringing other RRCs back within capacity gaps that our contracts added.

Mr. COMER. I am going to switch gears now. Next questions are going to be about drug abuse. How big a problem is drug abuse in the Federal prisons, and what are you doing to curb drug abuse and addiction in the Federal prisons?

Mr. INCH. Thank you for that question.

So in my experiences in corrections, certainly again that's been on the military side and then very active interaction with professional organizations in corrections. The aspect of decision-making is obviously influenced by—can be influenced by addictions, drug, alcohol, other addictions. And so, as I do an assessment of the Bureau's reentry programming writ large, you know, the aspect of cognitive behavioral therapy with other aspects, frankly, I'm very impressed with RDAP, the Residential Drug Abuse Program. We have both nonresidential, residential within the facility.

In my early visits to different facilities, I've made a point to go to both English and Spanish-speaking RDAPs and am impressed with the program both in my discussions with staff and the inmates.

Mr. COMER. What role do residential reentry centers have in inmates obtaining drug treatment?

Mr. INCH. Congressman, if it's possible if I could get back with you specifically on that?

Mr. COMER. Absolutely.

Mr. INCH. I think it ties in with our new statement of work, but I probably need to ——

Mr. COMER. Okay. No problem. My last question, how big of a challenge is preventing drugs or other contraband from entering into prisons, and what is the Bureau doing to prevent this?

Mr. INCH. Oh, thank you for that question.

It is a reality in the corrections profession since the start to this day, of course, is the aspect of countering the introduction of contraband. The seriousness of the type of synthetics primarily, not primarily, but certainly the seriousness of the introduction of synthetic drugs absolutely affects safety. And so our commitment to both using technological and procedural ways to address the introduction of contraband is a daily commitment and effort within the Bureau.

Mr. COMER. Thank you, Mr. Chairman. I yield back.

Mr. RUSSELL. The gentleman yields back.

And the chair now recognizes the gentleman from Pennsylvania, Mr. Cartwright.

Mr. CARTWRIGHT. Thank you, Mr. Chairman.

And I want to thank all the panelists for joining us today. We have had a fascinating discussion.

And I want to—I want to thank you, Ms. Roseberry, for mentioning our Secretary of Corrections in Pennsylvania, John Wetzel, who was appointed by a Republican governor and was kept on by the succeeding Democratic governor. I know Secretary Wetzel to be a very competent and capable head of our prison system in Pennsylvania.

And I also appreciate your mentioning, Ms. Roseberry, the importance of keeping correctional staff safe, and it is a particular concern of mine. We have had some ugly incidents in Federal prisons in Pennsylvania, and so I want to take it up with you, Director Inch, if I may? I realize you are still pretty new on the job, and maybe this is the right time to catch you while you are still wrapping your head around the process.

But this is something that I am very deeply concerned about. The Federal Bureau of Prisons has previously testified that the mission-critical staffing levels established by the Bureau are the bare minimum employment levels necessary safely to operate a prison.

Right now, the administration of the Bureau is mandating to all facilities that they must lower their staffing levels to 88 percent of mission critical. First off, were you aware of that?

Mr. INCH. Thank you, Mr. Cartwright.

First, just bringing to attention the issue and in terms of staffing levels, I am, yes, very aware of our staffing levels.

Mr. CARTWRIGHT. Okay. So why is the administration mandating reducing staffing levels to 88 percent of mission critical, which is defined as the bare minimum employment levels to safely operate a Federal prison?

Mr. INCH. Thank you, Mr. Cartwright.

So to—really to frame my answer, part of my first 90 days was actually to go to Pennsylvania. I was able to go to the regional headquarters that's in Philadelphia, to visit also Lewisburg and Allenwood. The—I also took the opportunity—and Mr. Don Williams was very gracious also to sit down with me and give a personal anecdote. For those who may not know Don Williams, his son Eric Williams was a Federal Bureau of Prisons correctional officer who was killed in the line of duty. And so I very much appreciated how gracious he was to meet with me.

So the aspect of staffing, as I've done staff recalls throughout those facilities I've been to in these first 90 days, and that's 5 out of 6 regions, that is a consistent concern of staff as well as the leadership of the facilities. Though I cannot specifically answer on the process that resulted in the mission-critical staffing positions by facility, it is certainly a priority that I've already set is a relook at our staffing numbers ——

Mr. CARTWRIGHT. Excellent. Excellent answer, and I want you to relook at that because we are talking about the safety of people like Eric Williams ——

Mr. INCH. Absolutely.

Mr. CARTWRIGHT.—and his coworkers. Now after the Federal hiring freeze policy was implemented, a large number of Federal Bureau of Prisons facilities are operating well below authorized strength. Many of these same facilities will, in the very near future, lose even more corrections officers and other critical staff due to normal attrition—retirements, relocation, things like that.

This situation leaves some institutions in a potentially dangerous situation without the ability to resolve it by hiring more staff. Does the Bureau currently have a plan to remedy this, and if not, why not?

Mr. INCH. Thank you.

So in the current hiring freeze, my ability to gain waivers back up to the cap, I believe it was January of 2017, we've been very successful in obtaining our waivers, are in that process. And with that process of achieving the waivers, of course, from the front end, that starts the aspect of going through, you know, initial training and the like.

But you're correct in identifying the importance of proper staffing in our facilities for safety and the—I would argue from a practitioner's, again, perspective is the challenge is it's facility by facility.

You know, you just can't cookie cutter this because our facilities were built over a 100-year period. And so the safe application of if we want to use the term "mission-critical positions" does have an impact of the facility as well as the type of prisoners and programs we have at those facilities.

Mr. CARTWRIGHT. Well, I thank you for that. And I want to just mention again. My other committee is Appropriations, and I am on the Commerce, Justice, and Science Subcommittee. We funded the Bureau's salaries and expenses funding level at just under 99 percent of what you asked for. So I urge you to do that relook on 88 percent of the bare minimum. By definition, that is woefully inadequate.

And I yield back, Mr. Chairman.

Mr. RUSSELL. The gentleman yields back.

And the chair now recognizes the gentleman from Wisconsin, Mr. Grothman.

Mr. GROTHMAN. Sure. I will start with Mr. Inch, but anybody else can jump in if they want to.

The first question, what percentage of inmates that you release have jobs within a month of their release?

Mr. INCH. Mr. Grothman, I don't have that statistic with me, but I'll work with staff and get that figure to you, your staff.

Mr. GROTHMAN. Hmm, does anybody know the answer to that question?

[No response.]

Mr. GROTHMAN. Within a month of when they were—people were—I don't know how you can solve a problem if you don't have the data.

But okay, next question. Among those people who get jobs, what type of jobs do they get? I mean, I was told—I was a legislator for a long time in Wisconsin, and we were told for a while that there were certain kind of tough jobs that, you know, employers were—would grab anybody coming out of prison to take because they couldn't find people to take these unpleasant jobs.

But could somebody comment on the type of jobs the average person coming out of prison is getting? Mr. Martin?

Mr. MARTIN. Thank you.

In my experience, particularly while I worked at a public interest law firm speaking to not just formerly incarcerated job seekers, but also employers who were interested in hiring them, typically they're low income. They're high turnover. There are no benefits. Retail ——

Mr. GROTHMAN. That is not answering what type of jobs they are getting.

Mr. MARTIN. I was getting there. I'm sorry. Mr. GROTHMAN. Okay.

Mr. MARTIN. Retail, construction, hospitality. However, I think the caveat there is that things change when the labor market gets tighter. So when it becomes a job seeker's labor market, I find that people have better opportunities. I also find that when people are credentialed, then employers are much more willing to consider a qualified applicant who has, say, a driver's license that has a certain credential that allows him to drive a truck.

If that person has a clean CDL is the name I'm looking for. Sorry, a clean CDL license, for instance, an employer is much more willing to give them consideration and puts less emphasis on the criminal record. But traditionally, it's the sort of jobs that I just mentioned in those industries.

Mr. GROTHMAN. Okay. Next question, I guess I wouldn't know how you would know this if you don't know what is going on in your own system. But do you know which State systems do the best job of getting people a job within 1 month after they leave incarceration? Does anybody know?

I mean, to me, it should be easy for the Federal Government to know what to do because we have 50 States out there who are operating things different ways. Does anybody have—take a shot at which States do a good job?

Ms. DOLEAC. Well, I don't know the answer to that question, but I think the real issue here is that the data that we would need to answer the questions that you're asking don't exist. We don't have data on—we don't have certainly at a national level criminal history data linked with employment data. And so we don't even know how many people in the United States have a criminal record, much less where they live or what jobs they have when they can get them.

Mr. GROTHMAN. Well, it is kind of appalling, isn't it? We have got all these universities, all this graduate student stuff, and we don't even know the—I mean, it is kind of almost pointless to even have the hearing unless we know the answers to those questions. We should know, you know, the percentage of people who leave Federal prison, a month out of prison, what job do they get?

We should know, we got 50 States, and this doesn't work in Tennessee or this does work in Iowa or whatever. And given the sea of money that is floating around here and the sea of money that we send to our colleges and universities to do studies, I just find it shocking that we don't have the most basic data that you need before you even address this problem. Isn't that kind of amazing? Kind of amazing.

Ms. DOLEAC. Could I comment on that? Mr. GROTHMAN. Yes.

Ms. DOLEAC. I mean, I think that the—this is a challenge for the Federal Government. Honestly, the data would need to be collected and—and investment needs to be made at the Federal level. I know the Census is working on this. They have people who are spending a lot of time and money trying to look at these datasets. This is not—not ——

Mr. GROTHMAN. But even they don't because they are not going to break it down by State, okay? We should say X number of people were released from Illinois State prison system last year, and X percent had a job

30 days after they got out. We should have that information, but apparently, we don't.

Looking—there have been some criticisms of the people, number of people in prison, and I want you to comment on this. I was just playing around because you have got everything on the Internet, and the murder rate kind of was really kind of wonderful like in the '50s in this country, and then it began to skyrocket up to the '80s. And then we began to put more people in prison, and the murder rate dropped again.

Is it possible one of the reasons we had such a drop in the murder rate from the early '80s to, say, 2013 or whatever is because we put more people in prison? That it wasn't entirely a bad thing to have more dangerous people in prison. Is that possible? Is that one of the reasons why the murder rate dropped so much in this country, more bad people were in prison? Anyone care to comment on that?

Mr. MARTIN. I'll take a swing at it. I live in New York, where we've cut our jail population in half in the last 20 years. We've cut our prison population by 28 percent, and our crime rate, particularly our violent crime rate, is down to levels of 1961. So I think that actually contradicts the idea that you put more people in prison, you get more public safety.

Having said that, I think your question was a little bit more nuanced about who we actually put in prison. I think that if we had more data, we'd be able to tell a story about whether locking up certain people for longer periods of time gets us better outcomes. But there is some research now that said—that says that there is the sort of law of sort of diminishing effect. The longer you have a person in prison, the more difficult time they have reentering society, and 95 percent of the people who go to prison come home at some point.

Mr. RUSSELL. The gentleman yields back.

The chair now recognizes the gentlelady from New Jersey, Mrs. Watson Coleman.

Mrs. WATSON COLEMAN. Thank you, Mr. Chairman.

Mr. Inch? Is it Inch? I am so sorry. I didn't hear them say your name.

Mr. INCH. It is. Mark Inch.

Mrs. WATSON COLEMAN. Inch at a time. Okay. Is it true that the majority of the prisoners in the Federal system are there for non-violent drug offenses?

Mr. INCH. Thank you for that question.

You know, during my opening statement, I identified the categories by which we had Federal inmates and recognized about 40 percent we have at a custody grade of medium or high based not only on their current conviction, but their histories of—histories of criminal history.

Mrs. WATSON COLEMAN. I am not sure you are answering. Could you just answer my question?

Mr. INCH. Yes. So in terms of the actual statistics, my staff can provide your office the exact statistics ——

Mrs. WATSON COLEMAN. Do you have any sense that the majority of the prisoners that are in the system are there for nonviolent drug-related offenses?

Mr. INCH. There's a philosophical aspect here is drug trafficking a nonviolent or a violent crime?

Mrs. WATSON COLEMAN. Okay. I can't have a colloquy with you. I am just going to ask you questions. You answer me questions.

Mr. INCH. Yes. Okay. That's ——

Mrs. WATSON COLEMAN. So I am just going to ask you, however you categorize those prisoners in your system, if you can't answer that question, could you please, through our chairman, supply that information?

Mr. INCH. Yes, I'll certainly supply the exact statistics of our inmate population.

Mrs. WATSON COLEMAN. Okay, thank you. All righty. Thank you.

What is your feeling about the change in the administration's position with regard to the use of private prisons?

Mr. INCH. Okay. Thank you for that, that question as well.

So within the Federal system, when I was in the military and doing military corrections, we did not use private prisons. So do not have an informed opinion from that experience.

Mrs. WATSON COLEMAN. Okay.

Mr. INCH. But I am obviously aware that we do use private prisons as one of the tools kind of in our toolbox addressed primarily to low inmates, alien low, though, of course, we also use a private facility for D.C. inmates.

Mrs. WATSON COLEMAN. Thank you.

My understanding is that there are other sort of entities and partners who look at this and observe this situation, including the IG, who said that these prisons, these private prisons are less safe, less secure, are more problematic for the safety and security of not only the inmate, but the staff. Do you have an awareness of that, and are you in agreement with that?

Mr. INCH. So I'm certainly aware of the report, the experience that we have on the Federal side with our contracts and with the population. The challenge, and I believe the report identified that, is the challenges of doing comparisons. When you try to compare different types of inmate populations, it's just an apples-to-oranges comparison.

Mrs. WATSON COLEMAN. So since you think that there are less violent, less problematic inmates placed in the private prisons, you would think that there would be less incidences of insecure activity. So I am going to ask Mr. Horowitz what your finding was?

Mr. HOROWITZ. Well, our private prison review, which identified a number of the issues that you reference, Congresswoman, caused us concern about BOP's oversight of the contract prisons, as you know from the report. Concerns about staffing that was going on at these private contract prisons not meeting the contractual requirements. The contracts not being reviewed for quality assurance purposes and those sorts of things.

So we found very significantly that, at a minimum, if private prisons were going to be used, BOP needed to do a better job of overseeing them.

Mrs. WATSON COLEMAN. Thank you.

You know, I have exactly one minute left. And this is an issue, this whole issue of prison, prison reform, criminal justice reform, reentry, making sure we have evidence-based programs that we are moving our inmates through so that when they come back—and the majority of them do come back—they are ready, willing, and able to take on their positions as good citizens.

Thank you, Mr. Martin. You are a fantastic witness. And thank you for your work.

And Dr. Doleac, is that right, Doleac? Your work concerns me, or your conclusions concern me because it is almost as if let us not do anything that makes sense for those who are vulnerable because that would just create greater discrimination against those who are vulnerable but have no record. And I say that has to do with the enforcement of the law against discrimination, and we ought to be more diligent and vigilant in that. And to do otherwise is to throw the baby out with the bath water.

And Mr. Chairman, I would just like to say that this is a very important hearing that we need to explore from various levels, from what is happening when you are in prison, how do you divert from the prison, and what do you do on the way out? And so I ask you, through my ranking member, that we devote a whole hearing to that.

And I thank you very much, and I yield back because I am over my time.

Mr. RUSSELL. And I thank the gentlelady. And I think, given the bipartisan interest in this matter, that we certainly could use a lot more time for deliberation. And the gentlelady yields back.

And the chair now recognizes the gentlelady from Florida, Mrs. Demings.

Mrs. DEMINGS. Thank you so much, Mr. Chairman.

And thank you to all of our witnesses who are here with us today.

First of all, I want to say I cannot agree more with my colleagues who talked about the importance of education and keeping persons from going to prison in the first place and, if they do, giving them a fighting chance once they are released from prison. As a former police chief, it is an issue that I looked at quite a bit, and I have asked the question over and over again, could reducing our prison population be as simple as ensuring that our young men in particular have the ability to graduate high school or receive an equivalent if they do not?

We have also talked quite a bit today about information, data, the importance of it or the lack thereof. You all know that last year, the Government Accountability Office released a report that basically said the Bureau of Prison lacks adequate information to effectively evaluate its programs. And based on the lack of answers that some of my colleagues were able to receive this morning, it looks like the GAO office is correct.

Ms. Mauer, I would like to ask you, how effective do you believe the Bureau of Prisons has been in collecting and tracking key program data?

Ms. MAUER. Thank you for that question.

We found that that's tended to vary depending on the type of program. As a general proposition, the BOP is very good at keeping track of the number of individuals they have within the system, where they're located, what their security level is, sort of the basic, fundamental information you need to run a correctional system.

However, where we—a common theme we found across a number of our reports is that BOP and the Department of Justice have often lacked the ability to assess the impact of their programs. They don't necessarily know whether they're working effectively. And we found that specifically when it came to residential reentry centers and home confinement, as well as reentry programming.

Mrs. DEMINGS. Director Inch, do you agree with those—with that statement?

Mr. INCH. Ma'am, I think it's a very compelling argument. I do understand the difference between a measure of performance. You know, we say this is what we do, and here is the facts, as opposed to a measure of effectiveness. It's a very legitimate comment.

Mrs. DEMINGS. How important—or has improve in oversight and accountability been part of your review of the major policies within the Bureau of Prisons?

Mr. INCH. Thank you, Congresswoman.

Yes. You know, within my first 90 days, the taking a very close look, especially within our Reentry Services Division, of how we not only address programs and focus the priorities of the program. I think the better way to describe it, though, is, and I'm just starting to spiral into that.

There's level upon level upon level because of the complexity, frankly, of that. But, yes, it certainly has my focus.

Mrs. DEMINGS. Ms. Roseberry, as a member of the task force, I know you all as well made several recommendations. How important do you believe those recommendations are to the overall success of what we are trying to do? And if you could talk a little bit about your perception of those recommendations that have been implemented or not?

Ms. ROSEBERRY. Thank you for that question.

We think that our recommendations are integral to the success of the Bureau of Prisons and ultimately to the citizens who matriculate through them. We've not found that many of them have been implemented up to this point specifically with respect to programming and individualized assessments, which, of course, has a direct impact on reentry.

We did find that one of the largest drivers of overincarceration were the low level or the nonviolent drug offenders and recommended that prison beds be reserved only for those who are very serious offenders and that we use diversion and other programs to provide corrections measures to people who have committed infractions.

Mrs. DEMINGS. I know one of your recommendations was to establish an oversight board. Has that board been implemented as of yet?

Ms. ROSEBERRY. It has not. And as I mentioned in my comments, transparency is an important part of our prisons. We need to know what's going on in our prisons.

I recently spokc with a professor who'd studied both French and American prisons who said to me that the only way we know what's going on inside American prisons is if some lawyer files a lawsuit or if a reporter takes a look at it. We deserve to know what is going on inside our prisons.

Mrs. DEMINGS. Director Lynch—or Inch, I am sorry, I know that 90 days can be a short time or a long time depending on where you are. But do you intend to implement this recommendation to have an oversight review board?

Mr. INCH. Thank you, Congresswoman.

Actually, that particular recommendation isn't for the Bureau of Prisons to implement. Certainly that would be a departmental decision above me.

Mrs. DEMINGS. What is your opinion of the oversight review board and the purpose that it would serve?

Mr. INCH. So my initial impression seeing that, one, this is my first hearing I've ever been at, and it's called an ——

Mrs. DEMINGS. Congratulations.

Mr. INCH. Yes. And it's called an oversight committee. I recognize I'm under oversight. The reports that I've certainly read by—from the Office of Inspector General and from the GAO, I find that they are very direct in their observations and very detailed, and I value that. I would argue that's oversight, and I can assure you my boss is involved in my life.

Mrs. DEMINGS. So you have not ruled out that possibility?

Mr. INCH. I have personally not requested an additional oversight mechanism, bureaucratic or otherwise, at this point.

Mrs. DEMINGS. Okay. Thank you. I have run out of time.

Thank you so much, Mr. Chairman.

Mr. RUSSELL. The gentlelady yields back.

The chair now recognizes the gentlelady from Illinois, Ms. Kelly.

Ms. KELLY. Almost done. Director Inch, I wanted to know, have recent cuts in halfway house services affected inmates' ability to transition back to their communities at a facility close to home?

Mr. INCH. Thank you again for the question on our residential reentry centers, a very important part of our program, and we are absolutely committed to it.

The reports, of course, of not executing option years or contracts of underutilized RRCs got a lot of attention in the past few months. That was primarily done for the efficiency of the system. You know, we have a clear spend plan. And the underutilized facilities are where we had facilities that were of a contractual type that was, frankly, not efficient, and we had other facilities within the region to pick up the requirements. I assure you it was not to signal any less commitment to the use of that program.

Ms. KELLY. Okay. And what is being done to ensure that inmates are sent to prison facilities within a reasonable distance of their home. I am from the State of Illinois, the Chicagoland area, even though mostly in the south suburbs of Chicago, and I hear that complaint a lot.

I am not just saying about Federal prisons, but a lot about there is a lot of people from the Chicagoland area that get sent downstate, and it is very difficult for their families to visit and a lot of different things that go along with that.

Mr. INCH. Thank you, Congresswoman.

Well, I grew up in Wheaton, and you'd probably call me downstate, too.

Ms. KELLY. No, I live in Matteson. So I don't ——

Mr. INCH. So, of course, with our array of Federal facilities, and in Illinois, I believe we have five, I've visited Thomson here in my first 90 days. But drawing back to the general, the whole aspect of inmate designation, we have consolidated that within the Bureau of Prisons, our designation center is actually in Texas, Grand Prairie. That takes into consideration absolutely the—well, a variety of aspects. But as you would expect, being close to home is a positive.

In my initial statement, I talked about one of our stakeholders being victims, and I divide the victims between victims of crime, and there is aspects of what we do that it relates to those victims. Victims among us. That's the staff and inmates that are victims. And what I would call, personal term is forgotten victims, and that's the family members of the offenders.

And so having very strong bonds between the offender and their family. Sometimes there's reasons why that can't be, but is important. So, but we look at programs, custody grade, health requirements. We have four levels of health requirements. It's quite complex. But the aspect of being close to family, that's one advantage of our Federal system of 122 facilities is it improves that capability.

Ms. KELLY. So, I mean, is it a very low percentage of people that aren't within the 500 miles or a great distance away, or do you feel like you have a handle on that issue?

Mr. INCH. So I feel we have a handle. But allow me to get back with—to staff on the exact statistics of the number of inmates that are within 500 miles, recognizing if they are outside that, there's often a very good reason for that.

Ms. KELLY. Did you want to say something?

Ms. ROSEBERRY. Yes. I'd like to just say that, you know, to these poor and marginalized communities, 500 miles might as well be 2 million miles away from home.

Ms. KELLY. I know. That is a long way.

Ms. ROSEBERRY. And also with respect to D.C. Code offenders who are housed within the Bureau of Prisons, they are typically farther away than 500 miles.

Ms. KELLY. Okay. Thank you.

And I think my colleague from Wisconsin brings up a good point.

I would like to know which States, you know, we feel have best practices. And when I think about Illinois, and you said you were from Wheaton. So there is something called the Safer Foundation, I don't know if you guys are familiar, that help people coming out of jail get jobs, and they seem to do a good job at that. And it seems like we need to study and research and analyze, you know, what is working because, I mean, it is ridiculous the amount of people we have in jail and the reasons, you know, they are in jail.

I think about the State of Washington and Colorado and what people are allowed to do there. Then we have people in jail, you know, for, you know, smoking marijuana. Now, you know, in some places, it is okay to do it.

So, but I do think we need to look at each State and look at best practices and what can be duplicated. Some things can't. Like in Illinois, we have ban-the-box, which I think is excellent that we did that. So, you know, that helps. But I think we definitely need to take a closer look and hear recommendations from you.

I yield back.

Mr. RUSSELL. The gentlelady yields back.

We do appreciate the panel being here today, and with six of you, obviously, we have been indulgent a little bit on time. So I appreciate you doing that, but you are not done yet. I have my own sets of questions.

But I am grateful. I think everybody here not only is committed to helping solve the problems. It might come from different viewpoints or angles.

And General Inch, thank you for your continued service to our country not only in your previous life, but now you are doing something easy like taking on the Bureau of Prisons. So we are grateful to your continued selfless service, and welcome to your first hearing.

It seems to me that coupled with recidivism, overincarceration, my State, in Oklahoma, we have one of the highest rates of incarceration per capita. But we also have, at least with State agencies, a ban-the-box provision, where we have tried to address and look at this. But I think coupled with that is—is our judiciary branch and its examination on how we look at sentencing. You know, we seem to have an incarcerative justice system rather than a restitutive justice system.

And until we address that—and then, as lawmakers, many times, I think we—wanting to be tough on crime and all of these things, I think oft times we tie the hands of the equal branch of Government being the judiciary, where judges can have latitude in their courts. Not every case is the same. Not every background is the same. Not every propensity for future criminal behavior is the same, even though the crimes might be identical. We have to take that on as well as a part of that.

I think, if I may start with you, Mr. Martin, and thank you for your work in highlighting these issues, you know, as a business owner that manufactures firearms, I have even made a hire where we had somebody with a criminal record, which is—you know, can be risk taking and complicated, given what we manufacture. You know, I am thinking as from an employer end, okay, say we have a ban-the-box provision, but then it is like, "Okay, Mr. Russell, tell me about your work history in the last 5 years." And then I am like, "Well, you know, I haven't been working in the last 5." "Well, why not? Where have you been?"

I mean, so how do we—yes, we have a ban-the-box type of provision. But at the same time, we also are kind of placing the applicant in a situation where really the applicant is going to have to divulge what has been going on if they are in that first 2-year at risk period trying to come out and look at employment. Could you address that?

Mr. MARTIN. Sure. So here is where I give credit for—to the Second Chance Act and the sort of reentry infrastructure that it's created around the country because programs like Safer, Fortune Society, a number of others around the country are in the business of helping job seekers understand how to have that conversation with employers. If you asked me if I were an applicant now for a job just out of prison, yes, I would take ownership over the conviction, but I'd spend a lot more time talking to you about what I've done since then by way of evidence of rehabilitation, whether it was drug and alcohol treatment programs or, in my case, access to a liberal arts degree or those sort of things.

So we're not going to solve all of the problems with ban-the-box, and I'm actually glad you brought up the fact that a conservative State has moved forward with ban-the-box because there's actually a number of more conservative States that have done so. But I think that, you know, we got here through a million cuts, and it's going to take probably just as many antidotes to get us out of this. And one of them is ban-the-box, but another one is investing—continuing to invest in reentry programs through the Second Chance Act that do the job of preparing people for that interaction.

And what I don't want to get lost in this conversation is something that the chairman said before he departed, which is let's talk about human beings and how they operate, right? Like we can look at the research, we can look at the data, but we also know that we have done a great job of dehumanizing the people that go into the system, whether it's violent, nonviolent, and everything else on the spectrum.

And that continued interaction between prospective employer and prospective employee, I think ultimately we will look back and realize that we have done a lot to rehumanize those folks, even if it means that every single person doesn't get the job.

Because people will—I visited 50 different employers. I guarantee you that maybe a third of them I probably wasn't even qualified, but just very desperate for a job opportunity. But at the same time, the interaction, I don't want to devalue the value of that.

Mr. RUSSELL. Well, thank you for that. And I do have some additional questions as we close out, but I will go ahead and yield back and recognize the gentleman from California, Mr. DeSaulnier.

Mr. DESAULNIER. Thank you, Mr. Chairman.

And let me first associate myself with the ranking member's beginning comments. I am afraid that historians will look back in our policy towards corrections and look at it like Michelle Alexander expressed in The New Jim Crow, that this is a period clearly driven by policy that had a lot to do with fear and racism and the challenge this country continues to have. And all, based in my opinion, on one very important political TV ad in a presidential campaign of which the author of, Lee Atwater, apologized on his deathbed.

So in that context where we have come to realize that we have made a mistake, I think, in a bipartisan way, Mr. Horowitz, having spent a lot of time in my previous job in California knowing that we were going to have a Supreme Court decision that said that we had to let 45,000 of our almost 200,000 State inmates out, knowing that the system was driving the State towards bankruptcy at that time, knowing that all the outcomes were bad, having spent time in various State correctional facilities and talked to people who would tell—who had worked there for 35 years and told me with pride what the department used to be like when they had vocation programs.

When, jokingly, people would want to get in a vocational program that was in a prison, and they would have to tell them the only way they could get in was to get arrested and sentenced to that facility. And then talking about how policy and politics changed those institutions.

And then because of that decision, we were required to change, and so far the history that we have done, based on everything I have heard from the panel today, is implementing evidence-based research, making sure that when those inmates go back to mostly urban counties that they have transitional housing, that they have behavioral health, that they have vocational training. And lo and behold, our recidivism rate is going down.

So how do we share that information? Part of what changed California was Washington State. So how does the Federal agencies look at what other countries and specifically what other States have done for 20, sometimes longer. In Washington State, we would bring their Institute of Public Policy down and tell California, its neighbor who was supposed to be so innovative, what we needed to do to change. And we pretty much just copied what we already knew worked in Washington State.

So how are we sharing all this robust information in a non-political, objective, and here is the real point, and doing it in a quick period of time? I am actually sort of shocked that California has done it as quickly as it has because changing those cultures is seems to me to be the largest obstacle. So can you tell me a little bit about how we share what should be obvious?

Mr. HOROWITZ. That's an excellent question, Congressman, and something we've been doing more of, and I think it's incumbent on the BOP to do more of, what we've talked about today. There are 50 State correctional systems out there, and frankly, many of them are far ahead—excuse me, far ahead of the Federal system.

One of the things our teams have been doing as we've been doing these reviews, and I know GAO does this as well, we're going to the largest State systems to see what they're doing, California generally being among them. But we've got Texas, Florida, Georgia, New York. I can go on and mention several other States that are both in more conservative parts of the country, less conservative parts of the country, and you see them moving forward on reentry programs.

Some of the programs the congressman just mentioned, Oklahoma, other States that are moving forward in the way that I think the Federal Government has not done a good job of recognizing, realizing are out there, and need to do. And we're certainly committed continuing to do that, whether it's on reentry, whether it's on preventing contraband. We've looked at also—I'll just add, we haven't talked much about this—Federal Prison Industries. Giving people a vocation.

We did a review on this a couple of years ago and the dramatic drop at the BOP in the use of the Federal Prison Industries. And study after study will tell you that giving inmates who've never had the kind of training we've all talked about, vocational skills is critical. Yet that program has not been sufficiently supported, and I'm not sure, frankly, the fault is entirely on the BOP.

I think there's a lot that needs to be discussed about that with Congress as well. That has been troubled and challenged because of various laws, funding, et cetera, but I don't—I don't think anyone would disagree that if people go to jail without a skill, it's in all of our interests to get them a skill.

Mr. DESAULNIER. I appreciate that. Thank you, Madam Chair— Mr. Chairman. I apologize for that. I yield back.

Mr. RUSSELL. The gentleman yields back.

And if I may, before I recognize the ranking member, Ms. Mauer, do you have some comments along that line as well? Because I know you all have been working hand-in-hand on a lot of that?

Ms. MAUER. Yes, absolutely. I definitely agree with what the Inspector General said. In the reviews that we've been doing at GAO on things like solitary confinement, correctional officer safety, overcrowding, we were looking predominantly at the Bureau of Prisons.

But as part of our audit work, we also looked at what the States were doing, and we found that that was valuable and insightful information.

I'd also like to give a shout-out at the Federal level to the Federal Interagency Reentry Council. You know, GAO doesn't typically issue reports where we talk strictly about good news, but we had a report about 3 years ago that looked at positive examples of interagency coordination, and that interagency council was one of four across the Federal Government that we highlighted as exemplary in terms of its best practices at coordination.

It brought together all the different Federal agencies who have some role in reentry. So I'd like to mention that as well. But I think the broader issue is definitely one I'd like to agree with, which is that there are a lot of innovative practices that are going on at the State level that can be instructive for the Federal prison system.

Mr. RUSSELL. Thank you for that.

And the chair now recognizes the ranking member for his additional comment.

Mr. CUMMINGS. Thank you very much.

I just—I want to go back to something, Mr. Chairman, if you don't mind. The halfway houses, it is my understanding that there is some efforts to cut back on halfway houses, and can you explain the rationale with regard to that, Mr. Inch?

You may have already said it. Maybe I was out of the room, but I didn't—I don't remember hearing it.

Mr. INCH. The—I did, but certainly saying it again. There is absolutely no intent to cut back in the program. It's an essential program to our system and reentry. The 16 facilities that were certainly reported in the media really was an aspect of creating efficiencies within the system.

These were aspects of not renewing option years or contracts that were not efficient in areas where we had capability in other facilities. Coupled with that, and this was, again, based on the Inspector General report, was that we need to do a better job of managing our contracts with the RRCs. So those 16 does not signal any lessening of our belief of the importance of the program, and I'm committed to running it very efficiently and to the capacity that is necessary for the population.

Mr. CUMMINGS. Well, the Baltimore RRC is the largest such facility on the east coast.

Mr. INCH. Yes.

Mr. CUMMINGS. And, but the occupancy has fallen sharply due to recent BOP cuts. The facility was given essentially no notice to prepare for these cuts. Now this facility is struggling to meet its costs.

Director Inch, can you explain the decision to cut services at the existing RRCs, such as Baltimore facility, and does the BOP intend to close more RRCs?

Mr. INCH. Again, thank you for asking that question. It's a very fair ——

Mr. CUMMINGS. Is that—that is where you visited, right?

Mr. INCH.—question, and I did visit it. And I have personal knowledge on that.

Mr. CUMMINGS. Okay, good.

Mr. INCH. So, first, is it our intent to cut back on our program?

Absolutely not. Specifically with the Baltimore facility, very impressed with the facility and the contract provider that runs that facility and others and fully recognize that that particular organization, of course, actually built a new facility to run their programs, and I think it's very well structured.

So the overbuilt capacity, and frankly, because we had poor management controls at a time, we overfilled the contractual capacity.

So we have in that particular facility, fully within the statement of work of the contract, we have brought it back down to that number. I suspect this is probably not an appropriate area to talk about actual contracting stuff.

Mr. CUMMINGS. No.

Mr. INCH. But I'd be happy to come by your office later ——

Mr. CUMMINGS. Yes, please do. Please do.

Mr. INCH.—and really talk. But you know, I think that is a great facility, and I really ——

Mr. CUMMINGS. I think so, too.

Mr. INCH.—appreciate the work they do.

Mr. CUMMINGS. All right. Let me close by saying this. I want to thank all of you for what you have had to say today, and I think that, you know, as I listen to the testimony, I think we all—we need to get back to the human side of all of this because it is extremely painful. It is extremely damaging to so many people.

And by the way, it is just not the former inmates. It is their families that suffer too, big time. And so we can look at statistics here and statistics there, but let us not forget the human element of all of this, you know? And I often tell my children whatever happens to you, whatever has happened to you—good, bad, or ugly—before this moment prepares you for this moment. And you know, as I am sitting here, I just remember I taught in the penitentiary, State penitentiary. I taught inmates that had very long sentences.

But I know, Mr. Martin, going back to something that you said, they had a sense of hope, and they got—I mean, these guys got degrees. Then we have Goucher, which is one of our small State colleges in Maryland, that has a program which I think President Obama started experimenting with using Pell Grants so that they could get their college degrees.

And when we went to visit them, we discovered that a lot of the inmates were just so excited because there were inmates that were already going through the program in their second or third year, and then other ones were saying you know what, we're going to do everything in our power to get in the program, too. So that, too, when we think about things like public safety, I mean the people have a sense of hope, and they can see an avenue to getting to where they have got to go.

And I believe—and just one second, Mr. Chairman, I will be finished. I believe that a lot of people are like going—our inmates, our former inmates are like going in circles. They come out, and they are on this circle, right? And they are looking for an exit to get to where they have got to go. They have dreamed dreams. They have said I am going to do better. I am going to take care of my family. I am going to do all these things.

And then when they get out, not only are they—as has already been said, not only are they facing a new world. I mean, in today's world, you can be in prison for 5 years and the world has changed drastically. But they come out and face a new world, but then they are not equipped to do anything. Many are not educated.

So some kind of way, I think it was Ms. Roseberry said we find a way to bring them down, but we don't find a way to bring them up. After we bring them—I mean, you get them there. And it is without a doubt, we become a part of the problem.

You know, you say you don't want recidivism. You don't want recidivism. Well, you send somebody out—you send—you go out there and not—and every employer turn you away. And let us say you don't have more than a 10th grade education. Try that one.

And then, and please don't be black. Try that one. Or poor. Try that one. And the next thing you know, you go—and so I have people come to me almost every—we do jobs fairs in my district. I have people come to me almost every week, probably sometimes three times a week, and this is what they say.

They say, "Mr. Cummings, Mr. Cummings, I can't get a job, man. I can't get a job. I want to do for my family. I can't get a job" because of a record or whatever. And so all I am saying—and these people—and I want to be clear because I know some people will say, oh, he doesn't care about public safety. I do care about public safety. There are some people that need to be in prison and probably for a very, very long time.

And the public needs to be protected, but at the same time, there are a lot of good people who make mistakes. All of us make mistakes at some point. Some of us just didn't get caught. And so, so we have got to figure out—figure this thing out.

Other than that, we are working against ourselves. We put them in jail. Then they come out, and there is absolutely nothing that they can do. So why is it that I see people at 2:00 in the morning selling drugs in 20-degree weather, probably not making much money. I mean, that is a job.

And so I beg you, as the new guy on the block, new head of the team, I hope that you will look at some of the things that are being done, some of the really constructive things. And you know, I want us to be effective and efficient in what we do. You know, we can go, I mean, forever and forever and forever, going in circles, and never achieving a damned thing except going backwards.

Thank you, Mr. Chairman. And thank you all very much.

Mr. RUSSELL. I thank the ranking member for his comments.

Along this theme of recidivism, one of the things that the Federal system has come under criticism on has been with faith-based educational and outreach opportunities. The States seem to do much better and are more open-minded toward these programs than we see in the Federal system or, by extension, the private prisons that are allowed to accommodate Federal.

What—and this would really just be a general question for those, but I would like to start with you, General Inch. Where will this go? Because when you examine the recidivism rates for these that have been engaged in these programs, whether it is educational or to a degree or towards others, they are actually much higher than the general, the general population. So they are obviously working, to some extent.

Could you comment on that?

Mr. INCH. Thank you, Congressman Russell. Great question.

So drawing back from previous experiences in military corrections, and I was the commandant of the disciplinary barracks, which is the Department of Defense's maximum security prison, we had a very robust volunteer program, both secular and faith-based.

And I saw great value in that.

The DB is kind of a one facility microcosm of what is now 122 facilities. And both through education programs, amazing treatment programs, vocational training, I've certainly seen a framework, and I would add in—and this harkens a little bit back to the issue of cross-fertilization—I've been very active in the American Correctional Association for much of my career and only recently active in the Association of State Corrections Authorities that do a lot of cross-fertilization of these programs. So I'm very receptive to these programs.

In my second week, when I was in Dallas visiting our regional headquarters, had the opportunity, for example, to go to the Texas Offender Reentry Initiative. I believe Bishop Jakes is—his church is the one that runs that particular one, just to see and learn. And I'm open to doing like things.

Mr. RUSSELL. Well, that is good to hear because I think, you know, as we explore all the possibilities, we certainly want to seize upon the things that work. None of them necessarily are compelled any more than, you know, some secular program. An inmate can choose not to get a GED completion, or he can choose not to get college courses. There is a number of things like that.

Mr. Horowitz, home confinement. Going back to the theme on the restitutive justice vice incarcerative justice that our Nation seems to be so enamored with, what is the maximum amount of time a person can serve outside of prison once sentenced? And maybe General Inch will know this, but—and then, whatever the answer is, in your studies, I know in your report, you had noticed an underutilization in home confinement. So could you speak to that?

Mr. HOROWITZ. Do you want to give the numbers first?

Mr. INCH. Yes. Certainly on the statutory aspect of the home confinement, it's 6 months or 10 percent of the sentence, whichever is less. So that kind of bounds it in there.

When you couple that with the residential reentry center, most programming that we target, though we can certainly take it up to a year, is a 4-month target. The idea is that in that 4-month period, it provides the opportunity to make that connection in the community and—and work to find a job, then with that amount, of course, basic math is 4/4/4. That's the three people participate in that program for one bed space of the contract per year.

Mr. RUSSELL. Okay. So ——

Mr. HOROWITZ. If I ——

Mr. RUSSELL. Yes, please.

Mr. HOROWITZ. Just briefly on the underutilization issue, BOP has three choices with regard to inmates whose sentences are close to expiration. Keep them in jail and release them straight into the community, send them to an RRC, or send them to their home with an ankle bracelet so they can reconnect to their community from home, as opposed to an RRC. That's obviously far cheaper than either prison or an RRC.

Our concern in our study was—in our review was that it seemed like the BOP's default was either keep people in jail or send them to an RRC even if there wasn't a demonstrated need for an RRC.

And the result being that important bed spaces in RRCs were being taken by people who were low need, low risk instead of thinking ——

Mr. RUSSELL. If you could pause just a moment? Whoever has that, please silence the ——

[Telephone ringing.]

Voice. Sounds Irish.

Mr. RUSSELL. Is that somebody here in the hearing? Yes, please turn it off. That is disrespectful to the witnesses.

I am sorry, Mr. Horowitz. Please continue.

Mr. HOROWITZ. Thank you.

The problem we saw was that the BOP wasn't thinking about who needed to be in which of the facilities. And so, in our view, they were sending people to RRCs who really should have been, it seemed to us, either staying in prison or going to home confinement. And the consequence of using the RRC was to take a valuable bed space for others who might need it, but never could be considered for it because the bed space was being taken by someone else in that position.

And frankly, and many of the studies show that low-risk individuals like white collar offenders who don't need the services of an RRC, sending them there with other individuals who do could actually be more harmful than helpful to those individuals, and so we were concerned about that as well.

Mr. RUSSELL. Yes, they would see it as a delay to the support base that they already have and don't have that need.

Ms. Maurer, would you care to comment on that as well?

Ms. MAUER. Yes, just very quickly. In some of our work, we were looking at the role the Federal judiciary can play in home confinement, and we found that there were instances where BOP had worked on an arrangement with the pretrial and probation services office at the Federal courts for the courts to provide home confinement services that at the time of our review seemed to be significantly less than what BOP was paying its contractors to provide home confinement services.

That's an option that could be explored for additional capacity and potential cost savings as well.

Mr. RUSSELL. Well, thank you for that.

And I will now defer and recognize the gentleman from Missouri.

However, this will be the last member that I will recognize out of respect to our witnesses and maybe their comfort. And so, with that, I recognize the gentleman from Missouri.

Mr. CLAY. Thank you, Mr. Chairman.

And thank the witnesses for your indulgence.

Director Inch, earlier this year, I joined several of my House and Senate colleagues in writing to you to request information about prison education programs, specifically the Second Chance Pell program and the Roadmap to Reentry Initiative. We received a response from BOP on October 27th, and Mr. Chairman, I ask unanimous consent that these two letters be made part of the official record of this hearing.

Mr. RUSSELL. Without objection.

Mr. CLAY. Thank you.

Director Inch, BOP's response indicated that some of those initiatives have been abandoned. Can you elaborate which initiatives have been eliminated and why?

Mr. INCH. Thank you, Congressman, for that question.

I believe the aspect of that, and certainly this was prior to my arrival, was the planning that had been done with the idea of creating at central office level of a kind of a school board type arrangement, probably about 40 people. The decision was made prior to my arrival to not grow the central headquarters by those numbers, to use that as a structure by which to work our education program.

So, for me personally, as I look at it, I'm absolutely committed to education. It's essential. It's important. You know, when I think of the story of Mr. Martin, and it's not the first time I've heard his story, it was absolutely inspiring that when he had an opportunity to speak to all the State corrections authorities last month and I was present, it was very inspirational.

The importance of education I'm absolutely committed to. In this first 90 days, in this first year, frankly, as we are organized within our Reentry Services Division, I'll use the assets, I'll understand the strengths and weaknesses. But my commitment to education, you know, please don't worry about that.

Mr. CLAY. So creating a school district concept was rather expensive, to say the least. And so I guess that it is about resources. How would you stand up a program? And maybe you could share with us how many resources you would need in order to stand up some type of effective educational program?

Mr. INCH. Sir, very fair question. I probably would not be able to do it any justice in my first 90 days.

Mr. CLAY. Okay.

Mr. INCH. This will take, as in all the programs that I've been observing and as I—though I'm not new to corrections, the profession, at all, I am new to the Bureau of Prisons. So ——

Mr. CLAY. Okay, that is fair. But now there was a person in place to oversee BOP's educational services, and have you all had— do you have a timeline for replacing Amy Lopez?

Mr. INCH. We do. The hiring process for our education director is ongoing, nearing—nearing completion.

Mr. CLAY. And so is that coming soon or ——

Mr. INCH. Yes, nearing completion. Yes, sir.

Mr. CLAY. And you have replaced Amy Lopez?

Mr. INCH. With the position and—in our current structure of how we supervise education, the senior person, that hiring action is ongoing right now.

Mr. CLAY. You know studies show that inmates who participate in correctional education programs have 43 percent lower odds of returning to prison than those who do not. Every dollar spent on prison education saves $4 to $5 on the cost of reincarceration. And so that should—should make you want to direct resources to effective education program, and hopefully, that is what your administration will be looking towards doing.

Mr. INCH. I'm absolutely committed to education.

Mr. CLAY. Let me ask Inspector General Horowitz, are you satisfied with BOP's progress to date on the recommendations that were made in a report?

Mr. HOROWITZ. I—I'm sorry.

Mr. CLAY. Go ahead. No, go ahead.

Mr. HOROWITZ. They are making progress. There are several more steps they need to take to effect implementation. We will continue to oversee it, but I will say that we have long had a very good, close working relationship with BOP and them being responsive to our recommendations. So we certainly look forward to continuing.

Mr. CLAY. All right. I see my time is up. I thank you, Mr. Chair-man. Thank the witness.

Mr. RUSSELL. The gentleman yields back.

And my final question, General Inch, you are uniquely suited, given your military experience, given your experience in corrections and then now on this side. States have been trying to deal with veteran incarceration a great deal, even on the judiciary side. Do we have special courts that deal with special sets of circumstances?

Do we look at the types of offenses and put that, you know, allowing once again our judiciary branch to have a little more latitude?

Do you have any plans in your goals and objectives, as you come in with this kind of understanding, to try to address some of the issues? And then how we would reenter those veterans who unlike in the military prison system, where they may actually lose rights of an honorable discharge or different things, many of them outside after being honorably discharged are still entitled to their benefits and their decorations and things of that nature. So they could reenter under a bit different circumstances than if they were incarcerated in the military.

Have you given much thought to this or about the direction to deal with that population?

Mr. INCH. Thank you, Congressman Russell. I have, and thank you for your service as well.

So I was actually pleased to find out that we have piloted a concept that in the corrections profession has been discussed for several years, and that's having veterans housing units. I had the good fortune, again in my previous life, but in association when I attended an American Correctional Association conference, that a facility—in this case, it was in the State of

Indiana—where I was able to see their program and see how they ran their program.

I spoke with the inmates in their housing areas. So I'm very interested in that program. I think, you know, in the aspects of treatment ——

Mr. RUSSELL. Would that be not the halfway houses, but actually

Mr. INCH. No, that's inside the facilities.

Mr. RUSSELL. Inside. So that you would ——

Mr. INCH. It would be an actual housing unit.

Mr. RUSSELL. Kind of like the commonality of barracks and routines and disciplines and that sort of thing?

Mr. INCH. So, anecdotal, it was when I spoke with the inmates at that one facility in Indiana, actually a privately run facility, that the inmates talked about the aspect of trust and that they were then able to focus on their programming. And several that had been in different environments in housing talked about how that was different for them.

So I think there's a lot of validity in looking at that concept. I'm always afraid to talk about that in the presence of a social scientist that will bring out the metrics. She intimidates me.

[Laughter.]

Mr. INCH. But that—but certainly, there is anecdotal aspects that are worth pursuing.

Mr. RUSSELL. And Ms. Doleac, you don't look terribly intimidating, but intellectually, we may all find ourselves on the wrong end, as the chairman has alluded to earlier. Would you like to comment on any of that?

Ms. DOLEAC. No, I defer. I defer to the expertise of the Director.

Mr. RUSSELL. Okay. Thank you.

Well, I want to say, you know, how grateful I am. This is a team effort. It is about our country. Mr. Martin, you bring out the human element of it, and I agree with the chairman and the ranking member that I think we forget that sometimes.

But this can't be the gift that keeps on giving. As people pay their debt to society, it truly needs to be a forgiven debt. But unfortunately, culturally, we have a lot of work to do there. As people reenter, they have paid that debt. It just can't be the gift that keeps on giving and puts them in a difficult position.

And with that, I would like to defer to the chairman for his comments.

Chairman GOWDY. Well, Congressman, I want to thank you for filling in so ably for me while I was next door.

I want to thank all of our witnesses. It is a super important hearing. I was bemoaning the fact next door that how important this issue is and how little attention there is in this hearing room. All of the attention is next door for important reasons, but this is important also.

Professor Doleac, I want to ask you to do one thing I couldn't do myself, which is you have access to the brain power and the studies. If what is being proposed does not or cannot accomplish what I think everyone agrees is the ultimate goal, then what will work?

Because I think there is a lot of sensitivity, regardless of politics, on helping people who have paid their debts to society have a chance to go on and have a constructive life that we all claim we want them to have. But if you can't get a job, all the other obligations in life are really hard to meet. So if this won't do it or can't do it, what can?

And with that, I don't want to single you out. Inspector General Horowitz, from what I read, you have been busy lately, too. So I appreciate you coming.

Everyone is busy. Everyone has very hectic schedules. I appreciate your expertise. I appreciate your comity with the committee and your collegiality and professionalism with each other.

And I thank you, Congressman.

Mr. RUSSELL. And with that, this hearing is adjourned.

Thank you.

[Whereupon, at 12:45 p.m., the committee was adjourned.]

APPENDIX. MATERIAL SUBMITTED FOR THE HEARING RECORD

Rep. Darrell Issa Statement for the Record "Oversight of the Bureau of Prisons and Inmate Reentry," December 13, 2017, Full Committee Hearing

Mr. Chairman, as the leading Republican sponsor of the Fair Chance Act, I want to emphasize that the issue that this legislation seeks to address is far from partisan.

In many states across the country, we have seen "ban the box" policies implemented and, like other criminal justice reform policies, they have enjoyed broad, bipartisan support. In states that include Indiana, Georgia, Kentucky, and Arizona, Republican Governors in recent years have championed the objectives that this bill seeks to achieve. Our counterpart bill in the Senate also enjoys Republican sponsorship from Senators Ron Johnson, Joni Ernst, and Rob Portman. And in the private business world, organizations ranging from Koch Industries to Walmart to Starbucks have all supported these policies and put them into practice.

Mr. Chairman, all of us who have worked in or ran businesses have witnessed the value and dignity that a job can bring to a person's life. The best way to prevent people from returning to lives of crime is to ensure that those leaving the criminal justice system have reasonable opportunities to become productive members of society.

When we shut the door on this group of individuals, the message we inadvertently send is that those who commit a crime will never be given a second chance. The Fair Chance Act will go a considerable distance in helping to break the cycle of crime, by restoring hope and giving many Americans opportunities to tum their lives around.

Mr. Chairman, it is time that the federal government caught up with many of the states and the business world and, for these reasons, I urge my colleagues to join us in supporting the Fair Chance Act.

Congress of the United States
Washington, DC 20515

October 3, 2017

General Mark S. Inch
Director
Federal Bureau of Prisons
320 First St., NW
Washington, DC 20534

Dear Director Inch:

We are writing to express our concerns regarding the implementation of programs that promote successful reentry, specifically prison education programs. Education programs have a documented record in reducing recidivism, yet educational opportunities are sorely lacking in federal prisons.

In 2015, the Department of Education (ED) created the Second Chance Pell program, a pilot program that reinstated access to Pel! Grant aid for eligible incarcerated students in Federal and State penal institutions. These incarcerated students-over 12,000 individuals-who otherwise meet Title IV eligibility requirements could access Pell Grants to pursue higher education or training. During the 2016 to 2017 academic year, 67 institutions of higher education partnered with over I 00 penal institutions-7 of which were Bureau of Prisons (BOP) facilities-to provide higher education for incarcerated students in over 28 states. Over 10 percent of these colleges and universities were Minority-Serving Institutions and about 37 percent were offering prison-based education for the first time.

In 2016, the Department of Justice (DOJ) announced its "Roadmap to Reentry" initiative to improve education, programming, and reentry preparation for people in federal prisons. The initiative included supporting the Second Chance Pell program. It also created a semi- autonomous "school district" within BOP that would offer better post-secondary education programs, as well as adult literacy and basic skills, high school diplomas, and expanded opportunities for individuals with learning disabilities.

To accomplish this goal, BOP hired Amy Lopez to be the first superintendent of its school district. Described by DOJ as a "veteran correctional educator" from the Texas prison school system, Ms. Lopez's hiring was announced in November 2016. Together, these actions by ED, DOJ, and BOP signaled their evolving views on the role of incarceration and the best ways to reduce federal prison spending without impacting public safety.

Education helps to ensure that when incarcerated people leave prison, they have the requisite tools to return successfully to their communities. Education for people in prisons has a clear public safety benefit, reducing recidivism rates by over 43 percent according to a 2010 Pew Charitable Trusts report. In addition, these programs are cost-effective: a 2013 RAND

Corporation report found that higher education in prisons offers a 400 percent return on investment over 3 years, saving taxpayers $5 for every $1 spent.

While the public safety and cost-saving benefits of prison education are clear, recent actions by DOJ signal a potential shift in policy away from promoting education in federal prisons. DOJ has not formally announced changes to the Roadmap to Reentry initiative, but in May 2017, Amy Lopez was fired from her position as superintendent. There has been little subsequent information regarding the terms and rationale for her firing, and neither DOJ nor BOP have issued a formal statement.

Considering these actions, we ask that you provide the following information regarding changes to BOP's prison reform efforts.

1) What is the status of the Roadmap to Reentry initiative? If there are changes to the BOP's prison education programs, what are those changes? What is the rationale for those changes?
2) Why was Amy Lopez fired? Is there a replacement for her position? If her position is not being filled, what is the rationale? Are there plans to abolish BOP's unified school district? If so, what is the rationale for such action?

3) How is BOP ensuring that people in federal prisons receive access to adequate secondary and post-secondary education, as well as adult literacy services and programs for people with disabilities? If BOP is not continuing its previous efforts to improve public safety and reduce prison spending by focusing on education and other reentry preparation programs, what is the rationale for this policy change?

Thank you for your attention to this matter and we look forward to your response.

Sincerely,

Brian Schatz
United States Senator

Danny K. Davis
Member of Congress

Richard J. Durbin
United States Senator

Yvette D. Clarke
Member of Congress

Jeffrey A. Merkley
United States Senator

WM. Lacy Clay
Member of Congress

Benjamin L. Cardin
United States Senator

Steven Cohen
Member of Congress

Elizabeth Warren
United States Senator

John Conyers, Jr.
Member of Congress

Christopher A. Coons
United States Senator

Elijah E. Cummings
Member of Congress

Sheldon Whitehouse
United States Senator

Mark Desaulnier
Member of Congress

Al Franken
United States Senator

Keith Ellison
Member of Congress

Cory A. Booker
United States Senator

Raul M. Grijalva
Member of Congress

Edward J. Markey
United States Senator

Colleen Nanabusa
Member of Congress

Patty Murray
United States Senator

Pramila Jayapal
Member of Congress

Richard Blumenthal
United States Senator

Marcy Kaptur
Member of Congress

Sherrod Brown
United States Senator

Barbara Lee
Member of Congress

Christopher S. Murphy
United States Senator

Sean Patrick Maloney
Member of Congress

Mazie K. Hirono
United States Senator

Gwen S. Moore
Member of Congress

Ron Wyden
United States Senator

Eleanor Holmes Norton
Member of Congress

Bernard Sanders
United States Senator

Bobby L. Rush
Member of Congress

Patrick Leahy
United States Senator

Tom Ryan
Member of Congress

Robert C. "Bobby" Scott
Member of Congress

Frederica S. Wilson
Member of Congress

U.S. Department of Justice
Federal Bureau of Prisons
October 27, 2017

The Honorable Elijah E. Cummings, Jr.
Member, U. S. House of Representatives

2163 Rayburn House Office Building
Washington, DC 20515

Dear Congressman Cummings:

Your letter dated October 3, 2017, was referred to me for response. You requested information concerning the Bureau of Prisons (Bureau) reentry initiatives focused on education.

The Bureau of Prisons remains committed to its mission to protect public safety and promote successful reentry. Education programs are one of the cornerstones of our reentry efforts and we continue to provide many effective reentry programs including GED, ESL, vocational training and apprenticeship programs. Additionally, we understand the difficulties faced by individuals with learning and other disabilities and fully acknowledge our responsibilities to address these needs.

The Roadmap to Reentry provided a framework for making a variety of changes in Bureau reentry programs including education. While we continue our efforts to expand and improve programs, some of the specific aspects of the Roadmap were impossible to pursue without significant resources that are not available to us. For example, the tablet computer-based pilot program was anticipated to cost as much as $1 billion. Those projected costs were prohibitive, so the project was cancelled. The adoption of a school district model contemplated the addition of many staff, a resource that is also not available to us. On the other hand, the Department of Education's Second Chance Pell Grant Pilot Initiative continues at the selected institutions.

Amy Lopez was hired to oversee educational endeavors specifically related to the Roadmap to Reentry. While it is true that a determination was made to terminate her limited term Senior Executive Service appointment, our work to enhance our educational services continues. We have an interim Education Administrator who has more than 15 years of correctional experience and a doctorate-level degree. The selection of a permanent replacement to oversee education programs is pending.

For inmates who require extra assistance in education and other programming, including inmates with learning disabilities, the Bureau employs 76 special education teachers who provide educational accommodations as appropriate. Also, we are evaluating a curriculum for inmates who function at lower educational levels, and we recently hired a National Disabilities Manager to coordinate services for inmates with disabilities.

The Bureau is continually assessing its education strategy and looks forward to working with Congress to support the educational needs of the inmate population. We remain committed to improving reentry outcomes for all inmates in the custody of the Bureau of Prisons. I trust this is responsive to your concerns.

Sincerely,
Hugh J. Hurwitz
Acting Assistant Director
Reentry Services Division

Response from Director Inch, Federal Bureau of Prisons, to Representative Grothman

December 13, 2017, Hearing: "Oversight of the Bureau of Prisons and Inmate Reentry"

This is in response to Cong. Grothman's question to Bureau Director Inch during the HOGR hearing on oversight of the Bureau. The Congressman asked about employment data for individuals who have released from the Bureau.

Currently, the Administrative Office of the United States Courts-Federal Probation- maintains employment data on released federal offenders who are on federal supervision (which is the vast majority of federal releases). This data is collected as part of their PICRA assessment tool. They would be best positioned to address employment data for federal releases at this time.

The Bureau has an ongoing project to merge Bureau inmate records with employment and earnings data for a subset of released federal offenders. This project involves access to several data files and therefore it is still in the planning stages. We are optimistic that it will be an important part of the process to understand post release employment for federal inmates. I trust this is responsive to your concerns. Please don't hesitate to contact me should you need anything additional.

Response from Director Inch, Federal Bureau of Prisons, to Representative Comer

December 13, 2017, Hearing: "Oversight of the Bureau of Prisons and Inmate Reentry"

This is in response to Cong. Comer's question to Bureau Director Iuch during the HOGR hearing on oversight of the Bureau. The Congressman asked, "What is the role of RRCs in obtaining drug treatment?"

Community-based drug treatment services are procured nationwide by the BOP specifically for inmates in Residential Reentry Centers (RRC) and on Home Confinement (HC). The primary role of the RRC contractors is to work collaboratively with the contracted drug treatment providers to ensure inmates are made aware of their treatment sessions, and are able to get to the treatment location, i.e., providing passes and/or, providing transportation, if applicable. BOP works in concert with the RRC staff to coordinate services for any inmates in need of treatment.

I trust this is responsive to your concerns. Please don't hesitate to contact me should you need anything additional.

Response from Director Inch, Federal Bureau of Prisons, to Representative Watson Coleman

December 13, 2017, Hearing: "Oversight of the Bureau of Prisons and Inmate Reentry"

This is in response to Cong. Watson Coleman's question to Bureau Director Inch during the HOGR hearing on oversight of the Bureau. The Congresswoman asked, "Are most inmates nonviolent drug offenders?"

Using snapshot data collected at the end of the calendar year, the Bureau was housing 183,951 inmates for whom drug and violence data were encoded (the total Bureau population was slightly higher, but we eliminated from the analysis those inmates for whom drug/violence data was missing).

Of those inmates, 73,729 were serving sentences for drug-related offenses - the vast majority of those (96%) were for drug trafficking charges. Of those offenders serving sentences for drug-related offenses, 39,989 were considered non-violent offenders.

I trust this is responsive to your concerns. Please don't hesitate to contact me should you need anything additional.

Questions for the Record, Bureau of Prisons, U.S. Department of Justice, Hearing before the Committee on Oversight and Government Reform, U.S. House of Representatives, "Oversight of the Bureau of Prisons and Inmate Reentry" December 13, 2017

Questions from Ranking Member Cummings

1. In a 2014 internal memorandum, the Bureau of Prisons (BOP) acknowledged that abstinence-based programs to treat drug addiction "only offer a 1in 10 chance of success for opiate-dependent participants."[65]

a. What are the current treatments provided to prisoners with opioid dependence?

Response: The Bureau of Prisons (BOP) drug abuse treatment protocol includes four programs: the Drug Abuse Education Course, the Non-Residential Treatment Program, the Residential Drug Abuse Program

---

[65] Prisons Are Making America's Drug Problem Worse, *Politico* (Mar. 11, 2015) (online at www.politico.com/magazine/story/2015/03/federal-bureau-of-prisons-medication-assisted-therapy-115998).

(RDAP), and Community Treatment Services. And, as recently announced by President Trump, BOP is implementing a medication-assisted therapy (MAT) program for releasing inmates in the near future.

b. To what extent does BOP provide prisoners with buprenorphine, methadone, suboxone, or other evidence-based medication-assisted therapies? *Hit* does not do so, why not?

Response: BOP supports evidence-based MAT for inmates as they transition to the community. Consistent with the recent Presidential announcement, BOP will use naloxone (brand name, Vivitrol), as it is not subject to diversion, and does not have high abuse potential. Vivitrol is also longer-acting than other MAT drugs and can reduce alcohol cravings. Methadone, buprenoiphine, and Suboxone can have abuse potential and therefore are not used in a Federal correctional setting.

2. Based on the findings of that internal memorandum, BOP has reportedly instituted a "field test" initiative for medication-assisted therapy (MAT) in federal prisons.

a. Please explain in detail the field test to provide MAT to inmates.

Response: BOP conducted a field trial in Fiscal Year (FY) 2015 to determine the feasibility of providing MAT for inmates transitioning to Residential Reentry Centers (RRCs or halfway houses). The field trial identified needed resources and operational requirements for providing MAT. The field trial was conducted in the Dallas/Fort Worth (DFW) area. Eligible participants at the Federal Medical Center Carswell and the Federal Correctional institutions in Fort Worth and Seagoville were transferred to either of two halfway houses in the DFW area. Overall, ten inmates were identified for the field trial.

b. How are opioid dependent inmates selected for this trial program? Response: individuals with a history of opioid abuse but who are riot currently opioid dependent, who were released from the three institutions listed above, and who were transferred to the two selected RRCs were interviewed and assessed by BOP's Chief Psychiatrist to determine appropriateness for the program. Additionally, the individuals were medically cleared for e program.

c. What findings have been produced from the trial to date?

Response: Several issues were identified during the trial, including staffing needs for clinical pharmacist telehealth appointments and coordination for the provision of the medication (to include shipment of the medication to the contractor who would administer the Vivitrol injection), scheduling the appointments for the injection and community treatment counseling services, and subsequent follow-up with the contractor providing those services.

d. Will this trial program be put in place permanently for inmates? *H* so, please provide a timeline for implementation.

Response: BOP has approved expansion of MAT treatment for the Boston area, with an expected implementation date of the Fall of 2018, and then, consistent with the recent Presidential directive, to all releasing individuals with a need who transfer to a RRC.

3. The criminal justice system is also a point of potential intervention for hundreds of thousands of Americans in need of mental health care, particularly for conditions like post-traumatic stress disorder.

a. Please detail the current tracking system for inmates with mental health concerns. Additionally, please provide a detailed description of the current transition services for those inmates with mental health concerns leaving prison.

Response: BOP's Mental Health Classification System is designed to promote accurate identification and tracking of mentally ill inmates and to facilitate the effective use of mental health resources in treating inmates. During initial designation of an inmate to BOP, BOP staff review available inmate records and determine a mental health screen assignment to ensure the inmate is matched with the institution best situated to meet their mental health needs. Upon arrival at the designated facility, the inmate meets with a psychologist who conducts an interview and record review. Based upon this, the psychologist assigns the inmate a mental health care level and documents clinical findings in the inmate's electronic medical record (Bureau Electronic Medical Record or BEMR). For inmates with mental health needs, a Diagnostic and Care Level Formulation note provides additional documentation of the record review and clinical interview, the diagnosis, and the mental health care level assignment.

A Mental Health Care Level 1 (CAREI-MH) inmate is a healthy inmate with a limited need for psychological services. A Care Level 2 (CARE2-MH) inmate is a stable mentally-ill inmate with a need for periodic, but not intensive, psychological services. A Care Level 3 (CARE3-MH) inmate is a seriously mentally-ill inmate with a need for intensive psychological services. In general, a CARE3-MH inmate requires weekly contacts with Psychology staff. A Care Level4 (CARE4-MH) inmate is acutely mentally-iii and in need of psychiatric hospitalization. Mental health care levels can only be changed by a psychologist, psychiatrist, or qualified mid-level practitioner. Inmates' mental health needs may be reassessed at any point and their mental health care levels adjusted to ensure they receive the proper frequency and intensity of care. Mental Health Care Levels are tracked in SENTRY, BOP's inmate management database. All treatment contacts are tracked in BEMR. These clinical notes and Mental Health Care Level system provide the ongoing tracking and treatment system during the inmate's term of incarceration.

Returning to the community can be a particularly stressful and challenging process for mentally-ill inmates. To meet the needs of inmates releasing to RRCs or home confinement, BOP enlists a comprehensive network of community-based providers who offer mental health evaluation and treatment on a contract basis. The following individuals warrant referral for community-based treatment services:

- Inmates who are taking psychotropic medications upon release from a BOP institution;
- Inmates who had regular contact with institution psychology, psychiatry, and medical staff for ongoing mental health concerns; and
- Inmates referred by institution or RRC staff.

The referral process begins before the inmate transfers from the BOP facility to the RRC (or home confinement). Psychology Services staff screen inmate records, including the Pre-· sentencing Report and BEMR, to determine appropriateness for referral. Ordinarily, inmates with advanced care level assignments are automatically referred for treatment. If an inmate meets the screening criteria, staff send a referral to the community-based treatment provider servicing the inmate's release destination. Based on the results of an evaluation, treatment services are arranged. Psychology Services staff monitor each inmate's clinical progress through frequent interaction with the contract provider and review of monthly progress reports until the inmate completes his or her RRC or home confinement placement.

b. What steps is BOP taking to ensure inmates who have mental health concerns are receiving proper care?

Response: BOP ensures inmates with mental health concerns receive proper care through a combination of quality control audits, clinical oversight, staff training, and evidence-based protocol development.

Psychology Treatment Programs, mental health interventions, and individualized treatment plans for inmates with mental illness rely on evidence-based clinical practices that reduce the symptoms of mental illness. Inmates with the most severe forms of mental illness are given priority treatment, though institutions provide a balanced offering of programs that address mental illness and criminal thinking for the entire inmate population.

Psychology Services staff also provide training for mental health treatment staff in- person, as well as via video, web-based training sessions, and a multitude of BOP online courses. Trainings are accredited by the American Psychological Association, the National Board of Certified Counselors, and the Association for Addiction Professionals.

BOP employs a rigorous quality assurance process known as Program Review. Each discipline operates under stringent guidelines intended to ensure compliance with agency policies, as well as correctional and discipline-specific best practices. Each institution's Psychology Services department is reviewed at regular intervals. Psychology Services Program Review Guidelines address a wide range of content areas, including treatment and care of the mentally ill, suicide prevention, mental health assessment and treatment, and specialized services such as treatment for substance abuse and sexual offending. The Program Review process includes scrutiny of clinical records, interviews of staff and inmates, and analysis of the SENTRY inmate records system.'

Psychology Services staff at BOP's headquarters ensure compliance with BOP policies and best practices for the discipline of psychology. They perform remote audits of inmate clinical records, to include suicide risk assessments, extended restrictive housing reviews, and Diagnostic and Care Level Formulation notes. The findings are used to intervene as needed and to develop or modify staff training plans. They also conduct peer reviews of all Chief Psychologists to assess clinical and leadership competencies.

Questions from Representative Hurd

1. What is the Administration's commitment to Re-entry services going forward? Recently, there have been closures of some Residential Re-entry Centers (RRCs) and a significant number of inmates whose referral dates to the Re-entry centers have been shortened or cancelled. The need for the Re-entry services continues to grow.

Response: BOP continues our long-standing commitment to providing transitional services to inmates as they are released back into our communities. BOP remains committed to providing quality inmate programs to reduce recidivism and prepare inmates for reintegration into the communities to include the use of RRCs. The recent closures were all for underutilized or inefficient locations and reflected less than one percent of our total RRC bed space.

2. In the past, BOP policy has been "everyone has the option of a Re-entry center placement." Has that policy changed? Has the number of inmates being denied consideration for a re-entry placement increased? What factors are impacting those decisions?

Response: All inmates are reviewed and considered for RRC placement. BOP has historically transferred approximately 77 percent of all eligible releasing offenders through RRC placements and expects no change in the placement rate. Those offenders who typically do not transition through RRCs include illegal aliens; individuals with detainers or active warrants from another jurisdiction; those who require inpatient medical, psychological, or psychiatric treatment; those whose current offense or behavioral history suggests a substantial or continuing threat to the community; and those individuals who refuse placement.

3. Your August 2016 report on alternatives to incarceration found that the Bureau of Prisons could better track and analyze data surrounding its use of Residential Reentry Centers and home confinement. Can you describe what that status was at the time you wrote the report and whether, since then, things have changed?

Response: In April2017, BOP implemented a new Statement of Work (SOW) for RRCs. This revised SOW includes the collection of data that BOP anticipates will assist us in tracking and analyzing statistical data surrounding RRC and home confinement use. This includes 16 discrete benchmarks, to include placement rates and average length of stay, staffing ratios, employment statistics both on arrival and on release, and average hourly wages earned.

Questions from Representative Lawrence

1. Treatment of women in immigration detention centers:

Non-citizens make up around 20 percent of the total Bureau of Prisons inmate population, but according to BOP, they are a majority of the 18,000-plns individuals held in BOP's privately operated prisons. AU 13 of BOP's privately-owned prisons as Criminal Alien Requirement (CAR) prisons, designated mainly for non-citizens who have entered the country without papers. Most of the roughly 23,000 immigrants held each night in CAR prisons have committed only the offense of crossing the border to escape often-dangerous situations in their home countries.

I am concerned about conditions in these facilities, particularly for pregnant women. An ACLU report revealed that some pregnant inmates face prolonged solitary confinement that adversely impacts the mother's health and endangers her pregnancy. Civil society groups have also revealed dangerous practices such as the shackling of pregnant women, including horrific instances of women shackled during labor. It has been reported that mothers are sometimes separated from their newborns less than 24 hours after birth. There are also concerns about lack of access to pre- and post-natal care, nutritious food, and vitamins.

a. Do you believe BOP has adequate guidelines and enforcement of policies to protect pregnant detainees and inmates?

b. How do those guidelines and policies address the issues raised in these reports, such as shackling, separation of mothers and newborns, and inadequate health services?

Female inmates and pre-trial detainees who are placed into the custody of BOP are housed in BOP-operated prisons, not in private contract prisons. BOP has policies that specifically guide our care and treatment of pregnant detainees and inmates, to include the extremely rare circumstances where shackling might be considered for safety of the inmate, the fetus, or staff. As a practical matter, BOP virtually never shackles pregnant females. BOP has an internal auditing process by which headquarters staff and subject matter experts do an in- person review of each institution housing females to ensure policy-mandates are being followed. Requirements include educating pregnant women about programs that will allow the mother and baby to stay together during critical early bonding periods (e.g., The Mother and Infants

Together and the Residential Parenting Program). Women in BOP custody have access to prenatal and post-natal care through qualified medical providers both within our facilities and at community-based hospitals and treatment facilities.

c. Do you have plans to change BOP policies to address these concerns? If so, what changes will you make?

It is BOP's understanding that the American Civil Liberties Union (ACLU) report was in reference to State prisons and jails, not BOP. As noted above, BOP has strict policies in place regarding shackling, use of restrictive housing, health care, and nutrition for our inmate population and specific guidance for pregnant females. Further, as noted above, BOP provides programs to allow for co-housing of mothers and their infant children.

2. On November 9, 2017, 31Members of Congress sent a letter asking the Government Accountability Office to report on the situation of pregnant women in BOP detention facilities. It asked GAO to address questions including: whether privately contracted prisons regularly provide data to BOP on conditions for pregnant women; whether BOP is complying with existing anti-shackling policies for pregnant women; and whether pre- and post-natal healthcare services are accessible to pregnant detainees.

a. How are you cooperating with GAO to report on the questions asked in the November 9 letter?

The Government Accountability Office (GAO) has not notified BOP of initiating an audit on these matters.

b. Are you conducting any further internal reviews of these matters, and if so, what are these reviews?

BOP does not house any women in privately-owned prisons. In BOP operated facilities, there are policies that protect pregnant detainees and inmates. These policies are enforced through the internal auditing process described above.

c. Please report or reference any data you currently have on conditions for pregnant women in BOP facilities.

As of March 15, 2018, there were 52 pregnant women in BOP custody. Under current policy, a social worker meets with the inmate upon notification of her pregnancy and educates her on available programs and services. Additional information about the BOP's policies for pregnant women can be found on the public website in Program Statement 5200.02, Female Offender Manual.

3. Second Chance Pell Grants: Education programs have a documented record in reducing recidivism, yet educational opportunities are sorely lacking in federal prisons. Education programs reduce recidivism by 43 percent and are cost-effective: higher education in prisons offers a 400 percent return on investment over 3 years, saving taxpayers for every $1 spent. The Second Chance Pen program, part of the Department of Education since 2015, reinstated access to Pen Grants for over 12,000 incarcerated students who are qualified for grants.67 higher education institutions partnered with 100 prisons, including 7 BOP facilities, to help students get a higher education and succeed after reentry. This includes 3 in Michigan, partnering with 19 facilities to provide Pen Grants to over 1,400 incarcerated students in 2016-2017. In my district, the Detroit Reentry Center partners with Jackson CoUrge to help students achieve certificates and associates degrees.

a. Do you support Second Chance Pell Grants? If not, why not? The Second Chance Pell experiment, which provides Pell Grant funds authorized by the Higher Education Act to eligible incarcerated individuals, is part of the experimental waiver authority administered by the Department of Education. Access to Pell Grants to participate in a postsecondary education program is an excellent opportunity for inmates. Approximately 260 BOP inmates are currently enrolled in certificate, two-year, or four-year programs. Eleven inmates were awarded an Associate of Science in Business degree in December 2017.

b. Do you plan any changes to the prison education programs, including Second Chance Pell Grants? If so, what is your rationale for those policy changes?

The Second Chance Pell experiment is administered by the Department of Education. BOP will continue to assess best practices and enhance our educational services for all inmates. BOP is committed to providing services not only at the post-secondary level, but is also working to strengthen high school equivalency and adult basic education services. Based upon current enrollments, additional inmates are anticipated to earn a post-secondary certificate or degree in FY 2018 and FY 2019 via the Second Chance Pell experiment.

c. Under your direction, how will BOP ensure that people in federal prisons receive access to adequate secondary and post-secondary education, adult literacy services, and programs for people with disabilities?

BOP recently hired a new National Education Administrator, who is assessing our current practices to ensure BOP is using the most innovative and evidence-based approaches. BOP also recently hired a National Disabilities Manager, who coordinates services for inmates with cognitive and other types of impairments. In addition to the educational programs offered to individuals with disabilities, BOP includes accommodations for communications with the community and/or modification of programs to increase accessibility.

4. If there is limited funding available for BOP reentry programs, we must also acknowledge that we do not need more funding for prison construction. In fact, the President's FY 2018 Budget proposed to rescind $444 million originally intended to construct a new high-security federal prison, and Deputy Attorney General Rod Rosenstein testified that there is no need for another such prison.

a. Do you agree that it is a higher priority now to invest in successful reentry programs rather than new prisons? If not, why not?

Reentry programming and prison construction come from two separate appropriations from Congress. The first is provided by Congress in BOP's Salaries and Expenses appropriation, and the second is provided by Congress in BOP's Buildings and Facilities appropriation. BOP continues to fulfill our mission and carry out Congressional directives.

b. How much will you spend on education versus on new prisons?

For FY 2018, BOP anticipates spending approximately $137.6 million on education. The anticipated expenditure for new prisons in FY 2018 has not yet been determined.

In: Bureau of Prisons (BOP)
Editor: Melody Kelley

ISBN: 978-1-53615-292-0

Chapter 2

REVIEW OF THE FEDERAL BUREAU OF PRISONS' MANAGEMENT OF ITS FEMALE INMATE POPULATION*

Office of the Inspector General,
U.S. Department of Justice

EXECUTIVE SUMMARY
REVIEW OF THE FEDERAL BUREAU OF PRISONS' MANAGEMENT OF ITS FEMALE INMATE POPULATION

Introduction

As of September 2016, the Federal Bureau of Prisons (BOP) incarcerated 10,567 sentenced female inmates, representing 7 percent of the total BOP sentenced inmate population of 146,084. Though female

* This is an edited, reformatted and augmented version of Office of the Inspector General, U.S. Department of Justice, Evaluation and Inspections Division 18-05 Publication, dated September 2018.

inmates compose a small percentage of the nationwide incarcerated population, correctional officials have recognized that in some areas female and male inmates have different needs and BOP has adopted gender-responsive programs and policies that account for these needs. As a continuation of prior U.S. Department of Justice Office of the Inspector General (OIG) reviews examining BOP's management of certain subpopulations of inmates, including aging inmates and inmates with mental illness in restrictive housing, OIG initiated this review of BOP's management of female inmates, specifically BOP's efforts and capacity to ensure that BOP-wide policies, programs, and decisions adequately address the distinctive needs of women. Our decision to initiate this review was also informed by members of Congress and public interest groups recently raising concerns about what they consider to be deficiencies in BOP's current management of female inmates.

Results in Brief

We concluded that BOP has not been strategic in its management of female inmates. We determined that BOP needs to take additional steps at the Central Office level to ensure that female inmate needs are met at the institution level. Our review identified instances in which BOP's programming and policy has not fully considered the needs of female inmates, which has made it difficult for inmates to access certain key programs and supplies. Further, while BOP is adhering to federal regulations and BOP policies requiring that only female Correctional Officers conduct strip searches of female inmates, BOP's method for ensuring compliance with these requirements assigns staff inefficiently. Finally, we found that BOP's conversion of Federal Correctional Institution (FCI) Danbury to house male inmates negatively affected certain female inmates who had been housed there.

BOP's Approach to Managing Female Inmates Has Not Been Strategic, Resulting in Weaknesses in Its Ability to Meet Their Specific Needs

We found that during the period of our review BOP could not ensure that its institutions adhered to policies pertaining to female inmates because BOP had only recently taken steps to formalize a process for verifying compliance. As of April 2018, BOP was drafting planning documents that it believes will enhance its ability to perform internal oversight of these policies and better ensure compliance with female inmate-focused policies and protocols.

Further, while BOP established a Central Office branch that serves as BOP's source of expertise on the management of female inmates in BOP custody, this branch may not have adequate staffing to fully fulfill its mission. Female inmates are just one of six special populations about which the Women and Special Populations Branch is responsible for providing national direction and subject matter expertise and for ensuring that the needs of each of these populations are met at BOP institutions. For example, this branch designs and delivers training to institution staff and ensures that programming run by other BOP divisions is responsive to the needs of each subpopulation. Given the branch's wide range of responsibilities, its four staff members may not be sufficient to accomplish its mission and to ensure that BOP adequately addresses the distinctive needs of women in its custody.

Additionally, BOP requires all staff in its female institutions to take training on the management of female inmates, as well as training in trauma-informed correctional care for the management of inmates who have experienced trauma. However, BOP does not require the same training for its Executive Staff and, as a result, National Executive Staff officials may develop policy and make decisions that affect female inmates without awareness of their needs.

BOP's Programming and Policy May Not Fully Consider the Needs of Female Inmates

We identified three areas in which BOP's programming and policy decisions did not fully consider the needs of female inmates: trauma treatment programming, pregnancy programming, and feminine hygiene.

BOP relies on research that shows that physical and emotional trauma affects as many as 90 percent of the female inmate population. Research also recommends that female inmates undergo trauma treatment early during incarceration to enhance their ability to benefit from all institutional programming. However, we found that BOP may not be able to provide its trauma treatment program to all eligible female inmates until late in their incarceration, or ever, because it has assigned only one staff member at each institution to offer this program. The lack of sufficient staff is most noticeable at larger female institutions, where inmates face delays in completing each of the program's two prerequisites, as well as the program's treatment phases.

In addition to female inmates being unable to use BOP trauma treatment programs, we estimate that only 37 percent of sentenced pregnant inmates participated in BOP's pregnancy programs between fiscal year (FY) 2012 and FY 2016. Further, we confirmed that these programs had additional capacity to include more pregnant inmates during this period. We believe that participation is low because BOP inmates and staff lack awareness of these programs. We also determined that BOP staff may apply eligibility criteria more restrictively than intended by BOP headquarters officials and that BOP lacks data to assess inmate interest and participation in its pregnancy programs.

In visits to several BOP institutions housing female inmates, we found that the distribution methods for feminine hygiene products provided to inmates varied by institution and did not always ensure that inmates had access to a sufficient quantity of products to meet their needs. BOP issued new guidance in August 2017 to standardize the range of products available free of charge. However, BOP still lacks a method to ensure sufficient access because the guidance did not address how products should be distributed to inmates.

BOP's Lack of Gender-specific Posts Results in Inefficiencies at Female Institutions

We found that BOP's practice of assigning Correctional Officers to posts solely by seniority has resulted in male Correctional Officers being assigned to posts at which staff must regularly conduct searches of female inmates. Because the *Prison Rape Elimination Act of 2003* and BOP policy prohibit cross-gender searches of female inmates, female Correctional Officers must leave other assigned posts to conduct these searches, leading to an inefficient use of Correctional Officer resources. Both female and male institution staff suggested that a small number of posts in female institutions, particularly some of the posts in the Special Housing Unit (SHU)—a unit used to separate inmates from the general population for protective or disciplinary purposes—and the visiting room, be reserved for female staff to ensure that they can conduct inmate searches without disrupting other operations. We agree that BOP should implement this or another approach to ensure the availability of female staff at locations in female institutions where inmate searches are common.

BOP's Decision to Convert Federal Correctional Institution Danbury to a Male Institution Negatively Affected Female Inmates Transferred to Metropolitan Detention Center Brooklyn

As a case study, we also examined BOP's 2013 decision to convert FCI Danbury from a female institution to a male institution as part of a larger plan to increase bed space for low security female and male inmates throughout BOP institutions. Although concerns were raised that the conversion would cause female inmates to be incarcerated farther from home, we found that, while 19 percent of U.S. citizen inmates were transferred farther from their homes, the overwhelming majority were transferred closer to their homes. The conversion resulted in 366 low security sentenced female inmates serving a portion of their sentences in Metropolitan Detention Center (MDC) Brooklyn, a detention center intended for short-term confinement. The National Association of Women Judges found that the conditions of confinement at MDC Brooklyn amounted to a violation of the American Bar Association Standards on

Treatment of Prisoners, as well as the United Nations Standard Minimum Rules for the Treatment of Prisoners. When we visited MDC Brooklyn, we found that BOP offered female inmates no access to outdoor space, less natural light, and fewer programming opportunities than what would otherwise be available to female inmates at BOP facilities designed to house sentenced inmates in long-term confinement. In addition, a separate OIG criminal investigation determined that, during the time that sentenced female inmates were assigned to MDC Brooklyn, multiple custody staff sexually assaulted female inmates, resulting in the convictions of two Lieutenants and a Correctional Officer. In December 2016, after reversing its decision not to house female inmates at FCI Danbury, BOP opened a new low security institution for female inmates at FCI Danbury. However, because FCI Danbury was constructed without a SHU, we found that managing female inmates who needed to be placed in a SHU disrupted institution operations because BOP had to transfer these inmates to Federal Detention Center Philadelphia for SHU placement.

Recommendations

In this chapter, we make 10 recommendations to improve BOP's management of its female inmate population. These recommendations include training executive leaders on issues important to managing female inmates, enhancing the capacity of BOP's trauma treatment program, communicating information about pregnancy programs, and clarifying guidance on the distribution of feminine hygiene products.

INTRODUCTION

Background

According to the U.S. Department of Justice's (Department, DOJ) Bureau of Justice Statistics, state and federal prisons had jurisdiction over more than 1.5 million inmates at the end of 2015. Of these inmates, approximately 111,500, or 7 percent, were female.[1] The percentage of female inmates in the Federal Bureau of Prisons' (BOP) custody as of September 2016 was also 7 percent (10,567) of BOP's total population of 146,084 sentenced inmates.[2] While female inmates compose a small percentage of the nationwide inmate population, BOP recognized that in some areas female and male inmates have different needs. Accordingly, BOP developed gender-responsive programs and policies to account for female inmates' distinctive needs.

As a continuation of several prior Office of the Inspector General (OIG) reviews examining BOP's management of certain subpopulations of inmates, including aging inmates and inmates with mental illness in restrictive housing, OIG initiated this review of BOP's management of female inmates.[3] Our decision to initiate this review was also informed by members of Congress and public interest groups recently raising concerns about what they considered to be deficiencies in BOP's current management of female inmates.[4]

In this chapter, we assess BOP's efforts and capacity to ensure that BOP-wide policies, programs, and decisions address the unique needs of female inmates. Specifically, we assess female inmates' access to BOP's

---

[1] DOJ Bureau of Justice Statistics, *Prisoners in 2015* (December 2016).

[2] For this review, we examined sentenced inmates incarcerated in BOP-managed institutions only. We excluded approximately 22,000 male inmates who were incarcerated in contract institutions, approximately 12,000 female and male inmates who were in halfway houses, and approximately 12,000 female and male pretrial detainees in the custody of the U.S. Marshals Service. BOP does not incarcerate female inmates in contract institutions.

[3] DOJ OIG, The Impact of an Aging Inmate Population on the Federal Bureau of Prisons, Evaluation and Inspections Report 15-05 (May 2015), and DOJ OIG, Review of the Federal Bureau of Prisons' Use of Restrictive Housing for Inmates with Mental Illness, Evaluation and Inspections Report 17-05 (July 2017).

[4] In July 2017, four U.S. Senators introduced legislation designed to increase familial visitation and female inmates' access to feminine hygiene products. See Dignity for Incarcerated Women Act of 2017, 115th Congress, 1st sess., S. 1524. The Arthur Liman Public Interest Program at Yale Law School also wrote about the management of female inmates affected by BOP's decision to convert Federal Correctional Institution (FCI) Danbury from a female to male institution in Dislocation and Relocation: Women in the Federal Prison System and Repurposing FCI Danbury for Men (September 2014). This issue was also discussed in "Female Inmates from Danbury Still in Limbo, Lacking Key Services," Slate Magazine, September 3, 2014, and "Female Inmate Transfers to Resume; Senators Say Relocation Disrupts Women's Lives, Vow to Fight Bureau of Prisons' Decisions; Danbury Federal Correctional Institution," Hartford Courant, October 5, 2013.

trauma treatment and pregnancy programs, which are significant for female inmates and their families and can play important roles in successful reentry into society. Additionally, we discuss BOP's gender-responsive policies and evaluate how they affect the conditions of confinement for female inmates. We pay particular attention to policies relevant to inmate access to feminine hygiene products and physical searches of female inmates. Lastly, we examine as a case study how BOP's decision to convert its low security institution in Danbury, Connecticut, from a female institution to a male institution affected female inmates.

Characteristics of BOP'S Female Inmate Population

As shown in Table 1, the overall population of sentenced female inmates decreased between fiscal years (FY) 2012 and 2016. The ratio of female inmates to male inmates has remained constant during this period and is approximately equal to the nationwide ratio, as mentioned previously.

Table 1. Female and Male Sentenced Inmate Population FYs 2012–2016

		2012	2013	2014	2015	2016
Female Inmates	Number of Inmates	11,737	12,154	11,868	11,214	10,567
	Percentage of BOP Population	7%	7%	7%	7%	7%
Male Inmates	Number of Inmates	152,803	152,676	149,663	143,655	135,517
	Percentage of BOP Population	93%	93%	93%	93%	93%
Total BOP Population		164,540	164,830	161,531	154,869	146,084

Source: BOP SENTRY.

BOP data shows that between FYs 2012 and 2016 the majority of both female and male inmates were incarcerated for drug offenses; but male inmates were much more likely to have been convicted of weapons, sex, or other violent crime offenses than were female inmates. Further, research shows that female inmates incarcerated for drug crimes were often accessories to the broader criminal activity of a male partner, rather than being the instigator of a crime.[5] Female inmates also tend to have shorter sentences than male inmates. For example, as of September 2016, the median total sentence length for female inmates in BOP custody was 5 years, whereas the median total sentence length for male inmates was 10 years.

BOP has four security classification levels for inmates: high, medium, low, and minimum. Nearly all sentenced female inmates are classified as low or minimum security. BOP does not classify female inmates as medium security but does classify a small number as high security.[6] BOP institutions are also assigned security levels, and BOP generally assigns inmates to institutions that correspond with their security level.[7]

Twenty-nine BOP locations throughout the United States house one or more female institutions.[8] BOP manages female inmates in 20 institutions designed for the long-term incarceration of sentenced inmates.[9] We describe these below:

---

[5] Darrell Steffensmeier and Emilie Allan, "GENDER AND CRIME: Toward a Gendered Theory of Female Offending," *Annual Review of Sociology* 22 (1996): 459–487. BOP cited this particular point as part of its own research, which found that gender is a powerful predictor of risk for serious violence and other serious misconduct while incarcerated. Miles D. Harer and Neal P. Langan, "Gender Differences in Predictors of Violence: Assessing the Predictive Validity of a Risk Classification System," *Crime and Delinquency* 47 (2001): 513–536. Because of this internal BOP research, BOP determines security levels for female and male inmates separately and, as a result, classifies nearly all female inmates as minimum or low security.

[6] Two officials in BOP's Designation and Sentence Computation Center, the BOP office responsible for determining where inmates should be housed, told us that nearly all female inmates can be managed in minimum security or low security settings because they are less prone to behaviors such as violence and escape attempts. The small number of female inmates who cannot be managed in these settings are designated as high security and housed in BOP's sole high security female unit at FMC Carswell.

[7] Throughout this chapter, we will use the term "female institutions" to refer to all of BOP's institutions designed to house sentenced female inmates, regardless of security level.

[8] During our fieldwork, BOP housed female inmates in 28 locations throughout the United States. BOP added a 29th location in late 2017 by converting a minimum security institution in Pekin, Illinois, which had formerly housed male inmates, into a female institution. Because Pekin did not house female inmates during the time we conducted the analyses used in our report, these analyses do not include data or information from Pekin.

[9] Eight of these female institutions are a part of larger facilities that also contain at least one other female institution. Such facilities include a low security institution and a minimum security institution in Aliceville, Alabama; a low security institution and a minimum security

- *Minimum security institutions,* also known as Federal Prison Camps (FPC), have dormitory-style housing and limited or no perimeter fencing. As of December 2017, BOP managed 13 of these institutions for female inmates.
- *Low security institutions,* also known as Federal Correctional Institutions (FCI) or Federal Satellite Lows, have perimeter fencing and either dormitory-style or cell-style housing. As of December 2017, BOP managed six of these institutions for female inmates.
- *Federal Medical Centers* (FMC) are used to treat sentenced inmates of all security levels who have serious or chronic medical problems. As of December 2017, BOP managed one medical center, FMC Carswell, for female inmates. This institution also housed the small number of BOP's high security female inmates.

In addition to these 20 institutions, BOP houses female inmates in 12 detention centers, which generally are designed for the short-term incarceration of pretrial detainees, as well as a transfer center that houses inmates in transit to other BOP facilities. Unlike institutions designed for long-term incarceration, detention centers and the transfer center house both female and male inmates.

Figure 1 shows the number of sentenced female inmates assigned to each of the three types of institutions described above. A map showing the locations of BOP's female institutions designed for long-term incarceration can be found in *Appendix 2*.

---

institution in Dublin, California; a low security institution and a minimum security institution in Danbury, Connecticut; and a minimum security institution and a female inmate medical facility in Fort Worth, Texas. As a result, BOP's 20 female institutions are in 16 locations throughout the country.

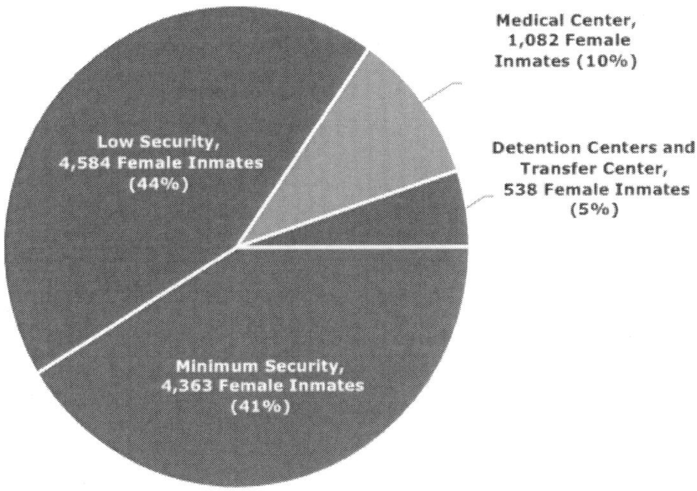

Source: BOP SENTRY.

Figure 1. Number of Sentenced Female Inmates, by Institution Type September 2016.

BOP Policy on the Management of Female Inmates

In August 1997, BOP developed a formal policy, known as a program statement, on the Management of Female Offenders. While this program statement recognized that BOP programs and services should meet the different physical, social, and psychological needs of female offenders, the Women and Special Populations Branch Administrator told us that this policy was not substantive and was difficult to enforce. In an effort to strengthen existing policy, BOP issued a new Female Offender Manual in November 2016.[10] The new manual expanded on the prior policy by incorporating gender-responsive language on how BOP should classify and designate female inmates; discipline female inmates; provide gender-responsive programming; and address birth control, pregnancy, child placement, and abortion.

The Female Offender Manual also identifies the Women and Special Populations Branch, within BOP's Reentry Services Division, as BOP's source of expertise on classification, management, and intervention

[10] BOP Program Statement 5200.02, Female Offender Manual, November 23, 2016.

programs and practices for females in BOP custody.[11] Further, the Female Offender Manual delegates a wide range of responsibilities to the Women and Special Populations Branch. For female inmates specifically, these responsibilities include advising BOP management and institution staff on issues affecting female inmates, developing staff training on these issues, and ensuring that programs managed by other BOP branches are gender responsive.[12] As of November 2017, the Women and Special Populations Branch comprised one Branch Administrator and three staff members.[13]

Gender-Responsive Approaches to Corrections

The BOP defines gender-responsive approaches to corrections as those that are based on an understanding of the ways female inmates are different from male inmates and that specifically aim to address those differences. In particular, BOP has established gender-specific policies pertaining to access to female and reproductive health services, to the provision of feminine hygiene products, and to the implementation of regulatory requirements that ensure female inmates are physically searched only by female BOP employees.[14]

---

[11] BOP's Reentry Services Division aims to prepare inmates for reentry by focusing on programming and community transition. The Reentry Services Division is composed of six branches: (1) National Reentry Affairs, (2) Education Services, (3) Chaplaincy Services, (4) Residential Reentry Management, (5) Women and Special Populations, and (6) Psychology Services.

[12] BOP also delegates to the Women and Special Populations Branch the responsibility of ensuring that BOP policy and practices are inclusive of the needs of other special populations. BOP identifies special populations to include female inmates, juvenile inmates, transgender inmates, inmates with disabilities, inmates who are parents, and inmates who are veterans. The Women and Special Populations Branch Administrator told us that she considers "special populations" to be any group of inmates that is not part of the male majority.

[13] In response to a working draft of this chapter, BOP stated that all four staff in the Women and Special Populations Branch, including the Branch Administrator, focus on program or training work.

[14] Federal regulations and BOP policies mandate that strip searches be conducted by a staff member who is the same gender as the inmate being searched. See 28 C.F.R. § 552.11(c) and BOP Program Statement 5521.06, Searches of Housing Units, Inmates, and Inmate Work Areas, June 4, 2015, 4. See also 28 C.F.R. § 115.15(a). Additionally, federal regulations and BOP policies mandate that only female staff can pat search female inmates. See 28 C.F.R. § 115.15(b); BOP Program Statement 5521.06, 3; and BOP Program Statement 5324.12, Sexually Abusive Behavior Prevention and Intervention Program, June 4, 2015, 17.

Trauma-informed Correctional Care

An important but less obvious difference between female and male inmates has to do with past traumatic experiences. While many studies support the conclusion that female inmates experience very high rates of trauma before incarceration, BOP used one particular study as a basis for emphasizing the need to account for past trauma in its management of female inmates. This study found that as many as 90 percent of women in prison have experienced trauma and that the most common type of traumatic experience for female inmates is repeated sexual violence, followed by intimate partner violence.[15] Male inmates are less likely to have been a direct victim of violence, but they more commonly have experienced or witnessed a singular traumatic event such as a shooting.[16]

Research also shows that the effects of trauma manifest themselves differently for female and male inmates. For example, female inmates who experience trauma can develop chronic depression, eating disorders, or difficulty managing emotions, while trauma in male inmates is more likely to manifest itself externally, resulting in emotional outbursts or violence.[17] Although female inmates are more likely to internalize their trauma, a Resolve Coordinator we interviewed told us that female inmates are generally more willing to discuss their trauma than are male inmates.

To address the effects of past trauma on inmates, BOP implemented a "trauma-informed correctional care approach." The BOP Psychology Services Branch describes trauma-informed care as a comprehensive approach to corrections in which all policies recognize, and actions of staff reflect, the concept that trauma is a "real and prevalent occurrence, and that any opportunity to avoid re-traumatizing an inmate is an opportunity for healing." The Psychology Services Branch stated that there is not a strict method for applying trauma-informed correctional care approaches, but it

---

[15] Niki A. Miller and Lisa M. Najavits, "Creating Trauma Informed Correctional Care: A Balance of Goals and Environment," *European Journal of Psychotraumatology* (2012): 2. BOP asserts that the 90 percent statistic is likely a low estimate because traumatic experiences are often underreported by victims.

[16] Miller and Najavits, "Creating Trauma Informed Correctional Care," 4.

[17] Miller and Najavits, "Creating Trauma Informed Correctional Care," 3.

identifies important principles for trauma-informed staff to consider. These principles include:

- ensuring physical, psychological, and emotional safety for inmates and staff;
- ensuring that, when practicable, staff interventions highlight strengths that can be used as a foundation for improvement, as opposed to focusing only on problems;
- ensuring that information and training about trauma are available to inmates and staff; and
- using communication methods that deescalate conflict and avoid triggering memories of past traumatic experience. (See the text box.)

Gender-Responsive Programs

Below, we highlight three gender-responsive programs because of their importance to female inmates and their families. These programs are administered by branches within the Reentry Services Division.

Resolve Program

The Resolve program, managed by BOP's Psychology Services Branch and offered at 14 of BOP's 15 female institutions, is a national treatment program for female inmates with a history of trauma-related mental illnesses.[18] According to the Psychology Services Branch, the objective of the Resolve program is to promote positive behavioral changes that decrease the incidence of trauma-related psychological disorders and improve inmates' level of functioning.[19] Psychology Services staff

---

[18] FCI Phoenix did not offer the Resolve program during the scope of our review because it had not been allocated a Resolve Coordinator position. Resolve is not offered at the 12 detention centers or the Federal Transfer Center because those institutions are exempt from most BOP programming requirements. As of September 2016, only 5 percent of the sentenced female inmate population was in a detention center or the Federal Transfer Center.

[19] BOP employs psychology, psychiatry, and mental health staff to offer services, beyond the scope of the Resolve program, to inmates who require mental health treatment.

emphasized the importance of this program because of the high number of female inmates with a history of trauma or victimization prior to incarceration. All inmates undergo an intake interview with a Psychologist at the beginning of their BOP incarceration.[20] If a female inmate describes a history of trauma during this intake interview, the Psychologist will recommend that she sign up for the Resolve program's introductory workshop. Participation in the Resolve program is voluntary.

Potential Effects of Past Trauma on Female Inmates

Awareness of how female inmates are affected by trauma is important in all aspects of BOP operations. For example, an inmate having her teeth cleaned is lying on her back, with someone leaning over her and something in her mouth that she cannot remove. These sensations can trigger flashbacks for victims of sexual abuse. It is therefore important for all BOP staff who work with female inmates to be aware of the potential for such reactions and how to respond to them.

Source: Interview with DOJ Civil Rights Division official.

All elements of the Resolve program, outlined in Table 2 below, are managed by a Resolve Coordinator, who is a Psychologist. One Resolve Coordinator is assigned to each of the 14 female institutions that offer the program.[21] According to BOP's program statement on Psychology Treatment Programs, inmates with a history of trauma or victimization initiate the Resolve program by taking the introductory workshop during the first 12 months of incarceration. BOP policy states that the Resolve program takes approximately 40 weeks to complete, but it also notes that scheduling conflicts may extend the length of the program.

---

[20] In this chapter, we use the term Psychologist to refer to a doctoral-level Psychologist.

[21] BOP operates multiple female institutions at 4 of the 14 locations where it offers the Resolve program to female inmates. BOP also offers the Resolve program, with a modified male-specific curriculum, to male inmates at two institutions.

Table 2. Structure of the Resolve Program for Female Inmates

Segment of Program	Name	Description
Prerequisites		
Introductory Workshop	Trauma in Life	Educational workshop that provides female inmates with psychological information on trauma and its potential impact in their lives
Screening	Psychological Testing	Psychological eligibility assessment to diagnose the related trauma[a]
Active Treatment[b]		
Phase I	Seeking Safety	Therapy group that emphasizes the acquisition of basic skills, with a focus on coping and interpersonal skills
Phase II	Cognitive Processing Therapy	Therapy group for inmates with a diagnosis of post-traumatic stress disorder, major depression, or substance abuse
	Dialectical Behavioral Therapy	Therapy group for treatment of inmates with borderline personality disorder
Post Treatment		
Maintenance	Maintenance Group	Skills group for maintaining treatment gains for inmates whose symptoms, if present, no longer interfere with daily functioning

Source: BOP.

Note: The Psychologist who performs the screening determines which version of the Phase II therapy is most appropriate for each inmate, depending on her specific diagnosis.

[a] In response to a working draft of this chapter, BOP stated that it completes psychological eligibility assessments to provide diagnostic clarity and accuracy prior to a formal diagnosis.

[b] In response to a working draft of this chapter, BOP stated that the group sessions used during the Active Treatment phases of the Resolve program are psychotherapy groups.

Female Integrated Treatment Program

In the fall of 2017, the Psychology Services Branch, in coordination with the Women and Special Populations Branch, piloted the Female Integrated Treatment (FIT) program at BOP's low security female institution in Danbury, Connecticut.[22] According to BOP, the FIT program offers evidence-based treatment for trauma, substance abuse, and mental health in a comprehensive, holistic program. The program begins with a 4-month educational curriculum that includes a Trauma in Life workshop as well as basic drug and mental health education. After completing the introductory portion of the program, each inmate participates in a treatment curriculum tailored to her individual trauma, substance abuse, or mental health needs. Inmates in FIT requiring trauma treatment take the Resolve curriculum described in Table 2 above. All female inmates designated to the low security female institution in Danbury participate in the FIT program.[23]

Mothers and Infants Nurturing Together Program

The Mothers and Infants Nurturing Together (MINT) program, managed by BOP's Residential Reentry Management Branch, is a community-based residential program in which pregnant inmates prepare for delivery and bond with their infant after giving birth.[24] According to BOP's Female Offender Manual, pregnant inmates in BOP custody are eligible to serve a portion of their sentence at a MINT program site if they are pregnant upon incarceration with an expected delivery date prior to release, have less than 5 years remaining on their sentence, are eligible for halfway house placement, and assume financial responsibility for their child's care.[25] Female inmates are generally eligible to transfer to a MINT

---

[22] The FIT program is available only for inmates in Danbury's low security female institution. Inmates in Danbury's minimum security female institution take the Resolve program instead.

[23] In response to a working draft of this chapter, the Administrator of the Women and Special Populations Branch elaborated on the terminology of this model, stating that "the entire facility operates as a 'modified therapeutic community.'"

[24] During the scope of this review (FYs 2012–2016), MINT program sites were located in San Francisco, California; Tallahassee, Florida; Phoenix, Arizona; Fort Worth, Texas; Springfield, Illinois; Hartford, Connecticut; and Hillsboro, West Virginia. As of December 2017, the sites in San Francisco and Hartford no longer accepted MINT inmates because they were unable to comply with some of the contract requirements for hosting the MINT program.

[25] The Female Offender Manual further states that inmates with more than 5 years remaining on their sentences, or who become pregnant while on furlough, or who plan to place their infants up for adoption are not eligible for the MINT program. BOP provides prenatal care

program site during the last 2 months of pregnancy. After birth, the Female Offender Manual requires BOP to allow participating inmates at least 3 additional months to bond with their infant, although the manual recommends 6 months. Once an inmate completes the MINT program, BOP returns the inmate to a BOP institution for the remainder of her sentence.

Residential Parenting Program

According to the Female Offender Manual, BOP's female inmates, no matter their location, may also participate in the Washington State Department of Corrections' Residential Parenting Program. In contrast to the MINT program, Residential Parenting Program participants and their infants reside in the minimum security unit of the Washington Corrections Center for Women in Gig Harbor, Washington, for up to 30 months after birth.[26] Female inmates who participate in this program receive credit toward their federal sentence for any time served at the Gig Harbor facility. BOP Social Workers are responsible for providing pregnant inmates with information about the two pregnancy programs.

Scope of the OIG Review

BOP has implemented gender-responsive policies and programs that affect the conditions of confinement for female inmates. OIG initiated this review to examine BOP's management of its female inmate population between FYs 2012 and 2016. We focused our analysis on how the Women and Special Populations Branch and other relevant BOP branches implement gender-responsive trauma-treatment and pregnancy programs.

---

and covers the financial costs associated with delivery for all pregnant inmates, regardless of whether they participate in this program.

[26] The eligibility requirements for the Residential Parenting Program are established by the Washington State Department of Corrections and are stricter than those for BOP's MINT program. For example, only minimum security inmates are eligible to participate in the Residential Parenting Program, whereas both minimum and low security inmates are eligible to participate in the MINT program. We discuss the eligibility requirements for the Residential Parenting Program in greater detail in a text box later in this chapter.

Additionally, we examined how BOP has implemented policies relevant to inmate access to feminine hygiene products and physical searches of female inmates. We also examined how BOP's decision to convert its low security institution in Danbury, Connecticut, from a female institution to a male institution affected female inmates transferred from Danbury. We held in-person, telephone, and video teleconference interviews with BOP officials responsible for or involved in the management of federal female inmates, as well as with state correctional officials to learn how non-federal correctional agencies manage their female inmates.

RESULTS OF THE REVIEW

BOP's Approach to Managing Female Inmates Has Not Been Strategic, Resulting in Weaknesses in Its Ability to Meet Their Specific Needs

We found that over time BOP has made efforts to improve its management of female inmates. However, we identified several additional steps BOP should take to ensure female inmate needs are addressed appropriately. First, BOP has only recently taken steps to formalize a process for verifying staff compliance with policies related to the management of female inmates. Second, we found that while BOP established a Central Office branch with responsibilities that include providing national direction and subject matter expertise on the treatment, management, and programming of female inmates, the branch may not have adequate staffing to fulfill its mission. Finally, while BOP requires all personnel working in female institutions to take training on current best practices in the management of female inmates, it does not require its National Executive Staff to take any training related to female inmates. As a result, National Executive Staff may develop policy or make decisions without awareness of female inmates' needs. As we will discuss later in this chapter, we also identified similar limitations in certain BOP programs and policies of significance to female inmates. For BOP to be fully effective at appropriately managing female inmates, we believe that it must take a holistic approach at the Central Office level to identify and address issues affecting this population.

BOP Has Not Fully Implemented Internal Controls to Ensure Institutions Follow Policies Related to the Management of Female Inmates

The Female Offender Manual is BOP's primary policy on the management of female inmates. The Assistant Director of the Reentry Services Division told us that it is important for institutions housing female inmates to be in compliance with the Female Offender Manual.[27] While BOP has recently taken its first initial steps to verify compliance with the manual, it has not yet fully implemented these efforts. Specifically, BOP is still in the interim stage of establishing a program review to evaluate the implementation of its Female Offender Manual.[28]

In 1997, BOP created its first policy on the management of female inmates.[29] This four-page policy only briefly described BOP's role in identifying the appropriate programs and services to meet the different physical, social, and psychological needs of female inmates; but it never explained what those needs were and it lacked specific guidance that would help institutions identify and address those needs. Further, BOP did not conduct program reviews to verify compliance with this policy.

To address the deficiencies in its initial policy concerning female inmates, BOP issued its Female Offender Manual in November 2016.[30] This manual is much more comprehensive than the 1997 policy in the topics covered, and it offers more guidance about how BOP should handle a range of policy and management issues pertaining to female inmates. For

---

[27] Subsequent to our interview, the Assistant Director of the Reentry Services Division was named the Acting BOP Director.

[28] BOP develops program reviews to assess an institution's internal controls, programs, and operations in a topic area. Most program reviews summarize the overall findings with a rating of Superior, Good, Acceptable, Deficient, or At Risk.

[29] BOP Program Statement 5200.01, Management of Female Offenders, August 4, 1997.

[30] BOP Program Statement 5200.02, Female Offender Manual, November 23, 2016.

example, it describes how BOP should classify and designate female inmates; discipline female inmates; provide gender-responsive programming; and address birth control, pregnancy, child placement, and abortion.[31] While the new manual is more comprehensive, we found that BOP has not yet finalized a mechanism to ensure that institutions housing female inmates comply with it.

During interviews, three managers in the Reentry Services Division emphasized the importance of establishing a program review to ensure institutions are managing female inmates consistently with the Female Offender Manual. For example, the Senior Deputy Assistant Director of the division described the establishment of a program review as critical for ensuring that BOP's female institutions are held accountable for how they manage female inmates. He and the Women and Special Populations Branch Administrator described the program review as the most important factor in ensuring compliance with the Female Offender Manual and said that the absence of a program review has weakened the branch's ability to ensure that institutions are implementing BOP's primary policy on the management of female inmates.

Program reviews are also important because BOP policy requires reviewed institutions to implement corrective action plans, monitored by the BOP Central Office, to correct any deficiencies identified during the course of the review. In response to a working draft of this chapter, the Senior Deputy Assistant Director of the Program Review Division described these follow-up requirements as critical aspects of all program reviews to ensure accountability.

We found that BOP had not begun to implement any review mechanism to evaluate institutions' compliance with the Female Offender Manual until November 2017, a year after its release, and, as of June 2018, BOP has not fully implemented these efforts.[32] According to a Senior Deputy Assistant

---

[31] BOP Program Statement 5200.02.

[32] In response to a working draft of this chapter, BOP stated that it began the process to establish this review mechanism in March 2017 by scheduling a management assessment, which initiates BOP's formal process for designing program reviews. BOP further stated that the management assessment was scheduled within the timeframe required by policy based on the release date of the Female Offender Manual. We focus on November 2017 in this

Director of BOP's Program Review Division, BOP created an interim program review in November 2017 with the intention of establishing a permanent program review in the near future.[33]

We reviewed BOP's interim program review plan and found that BOP conducted it entirely remotely, rather than on site at the institutions. We also learned that under the interim plan BOP did not intend to issue an institution a formal compliance rating at the close of the review. After BOP conducted its first remote program review, a Senior Deputy Assistant Director of BOP's Program Review Division told us that BOP intended to change its program review methodology to conduct future program reviews on site and provide the institution a rating on compliance with the Female Offender Manual.

We are encouraged that BOP plans to implement a rated, on-site program review. Although the Program Review Division's Assistant Director and Senior Deputy Assistant Director told us that on-site reviews may stretch limited resources, an on-site program review would allow BOP to assess compliance with the Female Offender Manual in part through direct observation, which BOP's Management Control and Program Review Manual describes as "the most dependable type of evidence, and...essential in determining the adequacy of internal controls."[34] Additionally, we believe that some of the criteria in BOP's interim program review guidelines and other guidance are particularly suited to direct observation.[35] For example, the interim program review guidelines

---

chapter because that was the date that BOP's Central Office notified the Wardens of the female institutions that a program review to evaluate institutions' compliance with the Female Offender Manual had been designed, and that the reviews would begin.

[33] The Program Review Division conducted its first program review of the Female Offender Manual in December 2017, using the interim program review plan, and provided results to the reviewed institution in January 2018.

[34] BOP Program Statement 1210.23, Management Control and Program Review Manual, August 21, 2002, Chapter 2, p. 8. This policy establishes BOP's standards for conducting program reviews.

[35] Officials in the Program Review Division told us that they could not create program review guidelines for all sections of the Female Offender Manual because some portions were too broadly written. The Women and Special Populations Branch Administrator said that some sections of the Female Offender Manual were written this way as a result of negotiations with the union before the policy was implemented. The Assistant Director of the Program Review Division said that a more detailed Female Offender Manual would allow for more robust oversight of how female institutions implement the policy.

for the Female Offender Manual require Program Review Division staff to assess whether institutions offer gender-responsive programs to inmates and whether institutions widely advertise those programs "in visible areas in the institution," such as bulletin boards, electronic message boards, and resource centers to assist in raising inmate awareness of the availability of those programs. In addition, BOP's August 2017 guidance on the accessibility and availability of feminine hygiene products, which we discuss in more detail later in our report, also lends itself to direct observation. We believe that a physical visit to the institution being reviewed would allow the Program Review Division staff to confirm that institutions are complying with BOP policy on the management of female inmates and to better identify any deficiencies that should be monitored through a corrective action plan.

BOP's Management Control and Program Review Manual generally requires that program reviews provide a rating that summarizes the review's findings and reflects the reviewer's overall judgment as to how well the institution accomplishes the program area's mission and objectives. Currently, all program reviews are rated except for the *Prison Rape Elimination Act of 2003* (PREA) program review.[36] The Senior Deputy Assistant Director for the Reentry Services Division said that it is important for the Female Offender Manual program review to be rated to ensure that the female institutions take the findings from the review seriously.

We agree that ratings would promote accountability, and we believe that ratings for the Female Offender Manual will make it easier for the Program Review Division to identify trends in an institution's results, potentially allowing BOP to identify deficiencies and systemic issues across BOP institutions over time.[37] The Senior Deputy Assistant Director

---

[36] Senior Deputy Assistant Director of BOP's Program Review Division said that the PREA program review does not receive a rating because the goal of the PREA program review is to help institutions prepare for the formal PREA audits conducted by outside auditors.

[37] We asked BOP whether program review ratings were taken into account during Wardens' annual performance evaluations. BOP's Management Control and Program Review Manual (Program Statement 1210.23) states that a program review rating is a measure of a program's performance, not directly related to a program manager's performance. BOP's Human Resource Management Division further reported that a program review rating was

for the Reentry Services Division said that it is important to rate female institutions on their management of female inmates so that the significance of meeting these standards does not get diluted across multiple reviews that cover items related to female inmates as well as items related to all inmates. He also said that a rated program review of the Female Offender Manual will make it easier for the Reentry Services Division to spot problems multiple institutions have in managing female inmates and identify areas where broader action is needed.

At the time of our review, BOP was in the early stages of implementing a system of formal oversight and enforcement for the Female Offender Manual. This accountability mechanism will provide BOP with a key tool for determining whether institutions are complying with policy governing the management of female inmates.

The Women and Special Populations Branch's Staffing May Not Be Sufficient to Fully Accomplish its Mission

BOP created the Women and Special Populations Branch in the Reentry Services Division of BOP's Central Office to address the needs of special populations, including female inmates.[38] However, we found that the number of staff members BOP allocated to this branch may not be enough to carry out all of the responsibilities it has given to the branch. In February 2014, the branch had only 1 staff position (of the Reentry Services Division's 247 positions). As of November 2017, the branch had four full-time employees, making up 2 percent of the Reentry Services Division's staffing.[39] The four staff members are responsible for six separate inmate special populations that, when combined, make up a large

---

taken into account only if it directly related to a specific performance measure described in a Warden's performance work plan As of April 2018, BOP had identified six special populations. We list these in the Introduction.

[38] As of April 2018, BOP had identified six special populations. We list these in the Introduction.

[39] The Women and Special Populations Branch Administrator is included in this staffing level. In response to a working draft of this chapter, BOP stated that all four staff in the Women and Special Populations Branch, including the Branch Administrator, focus on program or training work.

share of BOP's total inmate population.[40] While there is bound to be some overlap in the inmates that are a part of these populations, each population has distinct needs.

The Women and Special Populations Branch's responsibilities require it to coordinate regularly nationwide and across all BOP divisions at the Central Office and regional levels, at all female institutions, and with external organizations. The branch is required to perform a broad range of responsibilities for each special population, potentially independently of one another. For example, the following duties, among many others, demonstrate the broad scope of duties for this branch:

- developing, implementing, and maintaining national programs for female inmates, inmates with disabilities, children of incarcerated parents, and other special populations, which require extensive knowledge of mental health, case management, custody/discipline, vocational/workforce, education, life skills, release preparation, and community placement;
- representing BOP in the day-to-day dealings with outside agencies and with other BOP branches and institutions regarding female inmates or inmates from special populations; and
- serving as the BOP National Executive Staff's primary resource concerning female inmate and special population issues. The Women and Special Populations Branch also provides information and advice to other Branch Chiefs and management, including the BOP Director, regarding the needs of female or special population inmates and programs for these inmates.[41]

---

[40] Female inmates account for approximately 7 percent of the inmate population, as we state in the Introduction. We could not determine the number of inmates with disabilities from the BOP data we analyzed; but, in response to a working draft of this chapter, BOP estimated that inmates with disabilities account for approximately one-third of the inmate population.

[41] The items we highlight here represent just a fraction of the Women and Special Populations Branch's responsibilities. The Administrator's position description includes seven pages of responsibilities.

To accomplish these duties, the branch must collaborate with Health Services staff, Psychology Services staff, Education Services staff, and staff located in any other area of BOP, as necessary, to address the needs of female inmates. The Senior Deputy Assistant Director of the Reentry Services Division said that it is challenging for the branch to ensure institutions are complying with policy when the branch has only four staff, all of whom are located at Central Office. He noted that BOP might need to consider a variety of staffing arrangements, including placing staff at regional offices or individual institutions, as the branch continues to develop additional policies that each need to be implemented for different special populations.

The Women and Special Populations Branch Administrator told us that the branch's range of responsibilities and current level of staffing left it unable to provide training on current best practices for managing female inmates. She told us that she would like the branch to conduct more in-person, interactive trainings on the management of female inmates for staff at female institutions. In 2017, the branch conducted one such training at an institution; several Psychologists who attended told us that it was very useful because it enhanced staff members' understanding of trauma, how trauma impacts female inmates, and how to more effectively communicate with female inmates. A Social Worker at another female institution had not received in-person training but told us that given the mental health effects of abuse and the high rate of trauma in the female inmate population, Correctional Officers would benefit from increased training on effectively managing the needs of inmates with mental illness.[42]

As we described above, the Women and Special Populations Branch is responsible for overseeing BOP's management of multiple special populations, which includes coordinating across BOP's many divisions at the Central Office, as well as with individual institutions. Given these multiple responsibilities, we believe that BOP should evaluate the breadth

---

[42] OIG's review of BOP's management of inmates with mental illness in restrictive housing recommended additional mental health training for staff monitoring the behavior of inmates in restrictive housing. DOJ OIG, *Review of the Federal Bureau of Prisons' Use of Restrictive Housing for Inmates with Mental Illness,* Evaluation and Inspections Report 17-05 (July 2017), 66.

of the branch's mission and ensure that the branch has sufficient staff to accomplish that mission.

BOP Does Not Require Its National-Level Executives to Take Training on Managing Female Offenders

We found that while BOP has implemented mandatory training on the management of female inmates for staff who work in female institutions, BOP has not required its National Executive Staff to take this or other training pertaining to female inmates.[43] As a result, the officials who make decisions affecting the conditions of confinement for female inmates may not be fully aware of the unique needs of female inmates. According to BOP's primary training video on the management of female inmates, these unique needs include the prevalence of trauma in the female inmate population and how trauma affects female inmates' behavior; communication strategies that BOP recommends staff use when working with female inmates to avoid triggering memories of previously experienced trauma; BOP policies that impact female inmates differently, such as the inmate search policy; female inmate healthcare needs; relationships, especially relationships with their minor children; and educational and release needs. We will discuss actions BOP has taken to address some of these needs in later sections of this chapter.

BOP has made training on the management of female inmates mandatory only for staff who work in female institutions and directly with female inmates. When staff begin working at a female institution for the first time, they are required to take two trainings that were prepared by the Women and Special Populations Branch: a 1.5-hour video on the

---

[43] BOP's National Executive Staff consists of the BOP Director, Deputy Director, 6 Regional Directors, and 10 Assistant Directors in BOP's Central Office. The trauma-informed correctional care training video was incorporated into BOP's annual refresher training curriculum one time, in FY 2016, and all staff employed by BOP that year, including National Executive Staff, saw the video. BOP has an ongoing requirement that all staff assigned to a female institution for the first time take the trauma-informed correctional care training. However, because BOP does not also require this training at the time of promotion to BOP's National Executive Staff, it is possible for an individual to be promoted to an executive position without ever having taken the training. BOP reported to us that its National Executive Staff are required only to complete and maintain certification in a series of standard government manager and supervisory trainings.

management of female inmates, accompanied by discussions moderated by an on-site trainer, and a 24-minute video on trauma-informed correctional care.[44] Both of these trainings have been updated since 2016 to reflect BOP's current practices in the management of the female inmate population. A Correctional Officer who watched the trauma-informed correctional care video described the training as very powerful and said it made her more empathetic toward female inmates because it helped her understand how past traumas influence how female inmates express frustration and react to staff.

However, BOP National Executive Staff exposure to this training is ad hoc. One National Executive Staff member with decision-making authority over female inmates said that he had not received training on the management of female inmates because he had never worked at an institution that housed female inmates.[45] Another member of the BOP National Executive Staff told us that he had training on the management of female inmates in the 1990s because at that time he worked at an institution that housed female inmates. The Senior Deputy Assistant Director of the Reentry Services Division said that he believes it is important for Regional Directors to take this training because they oversee such institutions in their respective regions. He further recommended that the BOP Director take any training associated with a program statement he signs.[46] Although the Assistant Director of the Reentry Services Division told us that he does not believe that requiring National Executive Staff to take training on the management of female inmates is important, he also acknowledged that, if left to its own devices, BOP is not gender responsive. We are concerned that, without such training, members of the National Executive Staff who are in a position to make decisions that affect

---

[44] Three April 2018 program reviews of the Female Offender Manual conducted by BOP found that three different female institutions were failing to provide all institution staff with these trainings as required by BOP policy.

[45] During the course of this review, we interviewed three members of the BOP National Executive Staff who oversee aspects of BOP operations directly related to the management of female inmates.

[46] We note that the six Regional Directors plus the BOP Director account for more than a third of the BOP officials who make up the National Executive Staff.

the female inmate population may not be fully aware of female inmates' unique needs.

Individuals inside and outside BOP described training as an effective method for helping staff recognize the unique needs of female inmates, as well as an effective tool to convey support from agency leadership. A DOJ Civil Rights Division official who works closely with BOP on issues related to female inmates emphasized the importance of support from top BOP officials in ensuring that the incarceration of women is gender responsive in all areas. The Women and Special Populations Branch Administrator added that it is important for BOP leadership to be exposed to female inmate-specific issues so they understand the importance of those issues when making decisions. A Deputy Commissioner from the Alabama Department of Corrections told us that providing multidisciplinary training in gender-responsive corrections was "probably one of the most impactful" things the Department of Corrections has done to make its culture more understanding of female inmates. The Deputy Commissioner said that the training created significant buy-in from staff across all levels about understanding the unique needs of female inmates and recognizing the differences between female and male inmates.

Accordingly, we believe that BOP should ensure that all staff, including the National Executive Staff, who work with or have management decision authority over female inmates receive the current mandatory training on the unique needs of female inmates.

BOP's Programming and Policy May Not Fully Consider the Needs of Female Inmates

We identified concerns with the way BOP implements two programs for female inmates, as well as a concern with how BOP's implementation of its inmate grooming policy affects female inmates. First, BOP has not staffed its trauma treatment program for female inmates at a level that ensures that all female inmates who are eligible for the program can participate in it before they are released. Second, a lack of staff awareness and a lack of data may limit access to BOP's residential programs for pregnant inmates. Third, the distribution methods for feminine hygiene products did not always ensure that inmates had sufficient access to the quantity of products they needed.

BOP'S Trauma Treatment Program Is Inadequately Staffed Compared to the Level of Need

Based on research we previously referred to in the Introduction of this chapter, BOP's training materials acknowledge that the prevalence of trauma in the female inmate population is high—approximately 90 percent. Some of the inmates we interviewed described a range of traumatic experiences they had faced prior to incarceration, including homelessness, sexual abuse, and domestic violence. To treat the psychological and interpersonal difficulties that can result from traumatic life experiences, BOP offers the Resolve trauma therapy program at 14 of its 15 female institutions. One Resolve Coordinator said that the goal of the program is to help inmates improve their ability to function on a daily basis through treatment that reduces psychological symptoms, improves behavior, and decreases an inmate's need for medication. A BOP Mental Health Treatment Coordinator told us that, ideally, an inmate should take the Resolve program during the first 12 months of her sentence because the program can help the inmate adjust to being in an institution and prepare for other psychological programming, such as residential drug treatment. BOP Psychologists inform female inmates about the Resolve program at the start of incarceration and encourage all female inmates with a history of trauma to sign up for the introductory workshop. Participation in the Resolve program is voluntary.

Several of the inmates we interviewed who had taken Resolve told us that the program helped them come to terms with their past and prepare for life after prison. One inmate praised the Resolve program for helping her recover from severe domestic violence, saying, "I'm trying to better myself while in prison. I don't want to walk in here and walk out the same way." She also praised the Resolve Coordinator for helping her understand her marriage and how to heal from the abuse she suffered.

Although BOP considers Resolve to be an especially important program for female inmates, we found that due to current staffing BOP may not be able to ensure that all inmates who are eligible for the program can participate in it before their release from BOP custody. We learned that, regardless of the size of the institution's female inmate population, BOP allocates one position, known as a Resolve Coordinator, to administer and facilitate the Resolve program, its two prerequisites, and other tasks that are part of the program.[47] As we explain below in our discussion of the ramifications of BOP's current staffing model for Resolve, we estimate that the 40-week Resolve program can accommodate only 336 female inmates nationwide at a time, and 24 per institution at a time, representing roughly 3 percent of BOP's sentenced female inmate population.[48]

As a result of this limited staffing, inmates at larger institutions are often delayed from beginning each separate step of the program. This presents a challenge for BOP because female inmates generally have shorter sentences than male inmates. We also identified an unfilled need for trauma programming among non-English speaking inmates because BOP offers Resolve only in English. Finally, we found that Resolve's staffing level is significantly lower than several other BOP psychological treatment programs.

To determine an inmate's eligibility for the Resolve program, BOP policy requires that she complete two prerequisites: the Trauma in Life seminar and psychological screening tests (see Table 2 above). A Resolve Coordinator explained that the psychological screening tests determine whether an inmate meets certain traumatic stress criteria and is therefore eligible for the Resolve treatment. Typical diagnoses indicating eligibility include post-traumatic stress disorder, anxiety, or depression but may also include conditions such as schizophrenia if the condition is triggered or worsened by the traumatic experience. We found that inadequate staffing creates delays for inmates in completing the prerequisites, which may

---

[47] During the time of our review, BOP was piloting the Resolve program for male inmates at two institutions. At all other institutions, the Resolve program was available only to female inmates, even if the institution as a whole housed both female and male inmates.

[48] As of the end of FY 2016, there were 10,567 sentenced female inmates in the BOP's female institutions.

result in eligible inmates not being able to complete the treatment phases until later in their sentence, and possibly not at all. BOP cannot easily determine how many female inmates complete the Resolve program because, while BOP tracks completion of individual segments of the Resolve program, it does not track completion of the program as a whole.

Table 3. Trauma in Life Waiting Lists at All-female and Mixed-gender BOP Institutions, August 2017

Type of Institution	Average Female Population	Average Number of Female Inmates on a Trauma in Life Waiting List	OIG Estimate of Months Needed to Teach Trauma in Life to All Inmates on an Average Waiting List[a]
All female[b]	1,103	172	8
Mixed gender[c]	318	47	3

Sources: BOP data on Resolve program waiting lists; institution population data on BOP's website as of August 30, 2017; and OIG analysis.

Notes: The BOP's detention centers and Federal Transfer Center Oklahoma City all housed female inmates, but we excluded them from this analysis because they did not offer the Resolve program.

[a] BOP institutions told us that Trauma in Life courses can accommodate a maximum of 24 inmates at a time. Therefore, our analysis assumes that each Trauma in Life seminar can accommodate 24 inmates.

[b] The seven all-female institutions were Federal Prison Camp (FPC) Alderson, Federal Correctional Institution (FCI) Aliceville, FPC Bryan, Federal Medical Center Carswell, FCI Dublin, FCI Tallahassee, and FCI Waseca.

[c] The eight mixed-gender institutions were FPC Coleman, Federal Satellite Low and FPC Danbury, FPC Greenville, Secure Female Facility Hazelton, FPC Lexington, FPC Marianna, FPC Phoenix, and FPC Victorville. At these institutions, BOP housed female and male inmates in buildings separated by fences and enforced strict operational rules to keep female and male inmates apart at all times. We used August 2017 population data for this analysis to more accurately reflect the female population at the time we collected the waiting lists.

For example, the Trauma in Life seminar, the first prerequisite for determining eligibility in the Resolve program, is an 8-hour course and is typically taught in four 2-hour sessions over 4 weeks. Trauma in Life is intended to provide female inmates with information on trauma and its potential impact on their lives, as well as to identify inmates who need trauma treatment and to motivate them to participate in the Resolve program. As shown in Table 3 below, we found that waiting lists for Trauma in Life seminars can be lengthy, particularly in BOP's seven large, all-female institutions. We found this troubling because, as of September 2016, 70 percent of BOP's sentenced female population was in one of the seven all-female institutions.

We found that 6 of BOP's 15 female institutions had Trauma in Life waiting lists of 150 inmates or more. We concluded that inmates at the end of a waiting list of 150 could wait at least 6 months before they could take the first step toward determining whether they were even eligible for the Resolve program.[49] However, this may understate the amount of time that individual inmates must wait to enroll in the program because BOP organizes its program waiting lists by release date, not the date an inmate is added to the waiting list. A Social Worker told us that, as a result, female inmates with longer sentences may spend years rather than months on a program waiting list, including the Trauma in Life waiting list.[50]

After inmates complete Trauma in Life, they must undergo a psychological assessment to determine whether they have a psychological diagnosis related to a traumatic life event. Such a diagnosis is a requirement for inmates to begin Resolve's treatment phases. Making such a diagnosis requires the Resolve Coordinator to perform a screening assessment that includes several psychological tests and a review of the inmate's file. One Resolve Coordinator said that the process of interviewing an inmate, performing the psychological tests, and reviewing the inmate's file takes several hours for each inmate. Another Resolve Coordinator at a large female institution said that the amount of

[49] One institution reported to us that its Trauma in Life waiting list was 311 inmates. At this institution, we estimate the wait for the Trauma in Life course could be as long as a year.

[50] BOP policy states that inmates should enroll in the Trauma in Life seminar during the first 12 months of incarceration. An inmate was always placed on the Trauma in Life seminar's waiting list based on her release date, even if she did not sign up for the Trauma in Life seminar until after her first 12 months of incarceration. BOP policy does not establish a timeframe for completing the rest of the Resolve program.

psychological testing required for Resolve is a lot of work for a single staff member, especially given all of a Resolve Coordinator's responsibilities.

During our fieldwork, 5 of BOP's female institutions reported that 45 or more inmates were awaiting a screening assessment to determine whether they were eligible for Resolve. At 1 of these institutions, 180 inmates, representing 18 percent of the institution's population, were on the waiting list for screening.[51] The second-longest waiting list for screening assessments, 82 inmates, represented 5 percent of that institution's population.

After inmates complete Trauma in Life and receive a psychological assessment that results in a diagnosis related to a traumatic event, they are eligible to begin the Resolve program. However, according to BOP Psychologists, the single Resolve Coordinator running the program can manage a caseload of only 24 inmates at a time in the treatment phases. The caseload of inmates in the treatment phases does not include inmates who are taking the Trauma in Life seminar, are undergoing the psychological screening assessment, or have completed the treatment phases and are in the maintenance group. With a current staffing level of one Resolve Coordinator per institution, eligible inmates will not necessarily begin a Resolve program right after completing the two prerequisites.

Additionally, we found that the existing waiting lists for Resolve programming may underrepresent the actual level of need because Resolve is offered only in English and, therefore, waiting lists generally include only inmates who speak fluent English. BOP Psychologists at multiple institutions expressed concern that BOP is not able to provide sufficient trauma treatment for non-English speaking female inmates, specifically Spanish-speaking female inmates. While the fact that Resolve is taught only in English could be an impediment for any non-English speaking inmate, institution staff told us that Spanish is by far the most common non-English language spoken by inmates. A Warden and a Chief

[51] BOP's Chief of Mental Health Services attributed the backlog to the fact that the Resolve Coordinator position at this institution was vacant, noting that BOP has found it challenging to keep the Resolve Coordinator position filled at this rural institution.

Psychologist from two female institutions told us that their greatest unmet programming need was for Spanish Resolve. According to the Chief Psychologist, "There's horrific history, but we just can't get to them."

Psychological staff at multiple female institutions expressed concern that having only one position dedicated to administering all aspects of Resolve at each institution, regardless of the size of the institution, was inadequate. We note that this is particularly problematic for the three female institutions that have both a low security institution and a minimum security camp because security considerations require the low and minimum security inmates to be separated. The Resolve Coordinator from one of these institutions said that if she offered treatment to both low and minimum security inmates at the same time, she must do so in separate treatment groups. Another Resolve Coordinator worried that, as a result of low staffing levels, "you have people going home without the treatment, although we identified that they needed it."

The Chief of Mental Health Services described this staffing model as "not ideal" and noted that it worked better at camps, which typically have populations of around 300 female inmates, than at larger institutions. She further explained that BOP had not added staff to the Resolve program as of the time of our review because it had to balance competing priorities for psychological resources and had chosen in recent years to prioritize the treatment of serious mental illness.[52]

Finally, the Chief of Mental Health Services said that, because Resolve is run by a single coordinator in each institution, any time that position is vacant the program goes dormant until a replacement is hired. A September 2016 BOP statistical report summarizing staffing levels and inmate participation in psychology treatment programs showed that 5 of the 14 Resolve Coordinator positions in female institutions were vacant at that time. As a result, the Resolve program was not available to the female inmates at these institutions until the positions were filled.

---

[52] Based on concerns about insufficient mental health staff, OIG's review of BOP's management of inmates with mental illness in restrictive housing recommended that BOP prioritize and incentivize hiring mental health staff at institutions that have inmates with mental illness in longterm restrictive housing. DOJ OIG, *Use of Restrictive Housing,* 65.

We found that Resolve's staffing model allotted fewer staff than several of BOP's other psychology treatment programs, including the Residential Drug Abuse Program (RDAP), the Brave program, and the Challenge program.[53] BOP policy requires the RDAP, Brave, and Challenge programs each to be staffed by a Program Coordinator and multiple Treatment Specialists, allowing these programs to treat more inmates concurrently than Resolve can, as shown in Table 4 below, because each Treatment Specialist maintains a caseload of inmates. Meanwhile, Resolve is the only psychological treatment program with a capacity not established in policy, although BOP's Chief of Mental Health Services told us that the general expectation is that each Resolve Coordinator will treat 24 inmates at a time. The Chief Psychologist at a large female institution said that BOP does a great job treating substance abuse through RDAP because it allocates sufficient resources and staffing to RDAP; but it does not do the same for trauma treatment through Resolve.

RDAP, Brave, and Challenge differ from Resolve also because they are residential programs, meaning that all inmates in the program also live together in a single housing unit separate from the institution's general population. BOP residential programs are more intensive than non-residential programs, requiring more programming hours to complete.[54] Residential programs have more staff to account for these differences. While we recognize that residential programs are frequently of a greater intensity than non-residential programs such as Resolve, we believe that BOP's current approach to staffing Resolve does not take into account the importance of female inmates completing this program as close as possible to the beginning of their incarceration. For a description of a new trauma

---

[53] The Brave program is an institutional adjustment program for male inmates who are medium security, age 32 or younger, serving their first BOP sentence, and beginning a sentence of at least 5 years. The Challenge program is for male inmates who are high security and have either a history of substance abuse or a severe mental health diagnosis. BOP's program statement for Psychology Treatment Programs describes four additional programs for mental health treatment. We excluded these programs from our analysis because they are for inmates whose mental health diagnoses require intensive treatment services.

[54] Typical residential programs require inmates to participate in group sessions for 3–4 hours per day. Resolve consists of group sessions that meet for approximately 1–2 hours per week.

treatment program that BOP was piloting during the time of our review, see the text box.

Table 4. Psychology Treatment Program Average Participation Levels and Onboard Staffing Levels, September 2016

Program	Average Program Staff per Institution	Average Inmate Participants per Institution at a Time
Resolve	1	24
RDAP	6	118
Brave	5.5	75
Challenge	4	65

Source: OIG analysis of BOP data on psychology treatment programs.

Notes: We excluded three institutions from our analysis of Resolve program participation because the Resolve Coordinator positions at those institutions were vacant. The staffing levels of RDAP, Brave, and Challenge varied slightly, usually ranging between four and six staff per program location. Additionally, some BOP institutions operated multiple RDAPs at a single institution.

Female Integrated Treatment

BOP has taken a promising first step in its efforts to enhance the capacity of its trauma treatment programming at one female institution. The Female Integrated Treatment (FIT) program being piloted at the low security female institution in Danbury, Connecticut, has positions for a FIT Program Coordinator, two Psychologists, and four Treatment Specialists. BOP anticipated that, when fully staffed, FIT would be able to provide treatment to up to 96 women at a time. The capacity of the low security female institution in Danbury is 192 inmates, meaning that, unlike Resolve, the FIT program will be able to accommodate a relatively high proportion of Danbury's low security female population.

Sources: OIG interviews of BOP staff and BOP documents describing the FIT program.

A 2003 National Institute of Corrections report stated that "among women, the most common pathways to crime are based on survival (of

placement during and after pregnancy has helped them learn important parenting skills and develop a bond with their infants.

Despite the benefits that the MINT program can provide to pregnant inmates, we found that the program may be underutilized. Between FYs 2012 and 2016, there were 951 pregnant inmates in BOP's custody, 558 of whom were in institutions designed to house sentenced inmates. Of these 558 sentenced pregnant inmates, we estimate that only 204 (37 percent) participated in MINT or the Residential Parenting Program.[60]

We believe that the low levels of participation likely can be attributed to four causes. First, we found that pregnant inmates may not always be told about available pregnancy programs. Social Workers are responsible for informing inmates about these programs, but Social Worker positions are often vacant. In fact, we found that 5 of the 15 female institutions had Social Worker vacancies in September 2017. Additionally, underscoring the importance of program reviews, BOP's first review of its policies on the management of female inmates in December 2017 concluded that Social Workers at one institution were not meeting with pregnant inmates to discuss pregnancy programming, as required. Although we also found that some institution staff did not fully understand the eligibility criteria for the pregnancy programs, the Health Services Administrator of one female institution said that staff there inform pregnant inmates of either MINT or the Residential Parenting Program only if the staff believes that the inmate meets the eligibility criteria for those programs, to avoid disappointing inmates who are not eligible.

In addition to a lack of program awareness among inmates, we also found that BOP institution staff were generally unaware of the Washington State Department of Corrections' Residential Parenting Program, for which some BOP pregnant inmates were eligible. We believe that this general lack of awareness has, in part, contributed to low BOP inmate participation in the Residential Parenting Program. Specifically, only five inmates entered the program between FYs 2012

---

[60] For this review, we evaluated participation for those inmates who were in institutions designed to house sentenced inmates only. Additionally, BOP Program Statement 7310.04, Community Corrections Center Utilization and Transfer Procedure, December 16, 1998, states that pretrial detainees are not eligible for halfway house placement.

and 2016, most recently in FY 2013. This was the case despite the fact that Washington State Department of Corrections officials told us that the program had excess capacity. We describe the Residential Parenting Program, and its eligibility criteria, in the text box.

Residential Parenting Program

During the course of our review, we learned that BOP inmates may participate in the Washington State Department of Corrections' Residential Parenting Program. Unlike the MINT program, which provides a shorter period of mother-infant bonding time in a halfway house setting, the Residential Parenting Program offers 30 months of mother-infant bonding time in the minimum security unit of the Washington Corrections Center for Women in Gig Harbor, Washington. If an inmate is interested in the program after learning about it from a BOP Social Worker, the inmate's Unit Team submits a referral packet to BOP's Residential Reentry Management Branch for review and placement.

The eligibility requirements for the Residential Parenting Program are stricter than those for the MINT program. For example, only minimum security inmates are eligible to participate in the Residential Parenting Program, whereas both minimum and low security inmates can be eligible to participate in the MINT program. To be eligible for the Residential Parenting Program, inmates must meet certain disciplinary and work evaluation criteria and must have no history of violence, sex offenses, or child abuse. Inmates must also be eligible for release or home confinement within 30 months of their expected delivery date.

Sources: Washington State Department of Corrections officials, BOP officials, and BOP policies.

Third, we found that BOP institution staff may be applying policy more restrictively than intended by Central Office policymakers. BOP policy states only that inmates must be eligible for halfway house placement to participate in the MINT program and does not explicitly bar inmates from participation based on security level; however, we learned that some BOP institution officials may apply a more restrictive eligibility standard. For example, a Warden of a female institution told us that only minimum security inmates qualify for MINT, because, she believed, that low security inmates had not proven they were ready for halfway house style housing. However, the former Chief of BOP's Designation and Sentence Computation Center, which has responsibility for determining where inmates should be housed, told us that security level designation alone should not prevent an interested inmate from participating in MINT. BOP's policy on halfway house eligibility calls for case-by-case consideration of each interested MINT participant and her likelihood to pose a threat, rather than a blanket disqualification based on her security level.[61]

Fourth, we found that BOP does not collect data that would allow it to identify barriers to participation and monitor pregnant inmates' awareness of, interest in, and enrollment in the MINT program or the Residential Parenting Program. The Women and Special Populations Branch Administrator told us that collecting sufficient data on pregnant inmates historically has been a challenge for BOP. It was not until 2016 that BOP added a code to its inmate tracking system to indicate that an inmate is pregnant. Additionally, four of the interim remote program reviews that BOP conducted on Female Offender Manual compliance between December 2017 and May 2018 found inconsistencies in tracking pregnant inmates. During the time of our review, BOP did not track data that would allow it to ensure that pregnant inmates were informed about pregnancy programs, as required by the Female Offender Manual. Additionally, BOP did not collect data that would allow it to determine the specific eligibility criteria that preclude program participation, such as whether a pregnant inmate faced financial barriers to supporting her baby during mother-infant bonding time or planned to pursue adoption, either of which would render the inmate ineligible for participation in MINT.

Lastly, BOP did not track the length of time a pregnant inmate spent at a MINT program site. Tracking duration of stay could help BOP better determine the ideal amount of time an inmate should spend at a MINT

---

[61] BOP Program Statements 7310.04 and 5200.02.

program site to achieve the program's goals. During the time of our review, policy allowed institution staff to exercise discretion as to how long an inmate may stay at a MINT program site; inmates must be allotted 3 months after birth, but the policy recommended that inmates be allowed to participate for 6 months after giving birth.[62] Multiple MINT Coordinators told us that many inmates stay at the MINT program site for only 3 months after birth.

We learned from MINT capacity data and interviews with BOP and Washington State Department of Corrections officials that both the MINT program and the Residential Parenting Program can accept additional eligible BOP inmates. Therefore, we determined that low levels of inmate participation in pregnancy programs were not caused by limited program capacity. Instead, we found that low participation was likely due to BOP staff members' failure to fully communicate program opportunities and eligibility criteria to staff and pregnant inmates and to collect relevant data to assess pregnant inmates' interest and participation in the MINT program and the Residential Parenting Program. As a result, we believe that pregnancy program participation will remain low until BOP addresses these issues.

BOP Recently Implemented New Guidance on Access to Feminine Hygiene Products, but This Guidance Is Silent on How These Products Should be Distributed

In addition to managing female inmates' needs related to pregnancy, BOP must also appropriately manage female inmates' distinct needs related to feminine hygiene. During our fieldwork, we found that the distribution methods for feminine hygiene products and the type of products provided to inmates free of charge varied by institution and did not always ensure that inmates had access to a quantity of products sufficient to meet their needs. Even though BOP issued an Operations

---

[62] MINT Coordinators believe that when inmates participate in MINT for at least 6 months after birth, they are more likely to achieve the program's goals of learning parenting skills and bonding with their infants. One region's MINT program site allows any inmate who enrolls there to participate for 12 months.

Memorandum on the Provision of Feminine Hygiene Products (Operations Memorandum) expanding the availability of products, which appears to have made some important improvements, we note that the policy lacked specificity in how institutions should distribute the products.[63] Because our fieldwork ended around the same time as this policy was issued, we could not confirm that it has addressed our concern that some institutions were not making these products sufficiently accessible.

All BOP institutions that house female inmates provide some feminine hygiene products to inmates free of charge, as required by the BOP grooming policy, which states, "for women, products for female hygiene needs shall be available."[64] However, we found that distribution practices varied across institutions. All of the institutions we visited provided sanitary pads free of charge, and a few also provided tampons. Female inmates could also purchase at their own expense both pads and tampons at the commissary.

We found that the method of distribution generally varied by the type of institution. For example, minimum security institutions stored feminine hygiene products in central locations such as bathrooms or a container that was accessible to all inmates at all times. In contrast, at several low security institutions, BOP correctional staff issued each inmate a predetermined number of feminine hygiene products per month, usually 25 to 30, regardless of individual need. One BOP staff member we interviewed told us that the number of feminine hygiene products distributed was determined largely by dividing the number received from the warehouse by the number of inmates. One inmate we interviewed from an institution that issued a preset number of hygiene products said that the amount she received from the institution each month was not enough to meet her menstrual needs. At one institution we visited, officials told us that feminine hygiene products were centrally distributed because the inmates had been misusing them for

---

[63] BOP Operations Memorandum 001-2017, Provision of Feminine Hygiene Products, August 1, 2017.

[64] BOP Program Statement 5230.05, Grooming, November 4, 1996, is BOP's policy on standards of grooming for all inmates in BOP custody. The policy describes standards of grooming regarding bathing, clothing, and hygiene for all inmates. In addition, the policy states that BOP institutions are to provide feminine hygiene products free of charge to all female inmates.

purposes such as cleaning their cells.[65] Inmates told us that the centralized distribution was problematic because hygiene products were no longer accessible in the housing units and the amount inmates received was limited.

We also found that, if inmates needed more feminine hygiene products than were issued, their ability to receive additional products varied. At institutions where access was tightly controlled, inmates who needed additional feminine hygiene products had to request them from a counselor. One inmate we interviewed told us that she had requested additional sanitary pads from a counselor and the counselor told her that the amount she received should be enough. In other institutions, inmates must go to health services to request additional products and, in some instances, going to health services also required permission from correctional staff.[66] Inmates at these institutions indicated that they interpreted this as a quota system because they could not necessarily obtain additional hygiene products beyond the number issued, even if they asked for them; or if they asked, they might be questioned about why they needed more. We believe that any distribution method that tightly controls access to feminine hygiene products and requires inmates to request more from staff, with no guarantee that their requests will be granted, places an excessive burden on inmates and does not meet BOP's grooming policy requiring that such products "shall be available" to female inmates.

Advocacy groups also have stated that access to and affordability of feminine hygiene products has been a concern for incarcerated women. Feminine hygiene products are costly relative to the salary inmates earn in prison. Additionally, advocacy groups have raised concerns that limited access to feminine hygiene products creates anxiety and is dehumanizing for

---

[65] No BOP staff member told us that feminine hygiene products were misused in a manner that presented a security concern. When we asked the Women and Special Populations Branch Administrator whether making them accessible could be a security concern, she said that they could not be.

[66] We note that not all of the reasons for which a female inmate might need additional feminine hygiene products are indicative of a medical problem. For example, a female inmate whose menstrual period began as frequently as every 21 days would be considered medically normal. However, if she received feminine hygiene products every 28 days she would not have enough.

incarcerated women. Several U.S. Senators introduced legislation on this topic in 2017, as we discuss in the text box below.

2017 Legislation on Providing Feminine Hygiene Products for Inmates

In July 2017, four U.S. Senators introduced the "Dignity for Incarcerated Women Act of 2017." Among other provisions, the bill, if passed, would permanently prohibit federal prisons from charging female inmates for essential healthcare items, including sanitary napkins and tampons. The proposed legislation received widespread attention, and some states were reviewing their policies on sanitary napkins and tampons to make them more accessible for women.

In May 2018, the House Judiciary Committee passed the "FIRST STEP Act," a bill intended to improve the federal prison system through the implementation of corrections policy reforms. This bill included language that would require BOP to make sanitary napkins and tampons available for free, in a quantity that is appropriate to the healthcare needs of each inmate.

Sources: U.S. Congress website, media articles.

We found that some state correctional systems made feminine hygiene products more readily available for their inmates. Some states made the products freely available in several locations throughout the institution, including search areas, housing units, programming areas, and bathrooms, rather than distributing a preset number to each inmate per month. One state official we interviewed told us that at one time there were issues with inmates hoarding feminine hygiene products. He explained that the hoarding stopped once the inmates believed they would have regular access to the products for their menstrual needs. Other state officials told us that if inmates were misusing feminine hygiene products for other purposes, they would address the issue with the individual inmates rather than changing the distribution method for all inmates.

We believe that the Operations Memorandum that BOP distributed to all institutions in 2017 is a positive step in that it required all institutions to provide sanitary pads, tampons, and panty liners free of charge to inmates. Even though the Operations Memorandum did not explicitly address how products should be dispersed, BOP's Women and Special Populations Branch Administrator told us that the intent of the Operations Memorandum was to ensure that these products were freely available and that institutions should not be dispersing a preset amount of hygiene products to female inmates. She added that during the quarterly conference calls with Wardens of female institutions, she instructed them that placing quotas on or issuing a preset amount of feminine hygiene products was prohibited.

We could not validate that our concerns about inmates having insufficient access to products were addressed because the Operations Memorandum was issued at the end of our fieldwork.[67] Further, BOP's interim program reviews of the Female Offender Manual, implemented in November 2017, also assessed only whether an institution provided the products required in the Operations Memorandum, but did not assess the accessibility of the products to inmates.[68] Although the new guidance is in place and BOP has taken some steps to bring institutions into compliance, we are concerned that BOP still lacks a method to ensure sufficient access. As noted previously, in-person program reviews may provide a way to ensure institutions have implemented the Operations Memorandum as intended.

BOP's Lack of Gender-Specific Posts Results in Inefficiencies at Female Institutions

In addition to programming, pregnancy, and hygiene matters, another issue we identified in BOP's management of its female inmate population

---

[67] The Assistant Director of the Reentry Services Division told us that even after the new guidance was issued he became aware that six institutions had not implemented it as promptly as expected. He told us that the Regional Directors, who directly supervise the Wardens of each institution, had to intervene to bring those institutions into compliance.

[68] Program Review G5200I.01, Interim Remote Guideline Steps, November 2017, evaluated how well an institution was providing vital services to female offenders. The review included an assessment of the following: Classification, Staff Training, Inmate Programs, Pregnancy/Child Placement, Pregnancy/Programming, High Security Administrative Units, Trust Fund/Commissary, and Feminine Hygiene Products.

relates to BOP's policy prohibiting cross-gender searches. The *Prison Rape Elimination Act of 2003* (PREA) and BOP policy prohibit cross-gender searches of female inmates.[69] We found that BOP did not take this policy into account when assigning posts for its Correctional Officers. BOP assigned Correctional Officers to posts solely based on seniority, which resulted in male Correctional Officers being assigned to posts at which staff regularly conducted searches of female inmates. This means that female Correctional Officers had to leave other assigned posts to conduct these searches, which we found to be inefficient and disruptive. This problem is more acute at institutions where the inmate population is entirely female and female Correctional Officers must perform all inmate searches.

BOP policy requires that staff conduct strip searches of inmates in certain situations, most commonly when they enter or leave the Special Housing Unit (SHU) and before and after they have contact with the public, such as when they receive visitors in the institution's visiting room, appear in court, or have a medical appointment outside the institution.[70] Therefore, conducting strip searches is among the inherent duties of the Correctional Officer posts in those locations. However, BOP cannot currently ensure that there is a female Correctional Officer on each post where strip searches are required.

---

[69] In August 2012, the Department issued a final rule adopting national standards to prevent, detect, and respond to prison rape, as required by PREA. This rule banned male staff from conducting pat searches of female inmates (known as cross-gender pat searches) beginning in August 2015. See 28 C.F.R. § 115.15(b). BOP updated multiple policies to incorporate the ban after the rule was issued. See BOP Program Statements 5521.06, Searches of Housing Units, Inmates, and Inmate Work Areas, June 4, 2015, 3, and 5324.12, Sexually Abusive Behavior Prevention and Intervention Program, June 4, 2015, 17. The Department chose not to ban cross-gender pat searches of male inmates when promulgating the PREA regulations because it found that male inmates are less likely than female inmates to have a history of sexual abuse and are also less likely to experience re-traumatization as a result of a cross-gender pat search. Further, the Department concluded that in correctional agencies where the percentage of female correctional staff is substantial, but the percentage of female inmates is small, banning cross-gender pat searches of male inmates could have a significant adverse impact on employment opportunities for female staff.

[70] Federal regulations and BOP policies mandate that strip searches also be conducted by a staff member who is the same gender as the inmate being searched. See 28 C.F.R. § 552.11(c) and BOP Program Statement 5521.06, 4. See also 28 C.F.R. § 115.15(a).

The fact that every inmate search at BOP's female institutions—both strip searches and pat searches—must be done by female staff can be disruptive to operations when female inmate searches are needed at a post staffed only by male staff. Female Correctional Officers we interviewed at female institutions told us that in these instances they are required to leave their post and go to the post where the search is needed.[71] A female Correctional Officer at an all-female institution told us that in a recent 3-month period she was called to the SHU an average of 3 or 4 times each week to search female inmates because all of the Correctional Officers assigned to the SHU were male. Similarly, another female Correctional Officer told us that when all of the visiting room posts at her institution were filled by males she had to juggle the duties of her own post as well as theirs.

At BOP's mixed-gender institutions, the need for female staff to search female inmates is more manageable. While female Correctional Officers represent only a fraction of the staff, female inmates represent only a fraction of the population. The challenge at mixed-gender institutions is physical distance. BOP policy requires female institutions, including mixed-gender institutions, to have at least one female staff member on duty during every shift but does not specify where the female staff should be posted. Correctional Officers at mixed-gender institutions told us that, while there was always a female officer on duty, the duty location could be so far away that the female Correctional Officer would have to drive to respond to the search request.

In our interviews, BOP staff expressed widespread support for BOP requiring certain posts, such as in the visiting rooms and SHUs at female institutions, to be staffed by female Correctional Officers, citing as an impediment to operations the frequent need to call female staff from other

---

[71] BOP's policy on inmate searches states that except when circumstances are such that delay would constitute an immediate threat to the inmate, staff, others, property, or institution security, a female staff member should come to a post to pat search a female inmate rather than invoke an exemption in the PREA regulations that permits cross-gender pat searches in "exigent circumstances." BOP Program Statement 5521.06, 3. The PREA regulations define "exigent circumstances" as those that require immediate action in order to combat a threat to the security or institutional order of a facility. Institution staff did not describe to us any situations where they had to invoke the exemption.

posts to strip search and pat search female inmates.[72] Nearly two-thirds (15 of 23) of both supervisory and non-supervisory custody staff at female institutions with whom we discussed the topic were in favor of establishing a small number of gender-specific posts at female institutions.[73] This includes 9 of the 11 female custody staff, who are the most affected by BOP's current policies, and 6 of the 12 male custody staff we spoke to. The Women and Special Populations Branch Administrator echoed these views.

State correctional officials we interviewed told us that their agencies had recognized this issue and had taken several different approaches to address it. Officials from two of the five state correctional agencies told us that they had established gender-specific posts in specific areas of their female institutions, such as the SHU and the visiting room, to ensure that only female Correctional Officers search female inmates without interfering with operations.[74] Officials from two additional state correctional agencies told us that their agencies did not have any gender-specific posts in their female institutions, but that the institutions had enough female staff to handle all search needs. The fifth agency obviated the need for gender-specific posts by assigning only female staff to work at its female institution.

We found differences of opinion about whether the establishment of gender-specific posts is allowable under the Master Agreement that governs BOP labor practices and working conditions and even whether gender-specific posts are needed.[75] Specifically, BOP's Assistant Director

---

[72] These disruptions occur despite the fact that, on average, nearly 40 percent of Correctional Officers in BOP's seven female institutions are female.

[73] BOP staff specifically recommended that BOP require at least one of the Correctional Officers assigned to a female visiting room or female SHU be female. We reviewed the written directives describing the specific duties of these posts, known as post orders, from four of BOP's female institutions and found that the post orders anticipated that the Correctional Officers working the posts would routinely strip search and pat search female inmates.

[74] One of these two correctional agencies said that the agency had not faced challenges from male staff as a result of establishing gender-specific posts in female institutions, although the official we interviewed acknowledged that the agency's lack of a public sector union may also be a reason why the posts have not been challenged. See Appendix 1 for the methodology of our review, including the officials we interviewed.

[75] The current Master Agreement between BOP and the Council of Prison Locals, the union that represents BOP's bargaining unit employees, went into effect in July 2014. Master

of the Correctional Programs Division stated that the terms of the Master Agreement do not expressly allow for gender-specific posts and that he was not aware of any problems that would require the establishment of gender-specific posts.[76] He also expressed concern that having such posts could lead to an increase in staff complaints or grievances. Further, institution custody supervisors told us that they believed seniority was the only factor they could consider in determining assignments. They explained that Correctional Officers bid for their preferred posts quarterly in order of seniority and institution staff create a roster based on "reasonable efforts" to grant the requests. The Master Agreement defines "reasonable efforts" to mean that "management will not arbitrarily deny such requests."[77]

In contrast, BOP's General Counsel said that the Master Agreement could allow female institutions to establish a few gender-specific posts because, in his view, having enough staff on a post to complete the work efficiently is not arbitrary. Further, while in his opinion an institution could not establish a blanket rule that all posts in a particular location could be filled only by staff from one gender, institutions could require that a certain portion of them be filled by staff from one gender.[78]

We note that the Master Agreement went into effect in 2014, but the PREA regulations and BOP policies that ban cross-gender pat searches of female inmates did not go into effect until 2015. Given that cross-gender pat searches of female inmates were banned after the Master Agreement came into effect, BOP may need to reexamine its blanket ban on gender-specific posts. We recommend that BOP improve the availability of female staff at locations in female institutions where inmate searches are common, through the establishment of gender-specific posts or other methods.

Agreement between the Federal Bureau of Prisons and Council of Prison Locals, July 21, 2014–July 20, 2017.

[76] The Master Agreement does not discuss gender-specific posts. Instead, BOP's program statement on inmate searches prohibits the establishment of gender-specific posts and requires institutions to evaluate operational needs consistent with the Master Agreement and collective bargaining obligations. BOP Program Statement 5521.06, 3.

[77] Master Agreement, Article 18, Section d, para. 2d. This Master Agreement was in effect during the scope of our review.

[78] The post orders we reviewed indicated that visiting rooms and SHUs were staffed by multiple Correctional Officers.

BOP's Decision to Convert Federal Correctional Institution Danbury to a Male Institution Negatively Affected Female Inmates Transferred to Metropolitan Detention Center Brooklyn

Our broader evaluation of BOP's management of female inmates also encompassed a more specific review of the circumstances and results of BOP's decision to convert Federal Correctional Institution (FCI) Danbury to a male institution. We believe that the effects of this decision, described below, serve as a case study that highlights BOP's ongoing challenges in strategically managing its female inmate population.

In April 2014, BOP converted FCI Danbury, its low security female institution in Danbury, Connecticut, to a male institution.[79] As a result of the conversion, BOP eliminated its only low security female institution in its Northeast Region. Members of Congress and other stakeholders expressed concern that without a comparable facility in the region BOP would send local inmates to BOP institutions farther from their homes, making it difficult for families to visit inmates throughout their incarceration.[80] As a result of this concern, and the concern of other criminal justice stakeholders that following the conversion sentenced female inmates were housed in inappropriate conditions in Metropolitan Detention Center (MDC) Brooklyn, we examined how BOP's decision to convert FCI Danbury affected female inmates.

First, we found that, although the Danbury conversion resulted in 19 percent of U.S. citizen female inmates being transferred farther from home, far more were transferred to facilities closer to home. Second, we found that BOP offered female inmates at MDC Brooklyn no access to outdoor space,

---

[79] According to a September 2013 BOP projection, BOP would see a reduction in both the male and female low security overcrowding rates by opening FCI Aliceville as a low security female institution and converting FCI Danbury to a low security male institution. Specifically, BOP estimated that these changes would reduce the low security female overcrowding rate from 48 percent to 23 percent and the low security male overcrowding rate from 38 percent to 36 percent.

[80] In August 2013, Senators Christopher Murphy (Connecticut) and Kirsten Gillibrand (New York) sent a letter to then BOP Director Charles Samuels expressing concern regarding the conversion of FCI Danbury.

less natural light, and fewer programming opportunities than what would otherwise be available to female inmates at a BOP facility designed to house sentenced inmates for long periods of time. Third, although BOP opened a new low security institution for female inmates from the Northeast in December 2016, during the course of our fieldwork we found that BOP built the new institution without a SHU for female inmates, which has created challenges for disciplining female inmates. We discuss each of these findings below.

Most Female Inmates Transferred from FCI Danbury Moved Closer to Home

In response to congressional concerns that the conversion of FCI Danbury would cause female inmates to be housed farther from their homes, we analyzed the distances from home for female inmates transferred from FCI Danbury. We found that 81 percent of Danbury's U.S. citizen female inmates were transferred closer to or remained the same distance from home and 19 percent were transferred farther from home.

We further describe the outcomes of our analysis below in Table 5, which shows that of the 1,127 female inmates transferred or released from FCI Danbury, 497 were U.S. citizen female inmates who were transferred to other BOP institutions. Of those 497, we found that 401 were transferred to a BOP institution closer to their homes or were reassigned to a minimum security prison camp at FCI Danbury. Conversely, 96 were transferred to a BOP institution farther from home. Of those 96, 61 were from BOP's Northeast Region.[81] We did not consider the nonU.S. citizen inmates whom BOP transferred from FCI Danbury in this analysis because the BOP data we analyzed did not always include a U.S. residence for these individuals.

[81] These 61 inmates were transferred to 12 different institutions. BOP told us that it considered multiple factors when making each transfer decision. These factors include distance from home, availability of programming, and physical and mental health needs.

The Duration and Conditions of Confinement of Inmates Housed at MDC Brooklyn

After members of Congress expressed concern that the conversion of FCI Danbury would eliminate BOP's only low security institution for female inmates in the Northeast, in October 2013 BOP announced that it would open a new low security institution in Danbury in order to keep low security female inmates from the Northeast closer to home. While BOP was constructing the new institution, it decided to house many of the displaced inmates from the Northeast at MDC Brooklyn, a detention center designed and generally used for short-term confinement. BOP housed these inmates at MDC Brooklyn between March 2014 and December 2016, significantly longer than the 18 months it had initially anticipated.

According to the former Chief of the Designation and Sentence Computation Center, detention facilities such as MDC Brooklyn lack the physical infrastructure and programming opportunities appropriate for long-term incarceration. However, BOP officials decided that it would be better to house sentenced inmates at MDC Brooklyn in order to keep them closer to their families, as opposed to transferring them to institutions farther away from their homes that were suitable for long-term confinement.[82] The former Chief of the Designation and Sentence Computation Center stated that BOP officials chose the former in part because they estimated that the inmates would be housed there only on a temporary basis until the new institution at Danbury was complete.

In October 2013, BOP anticipated that the new institution would open 18 months later, in March 2015. However, the construction did not actually begin until June 2015, or 20 months later, and the new institution at Danbury did not open until December 2016, causing 70 of the 366 female

---

[82] We also note that, given the greater number of male institutions, BOP would be less likely to have to choose between institutions close to home and institutions suitable for long-term confinement if it had decided to convert or close one of its male institutions. For example, BOP operated four low security male institutions in its Northeast Region in 2013 (FCI Allenwood Low, FCI Elkton, FCI Fort Dix, and FCI Loretto), compared to one for women (FCI Danbury). Had the BOP decided to convert or close one of these low security male institutions at that time, the other three institutions would have remained options for low security male inmates from the Northeast.

inmates to remain at MDC Brooklyn for longer than 18 months, with the longest stay lasting 34 months.[83]

Table 5. Geographic Outcomes of FCI Danbury Female Inmate Transfers

Geographic Outcomes of FCI Danbury Female Inmate Transfers

1,127 Inmates Transferred or Released Between August 2013 and March 2014

- 675 U.S. citizens
- 445 non-U.S. citizens
- 7 U.S. citizens with incomplete data for geographical analysis[a]

675 U.S. Citizens

- 497 transferred to another BOP institution
- 45 released from BOP custody
- 133 transferred to a halfway house prior to release from BOP custody

497 Transferred to Another BOP Institution

- 373 transferred closer to home
- 96 transferred farther from home
- 28 not changed (transferred to Federal Prison Camp Danbury)[b]

96 Transferred Farther from Home

- 61 from BOP's Northeast Region[c]
- 35 from other BOP regions

Sources: BOP Sentry and SAS geolocation library.

[a] Of the 1,127 inmates BOP transferred or released from FCI Danbury, 682 were U.S. citizens. Due to data limitations, we were unable to conduct a distance analysis for seven of these U.S. citizen female inmates.

[b] BOP reduced the security level of these inmates to minimum and assigned them to the minimum security Federal Prison Camp Danbury, which is adjacent to FCI Danbury.

[c] For the purpose of this analysis, we used the 10 states that BOP designated as within its Northeast Region as our parameter for "Northeast." These states are Connecticut, Maine, Massachusetts, New Hampshire, New Jersey, New York, Ohio, Pennsylvania, Rhode Island, and Vermont.

Figure 2 provides a more detailed explanation of the period of confinement for sentenced female inmates at MDC Brooklyn.

---

[83] According to BOP, the March 2015 estimate was always subject to change. OIG is currently completing an audit of the FCI Danbury construction contract.

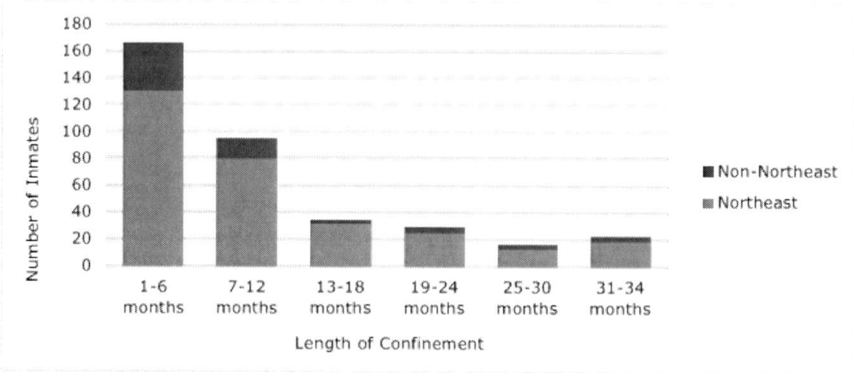

Source: BOP SENTRY.

Notes: For the purpose of this analysis, we defined 1 month as 30 days. This figure includes MDC Brooklyn's U.S. citizen and non-U.S. citizen sentenced female inmates. For the purpose of this analysis, we use the 10 states that BOP designated as within its Northeast Region as our parameter for "Northeast." These states are Connecticut, Maine, Massachusetts, New Hampshire, New Jersey, New York, Ohio, Pennsylvania, Rhode Island, and Vermont.

Figure 2. Length of Confinement for Sentenced Female Inmates at MDC Brooklyn.

Conditions of Confinement at MDC Brooklyn

Between March 2014 and December 2016, members of the National Association of Women Judges (NAWJ) visited MDC Brooklyn multiple times and issued two reports detailing its concerns about the conditions of confinement at the facility.[84] NAWJ reported that BOP housed female inmates at MDC Brooklyn without access to an outdoor recreation space that had fresh air and exposure to sunlight, which, NAWJ believed, amounted to a violation of both the American Bar Association Standards on Treatment of Prisoners and the United Nations Standard Minimum Rules for the Treatment of Prisoners.[85]

[84] NAWJ Women in Prison Committee, Visit to BOP's Metropolitan Detention Center (MDC), Brooklyn, New York (March 2015) and Second Visit to BOP's MDC, Brooklyn, New York (June 2016).

[85] In particular, NAWJ cited the *American Bar Association Standards on Treatment of Prisoners, Standard 23-3.1(a) 3rd edition,* 2011, which states that "a correctional facility should not deprive prisoners of natural light, of light sufficient to permit reading throughout prisoners'

During our visit to MDC Brooklyn in August 2017, we found that its female inmates had less access to fresh air and sunlight than what would have been available to them at FCI Danbury. Unlike female inmates at MDC Brooklyn, who rarely left the floor of their housing unit, low security inmates at FCI Danbury and those at most other BOP institutions designed for sentenced inmates have access to fresh air and sunlight not only during recreation, but throughout the day when they move from one part of the institution to another. Further, FCI Danbury and other BOP institutions have open outdoor recreation spaces, whereas the recreation space at MDC Brooklyn was directly attached to the female inmate housing unit and had only two caged sides exposed to sunlight.[86] Because male inmates in the facility had a direct sightline into the exposed sides of the women's recreation cage, MDC Brooklyn staff added metal sheeting to the exposed sides, which left only small portions, at the top and bottom, uncovered, further restricting the amount of natural light.[87]

Some BOP staff acknowledged that the limited access to sunlight for the sentenced female inmates was not ideal, and in our report on the *Federal Bureau of Prisons' Use of Restrictive Housing for Inmates with Mental Illness*, a BOP Psychologist explained that access to sunlight is important for an inmate's mental and physical well-being.[88] Although the

---

housing areas, or of reasonable darkness during the sleeping hours." Additionally, NAWJ cited a standard related to access to exercise and sports for inmates, which is outlined in the *UN Standard Minimum Rules for the Treatment of Prisoners,* 1977. The standard specifies that "every prisoner who is not employed in outdoor work shall have at least one hour of suitable exercise in the open air daily if the weather permits."

[86] These differences exist because MDC Brooklyn is a high-rise building, with all of its departments housed in a single building. As a result, inmates rarely leave the floor their unit is on. FCI Danbury and other institutions designed for sentenced inmates consist of multiple smaller buildings surrounded by a perimeter fence. Inmates in these types of institutions have access to the outdoors daily because they must go outside to get from their housing units to the cafeteria, the medical clinic, classrooms, and other departments.

[87] Judges belonging to NAWJ, who visited MDC Brooklyn in March 2015, estimated that there was an 18-inch opening at the top and a 6-inch opening at the bottom of the exposed walls. We did not take measurements at the time of our visit in August 2017 because most of the metal sheeting had been removed in late 2016.

[88] DOJ OIG, Use of Restrictive Housing, 23.

level of natural light in the recreation space was below the level BOP generally considers appropriate for long-term confinement, a February 2015 American Correctional Association (ACA) accreditation report on MDC Brooklyn did not identify natural light levels as a concern.[89]

We also found that female inmates assigned to MDC Brooklyn did not have the range of programming that is normally available at institutions for sentenced inmates. According to BOP's program statement on Education, Training, and Leisure Time, detention centers are exempt from providing the same education programs that are offered at other BOP institutions.[90] We believe that this exemption is reasonable when the only mission of a detention center is to provide short-term housing for pretrial inmates. However, in the case of MDC Brooklyn, the exemption limited the programming opportunities below the level BOP determined is appropriate for sentenced inmates.

Additionally, we found that MDC Brooklyn did not offer the Resolve program (discussed above) because it did not have a Resolve Coordinator on staff. We found this surprising given the emphasis that BOP places on trauma-informed care. MDC Brooklyn's Chief Psychologist told us that it was difficult to conduct those group psychology programs for which MDC Brooklyn did have sufficient staff because the population of sentenced inmates was too small to generate the number of interested inmates required for participation. When discussing the availability of programming at MDC Brooklyn, the Women and Special Populations Branch Administrator told us that in retrospect she believes that BOP

---

[89] The accreditation report determined that MDC Brooklyn was compliant with all relevant light access requirements outlined in ACA's Standards for Adult Local Detention Facilities. ACA's standards for access to light, as relevant to our review, are the same for both detention facilities and adult correctional institutions. However, ACA's accreditation report covers the institution as a whole and does not separately describe the female and male housing units. ACA, Standards for Adult Local Detention Facilities, 4th edition and 2012 Standards Supplement.

[90] BOP Program Statement 5300.21, Education, Training, and Leisure Time Standards, February 18, 2002.

should have better recognized the need to provide MDC Brooklyn with additional programming resources before it transferred sentenced female inmates there.

Although not directly related to the work of this review, a separate OIG investigation determined that, during the time that sentenced female inmates were assigned to MDC Brooklyn, multiple custody staff sexually assaulted female inmates.[91] We discuss the findings of this investigation of staff in the text box below.

While BOP recognizes that detention centers offer sentenced inmates less suitable recreation space and fewer programming opportunities than would be available in other institutions, we found that BOP does not have a policy that limits the amount of time sentenced inmates can be assigned to a detention center. We recognize that, in the case of FCI Danbury, BOP made a difficult decision either to transfer some female inmates to institutions that offer the appropriate type of recreation space and programming opportunities or to transfer female inmates to a detention center closer to their homes. However, we believe that BOP may continue to confine sentenced inmates for an extended period of time in conditions it recognizes as inappropriate unless it establishes a policy that defines how long a sentenced inmate can be confined in a detention center or ensures that the conditions of confinement at a detention center more closely approximate those of a non-detention center when sentenced inmates are housed there.

The Lack of a SHU for Female Inmates at Danbury Has Been Disruptive to Operations

During our fieldwork, we found that changes at FCI Danbury have created a separate challenge for BOP in enforcing discipline on female inmates.

---

[91] We note that as a result of OIG investigations, six BOP staff members from five additional female institutions have pled guilty to sexual abuse of a ward since January 2016.

OIG Investigation of Sexual Assaults at MDC Brooklyn

As a result of a nearly yearlong OIG investigation into allegations of sexual abuse of female inmates at MDC Brooklyn, the U.S. Attorney's Office for the Eastern District of New York filed indictments in May 2017 alleging that Lieutenants Carlos Martinez and Eugenio Perez and Correctional Officer Armando Moronta engaged in criminal sexual acts with female inmates between 2013 and 2016.

In January 2018, Martinez was found guilty on 20 counts that covered 4 sexual assaults between December 2015 and April 2016. The evidence at trial established that Martinez repeatedly raped a female inmate who spoke limited English and worked as a cleaner inside the prison. Specifically, Martinez raped his victim while she cleaned the Lieutenants' office on the weekends, when that area of the institution is generally empty, and monitored security video footage of the surrounding area to make sure no one would discover him committing sexual assault. Martinez also threatened his victim with placement in the SHU and additional jail time if she told anyone what he had done.

In May 2018, Perez was found guilty on 23 counts that covered sexual abuse of 5 women between January 2013 and September 2016. The evidence at trial established that Perez lured each of his victims into isolated situations by arranging for them to clean the Lieutenants' office at night and then used physical force and intimidation to compel the victims to engage in various sexual acts with him, including oral sex. Perez used his authority over the inmates to ensure they did not report the abuse.

In November 2017, Moronta pled guilty to four counts of sexual abuse of a ward. Specifically, between May and June 2016, Moronta engaged in criminal sexual contact and acts with three female inmates, including fondling a female inmate and causing inmates to perform oral sex on him while he was assigned to guard their unit.

Sources: U.S. Attorney's Office, Eastern District of New York, Press Releases, January 19, 2018; May 14, 2018; and November 8, 2017.

In particular, we found that BOP built the new low security female institution on the FCI Danbury campus without a SHU, a unit used to separate inmates from the general population for protective or disciplinary purposes.[92] Because BOP does not house female inmates and male inmates in the same unit, Danbury staff cannot use the SHU at the all-male institution to house female inmates for whom the SHU is appropriate. As a result, when Danbury staff determine that a female inmate should be separated from the general population, they must transport the inmate more than 150 miles to Federal Detention Center (FDC) Philadelphia.

We found that before construction on the new low security institution was completed, both the former and current Wardens of FCI Danbury expressed concern to BOP leadership that the construction plans did not include a SHU. They further explained that, without secure housing, Danbury staff would be forced to utilize secure housing in other facilities, which could cause operational problems. Despite these warnings, the BOP Central Office told OIG that it did not include a SHU in the construction plans because the new institution would have only a small number of low security inmates (its capacity is 192) and BOP did not believe this population necessitated the construction of a SHU.

Danbury staff told us that it is difficult to enforce rules and investigate misconduct at the institution given this arrangement. During our visit to FCI Danbury, we found that the operational challenges predicted by the former and current Wardens have manifested themselves. According to the current Warden, Danbury staff are less likely to recommend SHU placement for an inmate who misbehaves because of the challenges of transporting those inmates to FDC Philadelphia. The Warden also told us that the female inmates understand these challenges and, on occasion, are emboldened to misbehave.

FCI Danbury's Lieutenant for Special Investigative Services also told us that it is difficult to investigate inmate misconduct once the suspected inmates have been transferred to FDC Philadelphia because the Lieutenant

---

[92] With the opening of the new low security female institution, at the time of our review there were three institutions on the FCI Danbury campus: (1) FCI Danbury, a low security male institution that, prior to May 2014, was a low security female institution; (2) Federal Prison Camp Danbury, a minimum security female institution; and (3) Federal Satellite Low Danbury, the new low security female institution. We refer to BOP staff who work at any of the three institutions as "Danbury staff.

cannot conduct in-person interviews with Danbury inmates housed at FDC Philadelphia. Instead, he must rely on a Special Investigative Services investigator at FDC Philadelphia to conduct the interview. The Lieutenant said that, although he is satisfied with the quality of his FDC Philadelphia colleagues' investigative work, he would prefer to conduct the interviews himself because he is more familiar with the inmates and the situation he is investigating than his colleagues in other institutions.

The current Warden of FCI Danbury explained that in order to minimize the burden of transferring female SHU inmates long distances she was looking to identify a nearby jail that could house Danbury's female SHU inmates. This solution has been implemented by at least one other similarly situated institution, which we visited during our review. However, as of August 2017 the Warden had not yet identified an appropriate jail.

CONCLUSION AND RECOMMENDATIONS

Conclusion

Overall, we concluded that BOP has not been strategic in its management of female inmates. At the Central Office level, we found that BOP only recently took initial steps to implement oversight of the Female Offender Manual. We also found that BOP may not have allocated sufficient resources to the Women and Special Populations Branch to fulfill its complete range of responsibilities with regard to female inmates and that it has not ensured that BOP decision makers understand how female inmates' needs differ from those of male inmates. At the institution level, we identified deficiencies in how BOP staffs its trauma treatment program, makes staff and inmates aware of its pregnancy programs, distributes feminine hygiene products, and staffs correctional posts where female inmates are searched. Finally, we found that BOP's conversion of FCI Danbury from a female to a male institution negatively affected female inmates transferred to MDC Brooklyn. For BOP to be fully effective at appropriately managing female inmates, we believe that it must take a holistic approach at the Central Office level to identify and address issues affecting this population.

Recommendations

To ensure that BOP is better positioned to identify and respond to female inmates' needs at the Central Office level, provide female inmates with programming that addresses their unique needs, and consider female inmates' needs in policy and operational decisions, we recommend that BOP:

1. Fully implement ongoing plans to create a permanent program review for the Female Offender Manual that includes in-person visits and an institution-specific rating.
2. Determine the appropriate level of staffing that should be allocated to the Women and Special Populations Branch based on an analysis of its broad mission and responsibilities.
3. Ensure that all officials who enter into National Executive Staff positions have taken appropriate, current training specific to the unique needs of female inmates and trauma-informed correctional care.
4. Identify ways to expand the staffing of the Resolve program.
5. Improve the communication of its pregnancy program availability and eligibility criteria to relevant staff and pregnant inmates to ensure consistent understanding across BOP institutions.
6. Improve data tracking to allow it to more easily identify inmates who are aware of, interested in, eligible for, or participating in pregnancy programs, as well as to assess barriers to participation.
7. Clarify guidance on the distribution of feminine hygiene products

to ensure sufficient access to the amount of products inmates need free of charge.

8. Improve the availability of female staff at locations in female institutions where inmate searches are common, through the establishment of gender-specific posts or other methods.
9. Establish policy that determines how long sentenced inmates can be confined in a detention center, or ensures that the conditions of confinement and inmate programming at a detention center more closely approximate those of a non-detention center when sentenced inmates are housed there.
10. Explore options to procure female Special Housing Unit space closer to Federal Correctional Institution Danbury.

APPENDIX 1. METHODOLOGY OF THE OIG REVIEW

Standards

OIG conducted this review in accordance with the Council of the Inspectors General on Integrity and Efficiency's *Quality Standards for Inspection and Evaluation* (January 2012).

Purpose and Scope

OIG conducted this review to examine BOP's efforts and capacity to ensure that BOP-wide policies, programs, and decisions address the unique needs of female inmates. Our review analyzed BOP inmate population data, as well as BOP policies and programs from FY 2012 through FY 2016. We also included in our analysis the revised Female Offender Manual issued by BOP in November 2016, as well as new staff training materials that BOP launched in FY 2017, during the course of our fieldwork. We focused our analysis on how BOP's Women and Special

Populations Branch and other relevant BOP branches implement gender-responsive trauma treatment and pregnancy programs and examined how BOP has implemented policies relevant to physical searches of female inmates and inmate access to feminine hygiene products. Lastly, we examined how BOP's decision to convert its low security institution in Danbury, Connecticut, from a female institution to a male institution affected the female inmates who had been housed there. Our review focused on federal offenders incarcerated in the 28 BOP-managed institutions whose populations are all female or mixed gender. We excluded from our analysis inmates housed in contract halfway houses and contract state and local institutions. BOP does not house female inmates in private correctional institutions.

Methodology

Our fieldwork, conducted from July 2016 through September 2017, included interviews, data collection and analyses, and document reviews. We interviewed officials from six divisions of BOP's Central Office. We conducted site visits to 12 of the 28 institutions where BOP houses female inmates, including 5 institutions through video teleconference and 7 institutions in person. For each site visit, we interviewed institution officials and staff. For those institutions that we visited in person, we also interviewed inmates, toured housing units and programming space, and observed the physical landscapes. We visited all three types of BOP institutions for female inmates: minimum security, low security, and administrative. Our site visits also encompassed female institutions; mixed-gender institutions, including a detention center; and BOP's only Federal Medical Center for female inmates.

The seven sites that we visited in person were Federal Correctional Institution (FCI) Aliceville, Federal Medical Center Carswell, Federal Prison Camp (FPC) Bryan, FCI Dublin, Secure Female Facility Hazelton,

Metropolitan Detention Center (MDC) Brooklyn, and FCI Danbury. The five sites where we conducted video teleconferences were FPC Alderson, Federal Correctional Complex (FCC) Victorville, FCI Marianna, FCC Coleman, and FCI Phoenix.

Data Analysis

We analyzed both raw data and data reports provided by BOP, from its prisoner management system, SENTRY, to assess BOP's inmate population and pregnancy program participation. Additionally, to determine whether BOP housed an inmate closer to or farther from home following the inmate's transfer from FCI Danbury, we reviewed SENTRY zip code and transfer location data for the 1,127 inmates transferred from FCI Danbury between August 2013 and March 2014. We performed two SAS calculations to conduct this analysis. First, we calculated the distance between a transferred inmate's home zip code and FCI Danbury's zip code. Second, we calculated the distance between that inmate's home zip code and the zip code of the BOP institution to which that inmate was transferred.

We did not consider the 445 non-U.S. citizen inmates whom BOP transferred or released from FCI Danbury in this analysis because most of these inmates did not have a U.S. residence prior to incarceration. Due to data limitations, we were also unable to conduct a distance analysis for 7 of the 682 U.S. citizen female inmates transferred or released from FCI Danbury.

Interviews

We conducted 217 interviews during the course of this review. We interviewed Central Office officials, including the Assistant Director for the Correctional Programs Division, the General Counsel, a Senior Deputy Assistant Director for the Program Review Division, the Assistant Director of the Reentry Services Division, the Senior Deputy Assistant Director for the Reentry Services Division, the Women and Special Populations Branch

Administrator, the Residential Reentry Management Branch Administrator, the Education Branch Assistant Administrator, the former and current Chiefs and a Section Chief of the Designation and Sentence Computation Center, the Acting Chief of the Construction and Environmental Assessments Branch, the Chief of Mental Health Services, a Mental Health Treatment Coordinator, and two Social Science Research Analysts in the Capacity Planning Branch.

During our site visits, we interviewed 193 staff and inmates, including 10 Wardens, 6 Associate Wardens, 1 Executive Assistant, 1 Captain, 9 Lieutenants, 13 Correctional Officers, 5 Chief Psychologists, 1 Acting Chief Psychologist, 4 Resolve Coordinators, 3 Psychologists, 1 Female Integrated Treatment Program Coordinator, 1 Chief Social Worker, 5 Social Workers, 6 Health Services Administrators, 5 Assistant Health Services Administrators, 2 Clinical Directors, 1 Infectious Disease Coordinator, 1 Health Technician, 1 Pharmacy Technician, 10 Supervisors of Education, 2 Assistant Supervisors of Education, 1 Supervisor of Recreation, 1 Case Management Coordinator, 1 Assistant Case Management Coordinator, 3 Reentry Services Coordinators, 3 Unit Managers, 14 Case Managers, 14 Counselors, 1 Facilities Manager, 1 Maintenance Supervisor, 1 Supervisory Contract Specialist, and 61 inmates. Additionally, we interviewed the program coordinators from four different contract sites that operated BOP's Mothers and Infants Nurturing Together residential program as of December 2017.

Outside BOP, we interviewed a Section Chief from the DOJ Civil Rights Division, Special Litigation Section, as well as three judges from the National Association of Women Judges who were familiar with BOP operations related to female inmates.

Finally, we interviewed officials from the correctional agencies of four states (Alabama, Kansas, Washington, and Wisconsin), as well as the U.S. Navy, to discuss how those agencies meet similar challenges in the management of their female inmate populations. In the report, we refer to the four states and the Navy collectively as five state correctional agencies.

Appendix 2 Map of BOP Institutions for Sentenced Female Inmates

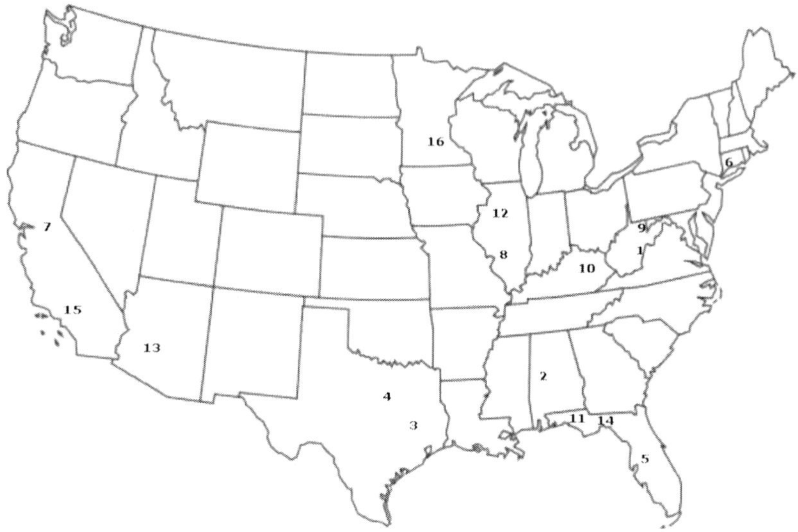

Key to the Map

#	Name	Number of Female Institutions on Site	Security Level(s) of Female Institution(s)
1	Federal Prison Camp Alderson	1	Minimum
2	Federal Correctional Institution Aliceville	2	Low and Minimum
3	Federal Prison Camp Bryan	1	Minimum
4	Federal Medical Center Carswell	2	Minimum and Administrative
5	Federal Correctional Center Coleman	1	Minimum
6	Federal Correctional Institution Danbury	2	Low and Minimum
7	Federal Correctional Institution Dublin	2	Low and Minimum
8	Federal Correctional Institution Greenville	1	Minimum
9	Federal Correctional Institution Hazelton	1	Low
10	Federal Medical Center Lexington	1	Minimum
11	Federal Correctional Institution Marianna	1	Minimum

#	Name	Number of Female Institutions on Site	Security Level(s) of Female Institution(s)
12	Federal Correctional Institution Pekin	1	Minimum
13	Federal Correctional Institution Phoenix	1	Minimum
14	Federal Correctional Institution Tallahassee	1	Low
15	Federal Correctional Institution Victorville II	1	Minimum
16	Federal Correctional Institution Waseca	1	Low

APPENDIX 3

U.S. Department of Justice

Federal Bureau of Prisons

August 30, 2018

MEMORANDUM FOR NINA S. PELLETIER
ASSISTANT INSPECTOR GENERAL
OFFICE OF THE INSPECTOR GENERAL
EVALUATION AND INSPECTIONS DIVISION

FROM: Hugh J. Hurwitz, Acting Director

SUBJECT: Response to the Office of Inspector General's (OIG) Draft Report: Review of the Federal Bureau of Prisons' Management of Its Female Inmate Population

The Bureau of Prisons (BOP) appreciates the opportunity to provide a response to the Office of the Inspector General's above referenced report. Therefore, please find the BOP's responses to the recommendations below:

Recommendation 1: Fully implement ongoing plans to create a permanent program review for the Female Offender Manual that includes in-person visits and an institution-specific rating.

Initial Response: The BOP agrees with this recommendation. The BOP will fully implement ongoing plans to create a permanent program review for the Female Offender Manual that includes in-person visits and an institution-specific rating.

Recommendation 2: Determine the appropriate level of staffing that should be allocated to the Women and Special Populations Branch based on an analysis of its broad mission and responsibilities.

Initial Response: The BOP agrees with this recommendation. The BOP will determine the appropriate level of staffing that should be allocated to the Women and Special Populations Branch based on an analysis of its broad mission and responsibilities.

Recommendation 3: Ensure that all officials who enter into National Executive Staff positions have taken appropriate, current training specific to the unique needs of female inmates and trauma-informed correctional care.

Initial Response: The BOP agrees with this recommendation. The BOP will ensure that all officials who enter into National Executive Staff positions have taken appropriate, current training specific to the unique needs of female inmates and trauma-informed correctional care.

Recommendation 4: Identify ways to expand the staffing of the Resolve program.

Initial Response: The BOP agrees with this recommendation The BOP will identify ways to expand the staffing of the Resolve program.

Recommendation 5: Improve the communication of its pregnancy program availability and eligibility criteria to relevant staff and pregnant inmates to ensure consistent understanding across BOP institutions.

Initial Response: The BOP agrees with this recommendation. The BOP will improve the communication of its pregnancy program availability and eligibility criteria to relevant staff and pregnant inmates to ensure consistent understanding across BOP institutions.

Recommendation 6: Improve data tracking to allow it to more easily identify inmates who are aware of, interested in, eligible for, or participating in pregnancy programs, as well as to assess barriers to participation.

Initial Response: The BOP agrees with this recommendation. The BOP will improve data tracking to allow it to more easily identify inmates who are aware of, interested in, eligible for, or participating in pregnancy programs, as well as to assess barriers to participation.

Recommendation 7: Clarify guidance on the distribution of feminine hygiene products to ensure sufficient access to the amount of products inmates need free of charge.

Initial Response: The BOP agrees with this recommendation. The BOP will clarify guidance on the distribution of feminine hygiene products to ensure sufficient access to the amount of products inmates need free of charge.

Recommendation 8: Improve the availability of female staff at locations in female institutions where inmate searches are common, through the establishment of gender-specific posts or other methods.

Initial Response: The BOP agrees with this recommendation. The BOP will improve the availability of female staff at locations in female institutions where inmate searches are common, through the establishment of gender-specific posts or other methods.

Recommendation 9: Establish policy that determines how long sentenced inmates can be confined in a detention center, or ensure that the conditions of confinement and inmate programming at a detention center more closely approximate those of a non-detention center when sentenced inmates are housed there.

Initial Response: The BOP agrees with this recommendation. The BOP will establish policy that determines how long sentenced inmates can be confined in a detention center, or ensure that the conditions of confinement and inmate programming at a detention center more closely approximate those of a non-detention center when sentenced inmates are housed there.

Recommendation 10: Explore options to procure female Special Housing Unit space closer to Federal Correctional Institution Danbury.

Initial Response: The BOP agrees with this recommendation. The BOP will explore options to procure female Special Housing Unit space closer to Federal Correctional Institution Danbury.

Appendix 4. OIG Analysis of BOP's Response

OIG provided a draft of this chapter to BOP for its comment. BOP's response is included in Appendix 3 to this chapter. OIG's analysis of BOP's response and the actions necessary to close the recommendations are discussed below. Please provide a status update on the 10 recommendations by December 31, 2018.

- *Recommendation 1:* Fully implement ongoing plans to create a permanent program review for the Female Offender Manual that includes in-person visits and an institution-specific rating.
  - *Status:* Resolved.
  - *BOP Response:* BOP concurred with the recommendation and stated that it would fully implement ongoing plans to create a permanent program review for the Female Offender Manual that includes in-person visits and an institution-specific rating.
  - *OIG Analysis:* BOP's planned actions are responsive to our recommendation. Please provide a copy of program review guidelines for the Female Offender Manual that include in-person visits and an institution-specific rating, as well as a schedule of Female Offender Manual program reviews by institution for calendar year 2019.
- *Recommendation 2:* Determine the appropriate level of staffing that should be allocated to the Women and Special Populations Branch based on an analysis of its broad mission and responsibilities.
  - *Status*: Resolved.
  - *BOP Response***:** BOP concurred with the recommendation and stated that it would determine the appropriate level of staffing that should be allocated to the Women and Special Populations Branch based on an analysis of its broad mission and responsibilities.
  - *OIG Analysis:* BOP's planned actions are responsive to our recommendation. Please provide a copy of the analysis BOP

performed of the branch's mission and responsibilities, including a conclusion about the appropriate staffing level for the work identified.

- *Recommendation 3:* Ensure that all officials who enter into National Executive Staff positions have taken appropriate, current training specific to the unique needs of female inmates and trauma-informed correctional care.
    - *Status:* Resolved.
    - *BOP Response*: BOP concurred with the recommendation and stated that it would ensure that all officials who enter into National Executive Staff positions have taken appropriate, current training specific to the unique needs of female inmates and trauma-informed correctional care.
    - *OIG Analysis:* BOP's planned actions are responsive to our recommendation. Please provide an update to the Bureau Mandatory Training Standards or other relevant policy showing how BOP will ensure that all officials entering into National Executive Staff positions have taken BOP's current training specific to the unique needs of female inmates and trauma-informed correctional care.
- *Recommendation 4:* Identify ways to expand the staffing of the Resolve program.
    - *Status:* Resolved.
    - *BOP Response:* BOP concurred with the recommendation and stated that it would identify ways to expand the staffing of the Resolve program.
    - *OIG Analysis:* BOP's planned actions are responsive to our recommendation. Please provide OIG with a copy of BOP's analysis of the Resolve program's staffing needs and the option BOP selected.
- *Recommendation 5:* Improve the communication of its pregnancy program availability and eligibility criteria to relevant staff and pregnant inmates to ensure consistent understanding across BOP institutions.

- *Status:* Resolved.
- *BOP Response:* BOP concurred with the recommendation and stated that it would improve the communication of its pregnancy program availability and eligibility criteria to relevant staff and pregnant inmates to ensure consistent understanding across BOP institutions.
- *OIG Analysis:* BOP's planned actions are responsive to our recommendation. Please provide a copy of any notices, operations memoranda, program statements, or other written materials used to communicate information about pregnancy program availability and eligibility criteria to inmates and institution staff. Please also include a description of how the materials were disseminated and a list of the institutions and position titles of the addressees who received them.

- *Recommendation 6:* Improve data tracking to allow it to more easily identify inmates who are aware of, interested in, eligible for, or participating in pregnancy programs, as well as to assess barriers to participation.
  - *Status:* Resolved.
  - *BOP Response:* BOP concurred with the recommendation and stated that it would improve data tracking to allow it to more easily identify inmates who are aware of, interested in, eligible for, or participating in pregnancy programs, as well as to assess barriers to participation.
  - *OIG Analysis:* BOP's planned actions are responsive to our recommendation. Please describe how BOP intends to track pregnant inmates to more easily identify inmate awareness of, interest in, eligibility for, participation in, and barriers to participation in BOP's two pregnancy programs.
- *Recommendation 7:* Clarify guidance on the distribution of feminine hygiene products to ensure sufficient access to the amount of products inmates need free of charge.
  - *Status:* Resolved.

- *BOP Response:* BOP concurred with the recommendation and stated that it would clarify guidance on the distribution of feminine hygiene products to ensure sufficient access to the amount of products inmates need free of charge.
- *OIG Analysis:* BOP's planned actions are responsive to our recommendation. Please provide a copy of BOP policy clarifying that female inmates should have sufficient access to the amount of feminine hygiene products they need, free of charge, and a description of how the policy was disseminated, including a list of the institutions and position titles of the addressees who received it.

- *Recommendation 8:* Improve the availability of female staff at locations in female institutions where inmate searches are common, through the establishment of gender-specific posts or other methods.
  - *Status:* Resolved.
  - *BOP Response:* BOP concurred with the recommendation and stated that it would improve the availability of female staff at locations in female institutions where inmate searches are common, through the establishment of gender-specific posts or other methods.
  - *OIG Analysis:* BOP's planned actions are responsive to our recommendation. Please describe the method BOP selected to improve the availability of female staff at locations in female institutions where inmate searches are common.
- *Recommendation 9:* Establish policy that determines how long sentenced inmates can be confined in a detention center, or ensures that the conditions of confinement and inmate programming at a detention center more closely approximate those of a non-detention center when sentenced inmates are housed there.
  - *Status:* Resolved.
  - *BOP Response:* BOP concurred with the recommendation and stated that it would establish policy that determines how long sentenced inmates can be confined in a detention center, or

ensures that the conditions of confinement and inmate programming at a detention center more closely approximate those of a non-detention center when sentenced inmates are housed there.

- *OIG Analysis:* BOP's planned actions are responsive to our recommendation. Please provide a copy of BOP policy that defines the length of time sentenced inmates can be confined in a detention center or describe how BOP would ensure that the conditions of confinement and inmate programming at detention centers more closely approximates those of a non-detention center when sentenced inmates are housed there.

- *Recommendation 10:* Explore options to procure female Special Housing Unit space closer to Federal Correctional Institution Danbury.
  - *Status:* Resolved.
  - *BOP Response*: BOP concurred with the recommendation and stated that it would explore options to procure female Special Housing Unit space closer to Federal Correctional Institution Danbury.
  - *OIG Analysis*: BOP's planned actions are responsive to our recommendation. Please describe the options BOP considered to procure female Special Housing Unit space closer to Federal Correctional Institution Danbury, research conducted by BOP to assess each option considered, and the option BOP selected.

In: Bureau of Prisons (BOP)
Editor: Melody Kelley
ISBN: 978-1-53615-292-0

Chapter 3

APPROPRIATIONS FOR THE BUREAU OF PRISONS (BOP): IN BRIEF*

Nathan James

SUMMARY

The Bureau of Prisons (BOP) is the largest correctional agency in the country in terms of the number of prisoners under its jurisdiction. BOP must confine any offender convicted and sentenced to a term of imprisonment in a federal court.

Changes in federal criminal justice policy since the early 1980s spurred growth in the federal prison population. The total number of inmates under BOP's jurisdiction increased from approximately 25,000 in FY1980 to over 192,000 in FY2016. While the federal prison population in FY2016 is nearly 7 times larger than what it was in FY1980, the number of inmates under the BOP's jurisdiction peaked in FY2013 at approximately 219,000 inmates. The federal prison population has decreased each fiscal year from FY2013 to FY2016.

BOP's appropriations increased by nearly $7.149 billion from FY1980 to FY2016, which was the peak of BOP's nominal

* This is an edited, reformatted and augmented version of Congressional Research Service Publication No. R42486, Updated January 29, 2018.

appropriations. Between FY1980 and FY2016, the average annual increase in BOP's appropriations was approximately $199 million. Its appropriations decreased by $340 million in FY2017.

BOP's annual budget is divided between two major accounts: Salaries and Expenses (S&E, i.e., the operating budget) and Buildings and Facilities (B&F, i.e., the capital budget).The nearly continuous increase in BOP's appropriations is in large part driven by a nearly unbroken year-by-year increases in the S&E account. Funding for the S&E account has continued to increase even though the prison population decreased from FY2013 to FY2016. An increasing per capita cost of incarceration might explain why funding for the S&E account has not decreased along with the prison population, but it might also be due to the fact that the prison population has not decreased to a point where BOP can reduce staff and shutter prisons.

The nominal per capita cost of incarcerating an inmate in the federal system has increased every fiscal year from FY2000 to FY2016, from approximately $22,000 per inmate to nearly $35,000 per inmate. After adjusting for inflation, the overall cost of incarceration was relatively flat from FY2000 to FY2012, but in recent fiscal years increases in per capita costs have started to outstrip inflation.

A comparison of requested and enacted funding for BOP's S&E and B&F accounts shows that Congress has been somewhat more likely to fund the Administration's request for prison construction and less likely to fully fund the Administration's request for operating the federal prison system. From FY1980 to FY2017, appropriations were lower than the Administration's request for the B&F account 16 times while appropriations were lower than the request for the S&E account 24 times.

One concern among some policymakers is that BOP's expanding budget is starting to consume a larger share of the Department of Justice's (DOJ's) overall annual appropriations. A review of funding for DOJ and BOP show that since FY1980 both BOP's total budget and the S&E account have, in general, encompassed a growing share of DOJ's annual appropriations.

INTRODUCTION

The Bureau of Prisons (BOP) is the largest correctional agency in the country in terms of the number of prisoners under its jurisdiction.[1] BOP

[1] E. Ann Carson and Elizabeth Anderson, *Prisoners in 2015*, U.S. Department of Justice, Office of Justice Programs, Bureau of Justice Statistics, NCJ 250229, Washington, DC, December 2016, p. 5.

was established in 1930 to house federal inmates, professionalize the prison service, and ensure consistent and centralized administration of the federal prison system.[2] BOP must confine any offender convicted and sentenced to a term of imprisonment in a federal court.

Changes in federal criminal justice policy since the early 1980s—enforcing a growing number of federal crimes, replacing indeterminate sentencing with a determinate sentencing structure through sentencing guidelines, and increasing the number of federal offenses subject to mandatory minimum sentences—led to rapid growth in the federal prison population. The total number of inmates under BOP's jurisdiction increased from approximately 25,000 in FY1980 to over 219,000 in FY2013.[3] Between FY1980 and FY2013, the federal prison population increased, on average, by approximately 5,900 inmates annually. However, since the peak in FY2013, the number of inmates in the federal prison system decreased each subsequent fiscal year to approximately 192,000 inmates in FY2016.[4]

Generally, the increase in the federal prison population necessitated an increase in appropriations for BOP's operations and infrastructure. In FY1980, Congress appropriated $330.0 *million* for BOP; by FY2016, the total appropriation for BOP reached $7.479 *billion*, which was the largest nominal appropriation ever for BOP. Appropriations for BOP have generally continued to increase since FY2013 (FY2017 was the exception) even though the prison population has decreased since that time. Increasing appropriations for BOP, despite the declining prison population, could be the result of a growing per capita cost of incarceration or BOP's need to maintain staffing levels commensurate with the size of the prison population.

This chapter provides an overview of BOP's appropriations since FY1980. Specifically, this chapter examines trends in BOP's total

---

[2] U.S. Department of Justice, Bureau of Prisons, *About the Bureau of Prisons*, p. 1.

[3] Data on the number of federal prison inmates can be found at https://www.bop.gov/about/statistics/population_statistics.jsp.

[4] In FY2013, the number of inmates under the BOP's jurisdiction was 219,298; in FY2014 it was 214,149; in FY2015 it was 205,723; and in FY2016 it was 192,170. At the time this report was updated, FY2016 was the most recent fiscal year for which federal prison population data were available.

appropriations, changes in funding for BOP's appropriations account, and trends in funding for the decision units under BOP's appropriations accounts. The report provides a brief analysis of how the Administration's requested funding for BOP compares to enacted appropriations. It also discusses changes in the per capita cost of incarceration and how appropriations for BOP have changed relative to those for the Department of Justice, both issues that have been of interest to policymakers.

APPROPRIATIONS FOR BOP

Trends in BOP's Total Appropriations

As shown in *Figure 1*, BOP's appropriations increased by nearly $7.149 billion from FY1980 to FY2016. FY2016 was the peak, in nominal terms, for BOP's funding. BOP's funding decreased by $340 million in FY2017. Between FY1980 and FY2016, the average annual increase in BOP's appropriations was approximately $199 million. The increasing appropriations for BOP generally coincided with an increase in the number of inmates under BOP's jurisdiction. This trend changed somewhat in recent years. BOP's appropriations increased each fiscal year from FY2014 to FY2016 even though the total number of federal inmates decreased in each of those fiscal years.

Figure 1 also shows that BOP's appropriations have increased at a rate that is significantly greater than inflation, as indicated by the positive slope on the inflation-adjusted line in the figure. In FY2017 inflation-adjusted dollars, BOP's appropriations increased 787% from FY1980 to FY2016. BOP's appropriations increased 732%, in inflation-adjusted dollars, when accounting for the decrease in appropriations for FY2017.[5]

It has been argued that even though appropriations for BOP are discretionary, they are effectively mandatory because "[b]y law, the BOP must accept and provide for all [f]ederal inmates, including but not limited

[5] Information on BOP's appropriations can be found in *Appendix A*.

to inmate care, custodial staff, contract beds, food, and medical costs. BOP cannot control the number of inmates sentenced to prison, and unlike other [f]ederal agencies, cannot limit assigned workloads and thereby control operating costs."[6]

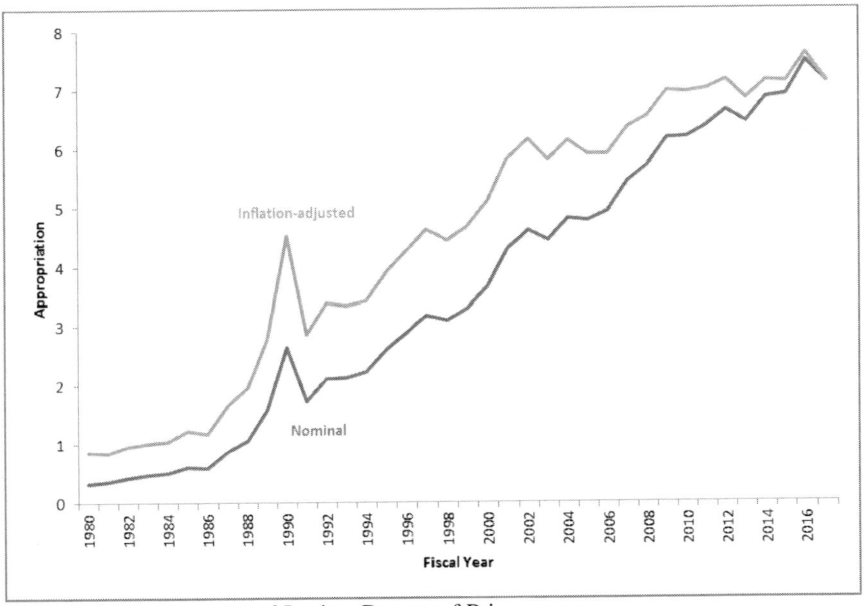

Source: U.S. Department of Justice, Bureau of Prisons.

Notes: Nominal appropriations were adjusted for inflation using the Gross Domestic Product (GDP) Chained Price Index presented in Table 10.1 of the FY2018 Budget of the U.S. Government. Inflation-adjusted amounts are presented in FY2017 dollars. The spike in BOP's funding for FY1990 was the result of Congress appropriating $1.512 billion for the B&F account (see Table A-1). The FY2013 enacted amount reflects the amount sequestered per the Budget Control Act of 2011(P.L. 112-25).

Figure 1. Nominal and Adjusted Appropriations for the Bureau of Prisons, FY1980-FY2017. (Appropriations in billions of dollars)

---

[6] U.S. Congress, Senate Committee on Appropriations, Subcommittee on Commerce, Justice, Science, and Related Agencies, *Departments of Commerce and Justice, and Science, and Related Agencies Appropriations Bill, 2013*, report to accompany S. 2323, 112th Cong., 2nd sess., April 19, 2012, S.Rept. 112-158 (Washington: GPO, 2012), p. 64.

Trends in BOP Appropriations by Account

Nearly all of BOP's operations are funded through annual appropriations provided by Congress.[7] BOP's annual budget is divided between two major accounts: Salaries and Expenses (S&E) and Buildings and Facilities (B&F). The S&E account (i.e., the operating budget) provides for the custody and care of federal inmates and for the daily maintenance and operations of correctional facilities, regional offices, and BOP's central office in Washington, DC. It also provides funding for the incarceration of federal inmates in state, local, and private facilities. The B&F account (i.e., the capital budget) provides funding for the construction of new facilities and the modernization, repair, and expansion of existing facilities.[8]

Two trends emerge from a review of BOP's appropriations from FY1980 through FY2017. First, while there has been a nearly continuous increase in the overall appropriations for BOP, it is in large part driven by an almost continuous increase in appropriations for BOP's Salaries and Expenses (S&E) account since FY1980 (see *Figure 2*). The one exception to this trend is the appropriation for FY2013, which is lower than the FY2012 appropriation due to the sequestration ordered pursuant to the Budget Control Act of 2011 (P.L. 112-25).

In general, appropriations for BOP's S&E account increased as the prison population increased, which is not surprising given that the S&E account funds the operation of the federal prison system, including the salaries and benefits of both correctional officers and other institutional employees.

---

[7] The operations of the Federal Prison Industries (FPI) are supported by revenue generated through the sale of prisoner-made goods to federal agencies. In addition, some programs, goods, and services (such as compensation for inmates participating in non-FPI jobs) are paid for by funds generated through the sale of goods to inmates through the prison commissary.

[8] In addition to appropriations for the S&E and B&F accounts, Congress usually places a cap on the amount of revenue generated by the Federal Prison Industries that can be used for administrative expenses in the annual Commerce, Justice, Science, and Related Agencies appropriations act. Although Congress does not appropriate funding for the administrative expenses of FPI, the administrative expenses cap is scored as enacted budget authority.

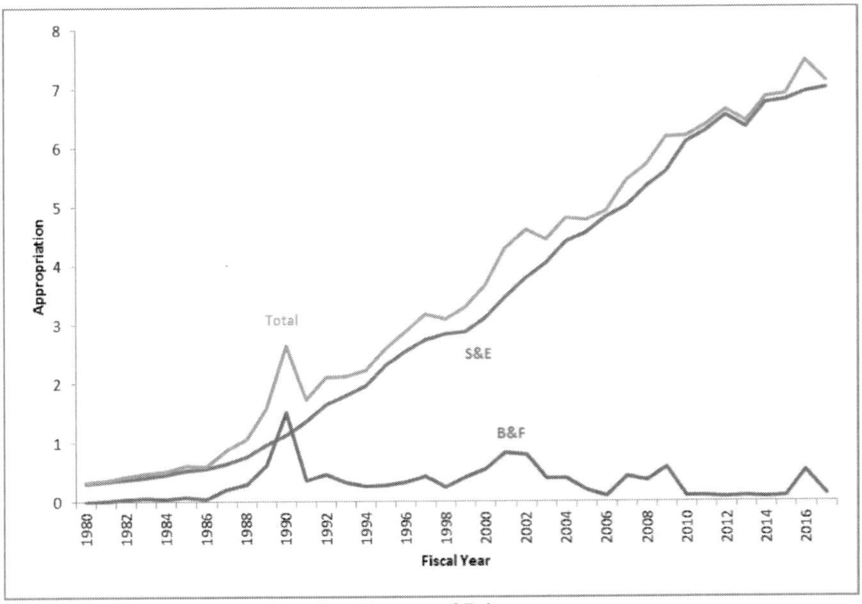

Source: U.S. Department of Justice, Bureau of Prisons.

Notes: Amounts in Figure 2 include all supplemental appropriations and any rescissions of enacted budget authority, but they do not include rescissions of unobligated balances. From FY1980 to FY1995, funding for the National Institute of Corrections (NIC) was included in a separate account. Since FY1996, funding for the NIC has been included in the S&E account. In this figure, funding for the NIC for FY1980-FY1995 was added to the S&E account to make funding for the S&E account comparable across fiscal years. The FY2013-enacted amount reflects the amount sequestered per the Budget Control Act of 2011(P.L. 112-25).

Figure 2. Appropriations for BOP, by Account, FY1980-FY2017. (Appropriations in billions of nominal dollars)

BOP hired more officers and other employees as it opened more prisons and supervised more inmates. However, funding for the S&E account has continued to increase, albeit at a reduced rate, even though the prison population has decreased each fiscal year from FY2013 to FY2016.[9] BOP has continued to request increased funding for the S&E account even though it is housing fewer inmates, and Congress has continued to increase

[9] On average, appropriations for BOP's S&E account increased by 10% each fiscal year from FY1980 to FY2013. In comparison, S&E appropriations increased by 7% in FY2014, by 1% in FY2015, by 2% in FY2016, and by 1% in FY2017.

appropriations, though generally below the level requested. BOP notes that additional funding is needed to cover the cost of pay raises and benefits for employees, as well as to cover growing costs associated with inmate health care, food, and prison utilities. Also, during some of these years, BOP requested additional funding to increase its capacity to provide programs and services for inmates (e.g., reentry programming and mental health treatment) and to hire more staff to increase institutional safety, something BOP might not have been able to do during the years when the inmate population was growing at a sustained clip and resources were dedicated to providing basic levels of care and security.[10] In addition, even though there are fewer inmates under the BOP's jurisdiction, the federal prison system is still operating over its rated capacity.[11] In short, the federal prison population has not declined enough that BOP could start to close prisons and reduce staff, which would help bring down the cost of the federal prison system.

Second, funding for the Buildings and Facilities (B&F) account is more irregular, with Congress appropriating more in some fiscal years and less in others. The irregularity in B&F funding is likely the result of the cyclical nature of the expansion of BOP's prison capacity as more offenders entered the federal prison system. Congress would appropriate funding to help boost bedspace in the federal prison system; BOP would use that funding to plan and construct new prisons. Upon completion of the new prison, BOP's capacity would expand, but it would need to expand again in later years as the prison population continued to grow, and the cycle would begin anew. In FY2017, a $400 million decrease in funding

---

[10] In a September 2012 report, the Government Accountability Office noted some of the effects that a growing prison population had on the BOP's operations, including waiting lists for rehabilitative programs and risks to institutional security resulting from increasing staff-to-inmate ratios. U.S. Government Accountability Office, *Bureau of Prisons: Growing Inmate Crowding Negatively Affects Inmates, Staff, and Infrastructure*, GAO-12-473, September 2012, pp. 48-63.

[11] BOP reports that at the end of FY2016, the federal prison system was operating at 16% over its rated capacity. However, this is down from 30% overcrowding at the end of FY2014. U.S. Department of Justice, Bureau of Prisons, *FY2018 Performance Budget, Congressional Submission, Salaries and Expenses*, p. 7.

for the B&F account was the primary reason why BOP's total appropriation decreased for FY2017.[12]

Trends in BOP's Funding by Decision Unit

Each of BOP's two appropriations accounts are divided into decision units, each of which fund specific aspects of BOP operations. The S&E account is divided into four decision units:

- *Inmate Care and Programs*: This decision unit covers the cost of inmate food, medical supplies, institutional and release clothing, welfare services, transportation, gratuities, staff salaries, and other operational costs directly related to providing inmate care. It provides funding for inmate programs, including education and vocational training, psychological services, religious programs, and drug treatment. This decision unit also covers costs associated with regional and central office administration and support related to providing inmate care.
- *Institution Security and Administration*: This decision unit funds institution maintenance, motor pool operations, powerhouse operations, institution security, and other administrative functions. It also covers costs associated with regional and central office administrative and management support functions such as research and evaluation, systems support, financial management, budget functions, safety, and legal counsel.
- *Contract Confinement*: This decision unit provides for the costs associated with the confinement of federal inmates in contract facilities, which include private prisons, Residential Reentry Centers (RRC), state and local facilities, and home confinement. It provides funding for the management and oversight of contract

[12] For FY2016, Congress appropriated $444 million under the B&F account for the construction of a new facility in Letcher County, KY. BOP's FY2018 budget justification included a proposal to rescind this funding.

confinement functions. This decision unit also provides funding for the National Institute of Corrections (NIC).

- *Management and Administration*: This decision unit provides funding for costs associated with general administration and provides funding for BOP's central office, regional offices, and staff training centers.

Since FY1999, approximately 80% of BOP's S&E funding has gone to combined appropriations for the Inmate Care and Programs and the Institution Security and Administration decision units. Funding for these two decision units has increased at about the same rate as funding for the S&E account overall. From FY1999 to FY2017, funding for the Inmate Care and Programs decision unit increased 141% and funding for the Institution Security and Administration decision unit increased 123%. In comparison, funding for the S&E account increased 143% over the same time period.

Funding for the Contract Confinement decision unit increased 295% between FY1999 and FY2017. The steeper increase in funding for the Contract Confinement decision unit comes as BOP has relied on confining more inmates in contract facilities, along with growing demand for RRC bedspace (a byproduct of more inmates being imprisoned and eventually released after serving their prison sentences).

While funding for the Contract Confinement decision unit outpaced the growth of funding for the S&E account overall, funding for the Management and Administration decision unit grew at a rate below that of the S&E account. From FY1999 to FY2017, funding for the Management and Administration decision unit increased 74%.

The B&F account is divided into two decision units:

- *New Construction:* This decision unit covers lease payments for the Oklahoma Transfer Center, the salaries and administrative costs of staff involved in new prison construction, construction of inmate work program areas and expansion and conversion projects (i.e., additional special housing unit space).

- *Modernization and Repair*: This decision unit provides resources to undertake essential rehabilitation, modernization, and renovation of correctional facilities and their grounds. This includes modifications to facilities to accommodate correctional programs, repair or replace utilities systems and other critical infrastructure, repair projects at existing institutions, and maintain all systems and structures in a good state of repair.

In 10 of the 19 fiscal years since FY1999, a majority of the funding for the B&F account has been dedicated for new prison construction. In fiscal years where funding for the B&F account increased, funding for new prison construction generally increased. On average, Congress appropriated $333 million for the B&F account from FY1999 to FY2017. Fiscal years in which funding for modernization and repair accounted for a majority of B&F funding were usually years in which funding for the B&F account was significantly below this average, usually when total B&F funding was less than $100 million.

Requested Versus Enacted Funding for BOP

A comparison of BOP's annual appropriations for its S&E and B&F accounts to the Administration's request for both accounts shows that Congress has been more likely to fund the Administration's request for prison construction and less likely to fully fund the Administration's request for operating the federal prison system (see *Figure 3*). The requested appropriation indicates what BOP believed it would need to properly manage the prison population each fiscal year. The data suggest that in many fiscal years BOP operated with a budget below what it felt was adequate.

The data presented in *Figure 3* show that from FY1980 to FY2017, Congress appropriated less than the Administration's request for the B&F account 16 times. Over the same time period Congress appropriated less than the Administration's request for the S&E account 24 times.[13] In contrast, however, the amount appropriated for the S&E account between FY2007 and FY2010 actually exceeded the Administration's request. The additional amounts provided by Congress during these fiscal years, as noted by the House Committee on Appropriations, were to compensate for underfunding BOP in previous years, which resulted in inadequate staffing levels and shortfalls in inmate programs.[14] In the past, both the House and the Senate appropriations committees reported that they felt the Administration's requests for BOP were inadequate, which did not allow BOP to meet its basic operational needs.[15] However, Congress has not raised similar concerns in more recent fiscal years. Appropriations for the S&E account have been below the Administration's request for six of the past seven fiscal years, by an average of $232 million.

PER CAPITA COST OF INCARCERATION

As noted above, appropriations for BOP have continued to increase even though the federal prison population has decreased in recent years. This trend might be partly explained by the increasing per capita cost for incarceration. As show in *Figure 4*, the nominal per capita cost of incarceration has increased from approximately $22,000 per inmate in FY2000 to almost $35,000 in FY2016, a 61% rise.[16] From FY2000 to

---

[13] Information on the Administration's requested funding for BOP can be found in **Appendix A**.

[14] U.S. Congress, House Committee on Appropriations, *Omnibus Appropriations Act, 2009*, committee print, 111th Cong., 1st sess., March 2009 (Washington: GPO, 2009), p. 274.

[15] Ibid. See also, U.S. Congress, House Committee on Appropriations, *Departments of Transportation and Housing and Urban Development, and Related Agencies Appropriations Act, 2010*, Conference Report to Accompany H.R. 3288, 111th Cong., 1st sess., December 8, 2009, H.Rept. 111-366 (Washington: GPO, 2009), p. 671; U.S. Congress, Senate Committee on Appropriations, Subcommittee on Commerce, Justice, Science, and Related Agencies, *Departments of Commerce and Justice, and Science, and Related Agencies Appropriations Bill, 2013*, report to accompany S. 2323, 112th Cong., 2nd sess., April 19, 2012, S.Rept. 112-158 (Washington: GPO, 2012), p. 65.

[16] BOP calculates the per capita cost of incarceration by dividing total obligations for the fiscal year by the average daily population.

FY2012, the per capita cost of incarceration roughly increased at the same rate as inflation. However, since FY2013 increases in the per capita cost have started to outstrip inflation.

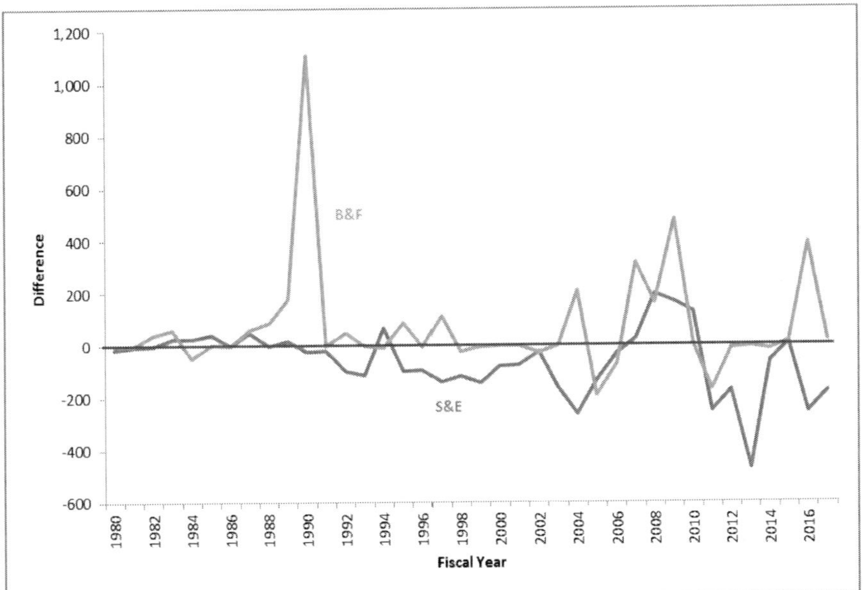

Source: Appropriated amounts were provided by the U.S. Department of Justice, Bureau of Prisons. The Administration's requested amounts were taken from the appendix to the Budget of the United States Government, for FY1980-FY2017.

Notes: Between FY1980 and FY1995, appropriations for the National Institute of Corrections (NIC) were provided in a separate account. After FY1995, the operating expenses for NIC are paid out of BOP's S&E account. Therefore, to make appropriations for the S&E account as comparable as possible, appropriations for the NIC for FY1980-FY1995 were added to appropriations for the S&E account. Between FY1996 and FY2000, BOP received an amount from the Violent Crime Reduction Trust Fund, which, according to BOP, was used for substance abuse treatment. As such, these amounts were also added to the S&E account.

Figure 3. Difference Between Appropriations and the Administration's Request for BOP's S&E and B&F Accounts. (Amounts in millions of dollars)

The increasing per capita cost of incarceration is partly due to inflationary pressures, such as the increasing cost of health care, food, clothing, and utilities.[17] However, it is notable that the per capita cost of incarceration has increased at a greater rate than inflation since FY2013, which coincides with the decreasing prison population.[18] Stable or increasing obligations combined with a decreasing prison population will result in increasing per capita costs because the shared inmate expenses are dispersed across fewer inmates.

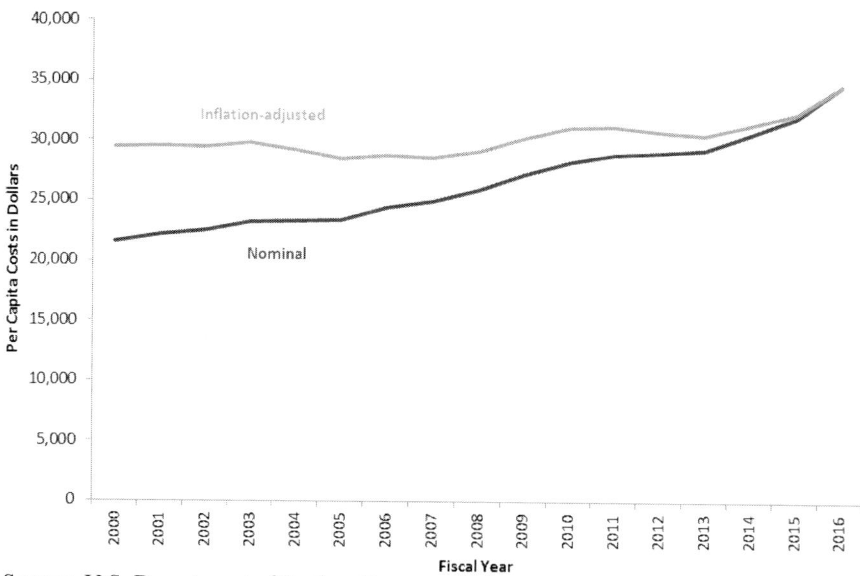

Source: U.S. Department of Justice, Bureau of Prisons.

Notes: Nominal appropriations were adjusted for inflation using the Gross Domestic Product (GDP) Chained Price Index presented in Table 10.1 of the FY2018 Budget of the U.S. Government. Inflation-adjusted amounts are presented in FY2016 dollars.

Figure 4. Per Capita Cost of Incarceration, FY2000-FY2016.

---

[17] For example, BOP reports that obligations for inmate medical costs increased from approximately $400 million in FY2007 to approximately $675 million in FY2016. U.S. Department of Justice, Bureau of Prisons, *FY2018 Performance Budget, Congressional Submission, Salaries and Expenses*, p. 24.

[18] On average, the per capita cost of incarceration increased by 2% each fiscal year between FY2000 and FY2013. The per capita cost of incarceration increased 5% in FY2014, 4% in FY2015, and 9% in FY2016.

Per capita costs are not equivalent to marginal costs (i.e., what it costs BOP to incarcerate one additional inmate). For example, if the per capita cost of incarceration is $22,000 per inmate and BOP's prison population decreased by 1,000 inmates, it does not mean that BOP would save $22 million. Per capita costs do not equate to marginal costs because per capita costs reflect the total amount BOP obligates in a fiscal year divided by that fiscal year's average daily population. Some costs (e.g., food and clothing expenses) would decrease if BOP incarcerated fewer inmates. However, obligations also account for items like staff salaries, which might not change until the prison population decreases to a point where BOP could close prisons and reduce staff. For example, if all of BOP's high security facilities hold 10% more inmates than their rated capacity and BOP's prison population decreases to a point where these facilities hold the same number of inmates as their rated capacity, it is likely that BOP would not reduce staffing at those prisons, which would mean that obligations for high security facilities for that fiscal year would not decline significantly.

APPROPRIATIONS FOR BOP RELATIVE TO THOSE FOR THE DEPARTMENT OF JUSTICE

One concern among some policymakers is that BOP's expanding budget is starting to consume a larger share of the Department of Justice's (DOJ) overall annual appropriations. *Figure 5* shows what proportion of DOJ's annual discretionary budget was dedicated to BOP. BOP's overall budget is more susceptible to fluctuations due to changes in year-to-year appropriations for BOP's B&F account. The trend lines (the dashed lines in the figure) show that since FY1980, both BOP's total budget and the S&E account have, in general, encompassed a growing share of DOJ's annual appropriations. The noticeable spike in BOP's share of DOJ's annual appropriations in FY1990 was the result of Congress appropriating more than $1 billion for the B&F account. In addition, the decrease in BOP's share of DOJ's appropriations observed in FY2009, a break in a general upward trend that started in FY2000, was the result of Congress appropriating an additional $4 billion for DOJ under the American Recovery and Reinvestment Act of 2009 (P.L. 111-5).

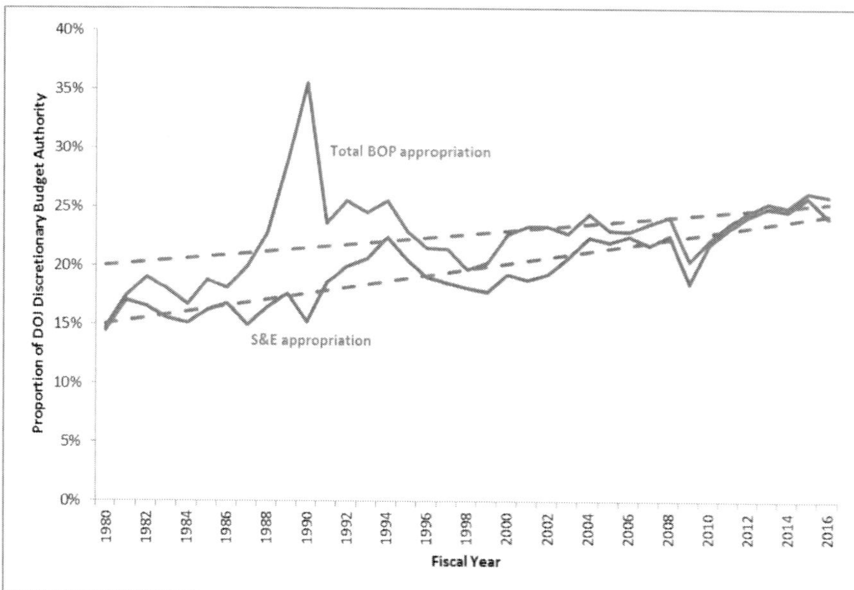

Source: BOP's annual appropriations data were provided by the U.S. Department of Justice, Bureau of Prisons. Annual discretionary budget authority data for the Department of Justice for FY1980-FY2016 were taken from Table 5.4 from the FY2018 Budget of the United States Government. Final FY2017 discretionary budget authority for DOJ was not provided in Table 5.4 of the President's FY2018 budget.

Figure 5. BOP's Appropriation as a Share of DOJ's Discretionary Budget Authority, FY1980-FY2016.

APPENDIX A. BOP APPROPRIATIONS: TOTAL AND BY DECISION UNIT

Table A-1. Requested and Enacted Appropriations for the Bureau of Prisons, FY1980-FY2017 (Appropriations in thousands of dollars)

Fiscal Year	Request			Appropriated		
	Salaries and Expenses	Buildings and Facilities	Total	Salaries and Expenses	Buildings and Facilities	Total
1980	$338,051	$5,960	$344,011	$323,884	$5,960	$329,844
1981	355,258	10,466	365,724	351,759	10,020	361,779
1982	377,267	14,731	391,998	378,016	56,481	434,497
1983	387,587	6,667	394,254	412,133	66,667	478,800
1984	437,928	97,142	535,070	464,850	47,711	512,561
1985	497,662	82,556	580,218	536,932	86,043	622,975
1986	560,004	46,063	606,067	561,480	44,082	605,562
1987	608,302	159,152	767,454	656,941	219,249	876,190
1988	771,360	210,334	981,694	772,013	297,076	1,069,089
1989	943,530	436,554	1,380,084	962,016	612,914	1,574,930
1990	1,162,666	401,332	1,563,998	1,138,778	1,511,953	2,650,731
1991	1,381,889	374,358	1,756,247	1,363,645	374,358	1,738,003
1992	1,748,056	411,593	2,159,649	1,649,121	462,090	2,111,211
1993	1,906,806	339,225	2,246,031	1,793,470	339,225	2,132,695
1994	1,895,214	276,850	2,172,064	1,962,605	269,543	2,232,148
1995	2,417,096	191,021	2,608,117	2,319,722	276,301	2,596,023
1996	2,640,417	337,228	2,977,645	2,546,893[a]	334,728	2,881,621
1997	2,888,316	320,924	3,209,240	2,748,427[b]	435,200	3,183,627
1998	2,965,642	278,057	3,243,699	2,847,777[c]	255,133	3,102,910
1999	3,032,494	413,997	3,446,491	2,888,853[d]	410,997	3,299,850
2000	3,191,928	558,791	3,750,719	3,111,073[e]	556,780	3,667,853
2001	3,545,769	835,660	4,381,429	3,469,739	833,822	4,303,561
2002	3,829,437	833,273	4,662,710	3,805,118	807,808	4,612,926
2003	4,208,459	396,609	4,605,068	4,044,788	396,632	4,441,420

Table A-1. (Continued)

Fiscal Year	**Request**			**Appropriated**		
	Salaries and Expenses	Buildings and Facilities	Total	Salaries and Expenses	Buildings and Facilities	Total
2004	4,677,214	187,900	4,865,114	4,414,313	393,515	4,807,828
2005	4,706,232	397,700	5,103,932	4,571,385	205,076	4,776,461
2006	4,859,649	170,112	5,029,761	4,830,160	99,961	4,930,121
2007	4,987,059	117,102	5,104,161	5,012,433	432,425	5,444,858
2008	5,151,440	210,003	5,361,443	5,346,740	372,720	5,719,460
2009	5,435,754	95,807	5,531,561	5,600,792	575,807	6,176,599
2010	5,979,831	96,744	6,076,575	6,106,231	99,155	6,205,386
2011	6,533,779	269,733	6,803,512	6,282,410	98,957	6,381,367
2012	6,724,266	99,934	6,824,200	6,551,281	90,000	6,641,281
2013	6,820,217	99,189	6,919,406	6,349,248	95,356	6,444,604
2014	6,831,150	105,244	6,936,394	6,769,000	90,000	6,859,000
2015	6,804,000	90,000	6,894,000	6,815,000	106,000	6,921,000
2016	7,204,158	140,564	7,344,722	6,948,500	530,000	7,478,500
2017	7,186,225	113,022	7,299,247	7,008,800	130,000	7,138,800

Source: U.S. Department of Justice, Bureau of Prisons.

Notes: Amounts in Table A-1 include all supplemental appropriations and any rescissions of enacted budget authority, but they do not include rescissions of unobligated balances. From FY1980 to FY1995, funding for the National Institute of Corrections (NIC) was included in a separate account. Since FY1996, funding for the NIC has been included in the S&E account. In this table, funding for the NIC for FY1980-FY1995 was added to the S&E account to make funding for the S&E account comparable across fiscal years. The FY2013-enacted amount reflects the amount sequestered per the Budget Control Act of 2011(P.L. 112-25).

[a] Includes $13.5 million appropriated from the Violent Crime Reduction Trust Fund (VCRTF).

[b] Includes $25.2 million appropriated from the VCRTF.

[c] Includes $26.1 million appropriated from the VCRTF.

[d] Includes $26.5 million appropriated from the VCRTF.

[e] Includes $22.5 million appropriated from the VCRTF.

Table A-2. Appropriations for BOP, by Decision Unit, FY1999-FY2017 (Appropriations in thousands of dollars)

Fiscal		Salaries and Expenses			Buildings and Facilities	
Year	Inmate Care and Programs	Institution Security and Administ-ration	Contract Confine-ment	Management and Administ-ration	New Construction	Moderni-zation and Repair
1999	$1,090,148	$1,401,349	$255,062	$142,249	$322,963	$88,034
2000	1,123,856	1,494,809	344,773	147,635	441,003	115,777
2001	1,208,480	1,601,518	511,579	148,162	710,816	123,006
2002	1,311,335	1,722,567	620,145	151,071	675,040	132,768
2003	1,454,481	1,868,538	567,365	154,404	262,956	133,676
2004	1,624,308	2,050,417	574,473	165,115	177,620	164,000
2005	1,682,656	2,094,917	627,135	166,677	25,372	179,704
2006	1,740,011	2,227,223	683,031	179,895	48,115	51,846
2007	1,774,048	2,297,055	757,851	183,479	368,875	63,550
2008	1,942,077	2,409,112	814,529	181,022	302,720	70,000
2009	2,070,002	2,495,196	840,933	194,661	465,180	110,627
2010	2,215,992	2,708,651	981,112	200,476	25,386	73,769
2011	2,294,174	2,783,664	996,772	207,800	25,335	73,622
2012	2,421,272	2,880,290	1,040,213	209,506	23,035	66,695
2013	2,424,620	2,717,938	1,017,297	189,393	23,649	71,707
2014	2,525,039	2,966,364	1,074,808	202,789	22,852	67,148
2015	2,587,936	3,002,827	1,011,505	211,347	25,000	81,000
2016	2,679,562	3,025,209	1,015,739	227,990	444,000	86,000
2017	2,625,439	3,129,075	1,006,522	247,764	50,000	80,000

Source: U.S. Department of Justice, Bureau of Prisons.

Notes: Amounts in this table include all supplemental appropriations and any rescissions of enacted budget authority, but they do not include rescissions of unobligated balances. The FY2013-enacted amount reflects the amount sequestered per the Budget Control Act of 2011(P.L. 112-25).

APPENDIX B. BOP PER CAPITA COSTS

Table B-1. Per Capita Cost of Incarceration in the Federal Prison System, FY2000-FY2016 (Security Level)

Fiscal Year	All of BOP	High	Medium	Low	Minimum	Federal Correctional Complexes[a]
2000	$21,603	$26,518	$21,417	$18,407	$17,452	$21,360
2001	22,175	26,135	21,806	18,846	17,788	20,543
2002	22,518	27,456	21,473	19,228	18,770	21,538
2003	23,180	26,461	21,946	19,480	18,136	21,948
2004	23,267	26,951	21,896	19,242	17,647	21,764
2005	23,431	26,377	21,718	19,193	17,478	22,458
2006	24,439	25,398	23,648	20,834	17,291	23,152
2007	24,923	26,109	23,492	21,922	17,812	22,804
2008	25,895	27,924	24,065	23,373	19,635	23,958
2009	27,251	32,119	25,442	24,087	20,772	25,750
2010	28,282	33,858	26,248	25,377	21,005	27,267
2011	28,894	34,629	26,852	26,853	21,286	27,516
2012	29,027	34,046	26,686	27,166	21,694	27,683
2013	29,291	33,887	27,278	27,386	21,960	28,330
2014	30,621	35,718	28,536	28,425	23,232	29,617
2015	31,976	36,690	29,475	29,273	24,149	31,528
2016	34,703	39,716	32,614	31,991	27,295	33,589

Source: U.S. Department of Justice, Bureau of Prisons.

Notes: The per capita cost of incarceration for all of BOP includes direct costs for federal detention centers, administrative security facilities, medical referral centers, privately operated institutions, residential reentry centers, and contracts with state and local institutions. It also includes support costs for federal detention centers, administrative security facilities, and medical referral centers.

[a] Federal correctional complexes (FCC) contain two or more facilities with different security levels on the same grounds. For example, FCC Allenwood (PA) contains high-, medium-, and low-security facilities.

INDEX

A

B

C

D

E

F

G

H

L

M

N

O

P

R

S

T

U

V

W

The Federal Bureau of Prisons' Compassionate Release Program

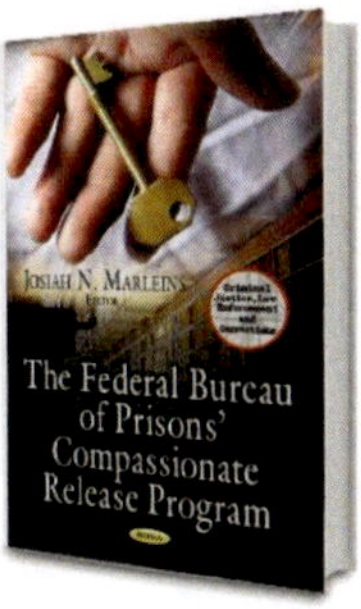

Editor: Josiah N. Marleins

Series: Criminal Justice, Law Enforcement and Corrections

Book Description: This book assesses the BOP's compassionate release program, including whether it provides cost savings or other benefits to the BOP.

Hardcover ISBN: 978-1-62808-318-7
Retail Price: $130

Inmate Populations in Federal Prisons: Buildup Issues and Policy Options

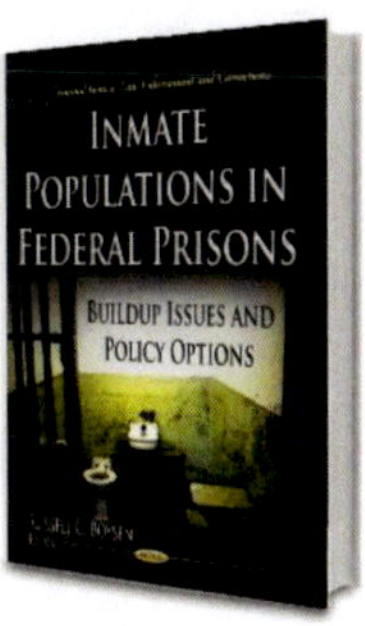

Editor: Russell C. Boysen

Series: Criminal Justice, Law Enforcement and Corrections

Book Description: This book explores the issues related to the growing federal prison population, with a focus on the Bureau of Prisons (BOP) operations and budget; federal mandatory minimum sentences; maximum fines and terms of imprisonment for violation of the Federal Controlled Substances Act and related laws; and a statistics report of prisoners in 2011 from the Bureau of Justice Statistics.

Hardcover ISBN: 978-1-62618-341-4
Retail Price: $179

Criminal Justice Issues in the United States

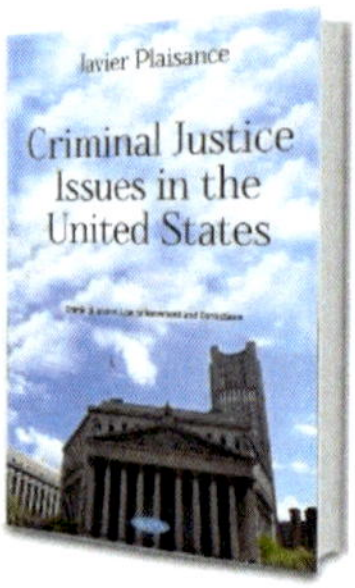

Editor: Javier Plaisance

Series: Criminal Justice, Law Enforcement and Corrections

Book Description: The CRS Reports that comprise this book examines criminal justice issues we are currently facing in the United States.

Softcover ISBN: 978-1-53613-819-1
Retail Price: $95

Corrections and Criminal Justice Reform: An Economic Perspective and Educational Comparisons

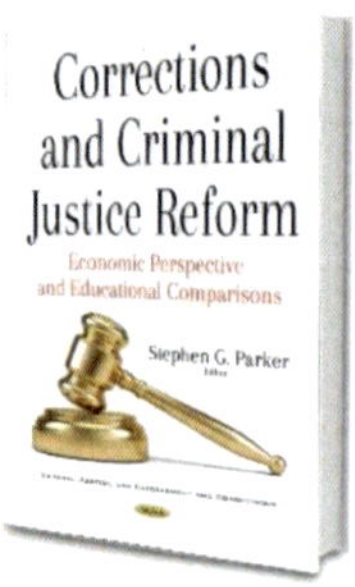

Editor: Stephen G. Parker

Series: Criminal Justice, Law Enforcement and Corrections

Book Description: Calls for criminal justice reform have been mounting in recent years, in large part due to the extraordinarily high levels of incarceration in the United States.

eBook ISBN: 978-1-53610-078-5
Retail Price: $95